Th

GRAPHIC NOVELS FOR CHILDREN AND TWEENS

David S. Serchay

Neal-Schuman Publishers, Inc.
New York   London

Published by Neal-Schuman Publishers, Inc.
100 William St., Suite 2004
New York, NY 10038

Printed and bound in the United States of America

The paper used in this publication meets the minimum requirements of American National Standard for Information Sciences-Permanence of Paper for Printed Library Materials, ANSI Z39.48-1992.

Library of Congress Cataloging-in-Publication Data

Serchay, David S., 1971-
   The librarian's guide to graphic novels for children and tweens / David S. Serchay.
      p. cm.
   Includes bibliographical references and index.
   ISBN 978-1-55570-626-5 (alk. paper)
   1. Libraries—Special collections—Graphic novels. 2. Graphic novels—United States. 3. Children—Books and reading—United States. 4. Preteens—Books and reading—United States. I. Title.

Z692.G7S47 2008
025.277415—dc22

                                                        2008006487

This book is dedicated to my parents
and to my wife, Bethany,
for their love, their support,
and for putting up with
an ever-growing comic book collection.

Contents

Part II: Building a Graphic Novel Collection

List of Figures and Exhibits

Preface

The general acceptance of graphic novels into library collections has enjoyed a remarkable transition. Looking through a 1941 issue of the *Wilson Library Bulletin*, I discovered an article quoting a librarian who bemoaned that her board of directors ordered her to provide comic books in her children's room. Now, barely 65 years later, librarians around the country actively encourage teens to "get graphic @ your library." Graphic novels now enjoy a major presence in libraries, bringing in new readers and increasing circulation. For busy and active professionals serious about serving the needs of their patrons, it has quickly become a key area to embrace and understand.

The Librarian's Guide to Graphic Novels for Children and Tweens begins by clarifying one major misconception: The "graphic novel" is a book format, not a genre. In fact, the format comes in all manner of genres—superhero, action, mystery, crime, true-crime, science fiction, fantasy, horror, religion, history, biography, education, science, romance, literary—all of the genres you will find in your library in fiction (and in many cases, nonfiction) can also be found in graphic novels.

Another crucial concept to grasp: some graphic novels are for all ages, while others are very age-specific. Employing movie terms, they can be G, PG, PG-13, R, or even NC-17. Because of this, many excellent, acclaimed, and award-winning titles should not be read by any patron under high school age. Most people do not realize that the average comic book reader is in his or her twenties and thirties and that many of the more mainstream titles, such as books in the superhero genre, are written to appeal to an older audience. How can a librarian who is not a regular reader of the format be certain what materials are proper to purchase? This question becomes especially important if the librarian works mainly with children or tweens. In other circumstances, a librarian who works primarily with adults finds it difficult to determine what titles are proper to offer or suggest to the tweens who are coming to their library.

Some facts are certain: Graphic novels are both important and entertaining. Perhaps most important, they are here to stay! Children and tweens will come in looking for these books, sometimes by title, sometimes simply asking for graphic novels or even manga. No one wants to mistakenly provide them with an inappropriate book.

After reading *The Librarian's Guide to Graphic Novels for Children and Tweens*, you will know all about these basic issues as well as the answers to other vital questions.

In Part I, "Exploring and Understanding Graphic Novels":

- What exactly are graphic novels?
- What is the difference between comic book and graphic novels?
- What are the most important genres?
- What are the distinctions between fiction and nonfiction?
- What is manga?

In Part II, "Building a Graphic Novel Collection":

- What are the reasons my library needs to offer them?
- How do I purchase this format?
- Who should I buy from?
- What should I collect and *not* collect?

In Part III, "Managing, Promoting, and Maintaining a Graphic Novel Collection":

- How do I catalog?
- How do I weed and replace?
- How do I avoid theft and vandalism?
- How do I display?
- How do I promote?
- How might I integrate the collection into classrooms?

Three appendices provide a wealth of ideas for current and future work:

- An annotated list of suggested graphic novels
- A bibliography of non–graphic novel titles for children and tweens as well as further reading about graphic novels
- A rich list of online resources

I have read comic books all of my life. Unlike some, I confess that I cannot name the first comic book that I ever read, but I have fond memories of the free *Archie* comics my dentist would give out, and of going to the Superhero Shop at my local mall. I used comic book examples in papers for high school and college, and when it came to library school, I found out that libraries could have comics too, and I wrote about this.

Once I became a librarian, I encouraged my system to purchase more graphic novels, gave talks about the subject, recommended what to purchase, and finally found myself as one of the people who decided what graphic novels would be in the system.

Although I have previously written on comics, graphic novels, and libraries, *The Librarian's Guide to Graphic Novels for Children and Tweens* is the culmination of what I have long wanted to do. I hope that it will be helpful to you in your decisions to purchase graphic novels for your library or your media center, so that a new generation of readers can learn to love comics.

Enjoy!

If you have any questions or comments, please contact me at davidserchay@yahoo.com.

Acknowledgments

I have to give thanks to all who have helped me to create this book, especially Lucia LaPardo, Carole Fiore, Arlene Garcia, Susan Hodos; my editors at Neal-Schuman Elizabeth Lund, Paul Seeman, and Charles Harmon; my wife Bethany; the people at GNLIB-L, especially Kat Kan, Mike Pawuk, and Robin Brenner; and all of the writers, artists, editors, and publishers who have answered my questions and provided me with materials for review.

PART I

Exploring and Understanding Graphic Novels

Chapter 1

What Are Graphic Novels?

The use of pictures to tell stories, or sequential art, goes back thousands of years. Cave paintings, hieroglyphics, and certain examples of ancient artwork show this. In 1983, Italian archeologists found a 5,000-year-old goblet in a grave in Burnt City in the Southeastern Iranian province of Sistan va Baluchestan. The goblet had a design with several pictures of a goat and a tree. In each picture the goat is closer to the tree, so even this goblet was an example of sequential art. In more recent centuries, the works of such artists as William Hogarth, Rodolphe Töpffer, Thomas Rowlandson, and James Gillray established art styles that are the ancestors of modern comics.

Comic Books: A History

Long before there were graphic novels there were comic books. Comic books are often not very "comic," and they are certainly not books, but without them we wouldn't have graphic novels. The earliest American comic books were created in the nineteenth century, though they were different from what we know as comic books today. Comic historians call this period (circa 1842–1933) the "Platinum Age." The first comic is considered by many to be *The Adventures of Mr. Obadiah Oldbuck*, an unauthorized translation of Töpffer's *Historie de M. Vieux Bois*, which appeared as a supplement in the September 14, 1842, edition of the New York newspaper *Brother Jonathan Extra*. Over the next 60 years, other early versions of comic books came out both in the United States and elsewhere, with such titles as *The Mischief Book* (1880), *Plish and Plum* (1883), and *The Girl Who Wouldn't Get Married* (1890).

In 1897, *The Yellow Kid in McFadden Flats* was published. This 196-page hardcover (cardboard) book reprinted the *New York Journal*'s popular comic strip. The term "comic book" was coined here, printed on the back cover (Russell, 2005). This book was soon followed by other titles that are still known a century later, including *Buster Brown, Mutt and Jeff, The Katzenjammer Kids*, and *Little Nemo in Slumberland*. Other comics from the early twentieth century include

The Adventures of Willie Winters (1912), which was published by Kellogg's, *Foxy Grandpa Visits Richmond* (1920), a hotel giveaway featuring a well-known comic strip character, and *Comic Monthly*, which came out 1922 and was the first magazine format collection of comic strips to come out on a regular basis. This title, which cost a dime and contained black-and-white reprints of such popular strips as *Barney Google*, lasted for 12 issues (Goulart, 2004: 96).

Another precursor to the modern comic book was *The Funnies* (1929). Its format was closer to the Sunday comics supplement than to modern comics, but it contained original color comic strips and not reprints. It also lasted only one year, but a revived version in a new format (and a later title change) ran from 1936-1962 and featured such characters as Raggedy Ann and Andy and Woody Woodpecker (Goulart, 2004: 163).

In 1932, the Whitman division of Western Publishing put out the first of the Big Little Books, which, although not a comic book, has been considered to be a forerunner. The books were roughly 4" × 4" × 1½" with cardboard covers and anywhere from 240 to 320 pages of pulp paper that alternated between text and art. The first book was *The Adventures of Dick Tracy, Detective*, which took art from the comic strip but removed the captions and word balloons. Besides original material, other comic strips featured in The Big Little Books were *Mickey Mouse, Little Orphan Annie*, and *Buck Rodgers*. Western Publishing would later produce comic books.

The following year saw the debut of *Funnies on Parade*, which contained reprints of Sunday color comics and is considered by many to be the first modern comic book. It was a giveaway from Procter & Gamble, which customers could get by redeeming a coupon. Within weeks, the print run of 10,000 copies was gone, and similar books were soon created for Canada Dry, Kinney Shoes, Wheatena, and other companies. In 1934, another reprint title, *Famous Funnies* appeared. It ran for 218 issues, sold very well, and was the first monthly comic book in the "current" format (Inge, 1990: 140).

In 1935, Major Malcolm Wheeler-Nicholson's National Allied Publishers (the forerunner of today's DC Comics) developed the idea of publishing original material and created *New Fun* (Inge, 1990: 140). The series, which was at first oversized in black and white and sold for a dime, contained stories in a variety of genres (including "Don Nogales, Cattle Rustler," "Sandra," "2023: Super Police," and "Oswald the Rabbit"). The first issue of *New Fun*, which, with some title changes, would run until 1947, is generally considered to be the start of the "Golden Age" of comics, which is commonly regarded to have ended around 1949. The next major age, the "Silver Age," began in 1956 (see the entry on DC Comics in Chapter 6) and ended, depending on who you ask, anywhere between 1969 and 1985. The names and periods of the other ages have been debated among comic fans and historians.

The next 60 years would see many changes in comic books, some of which are covered throughout this book. The size would slightly change, as would the quality of the paper and of course the price. The industry has had its ups and downs, with sales skyrocketing and falling and publishers beginning and ending. Today, most American comic books—also called simply comics, comic magazines, and, more recently, "floppies" and "pamphlets," to differentiate them from the booklike graphic novels—are 6⅝" by 10⅛", between 24 and 64 pages, and cost between $2.00 and $7.00, with $2.99 the average price in 2006 (Jones, 2006). The type of paper varies from book to book, and they generally have a stapled binding called "saddle stitch." The inside of a comic book may have one story or multiple stories, or even a full issue of one-page "pinups." An issue may also contain advertisements (for other comics, movies, and various products, ranging from candy to cars), text pages (often a column or information from someone at the comic company), and/or letters' pages (letters from fans about previous issues).

How Are Comic Books Made?

Many jobs contribute to a comic book story, or a graphic novel story for that matter, including the writer, the penciler, the inker, the colorist (when needed), and the letterer (Gertler and Lieber, 2004: 26–29, 70–72). Sometimes one individual will handle more than one of these positions, and on other occasions more than one person will be responsible for a particular area.

Writers and Artists

The writer is responsible for writing the story, including the plot and dialogue. The penciler is the primary artist on the story and creates the layout and the look of the story, even though much of what he or she draws is later covered up or erased by others, especially the inker. The inker enhances the art by going over the penciler's drawings with ink, since the light pencils of the original drawings do not reproduce very well. The inker's work provides the shape and width of the penciled line, which then helps to create depth and also shading. A good job by an inker can improve the penciler's work, whereas a poor job can hurt it.

The working relationship between writer and penciler, when they are not the same individual, varies from work to work. In some cases, known as "full script," the writer's script is extremely detailed, with every panel—defined as "a box that contains a given scene"—fully described for the artist. Other panel-related terms are border—"the outline of the panel"—and tier—"the row of panels on the page" (Eisner, 1985: 157).

If the writer has any artistic talent, then he or she may create a "layout" or "drawn" script providing rough preliminary sketches to guide the artist. In other cases, the writer will provide the penciler with a basic plotline that describes the story and actions, which the artist then uses to create his or her work. This gives the artist more input into the creation of the story. Some artists like this method, since it gives them more creative freedom, while others feel that it forces them to do the writer's job (Gertler and Lieber, 2004: 70–72).

In this type of script, the writer, after seeing the penciler's work, may revise the story so that it better fits with what the artist drew. This is sometimes known as "the Marvel method," since it was the style that Stan Lee, who in the 1960s was editor and main writer for most of Marvel Comics' titles, would use. Luckily, he had artists such as Jack Kirby and Steve Ditko who were masters at using their art to tell a story. This method does not work as well if the artist does not have the knack for graphic storytelling (Gertler and Lieber, 2004: 72). In any case, a good relationship between writers and artists helps create a good comic. Thanks to modern technology, the writers and artists never have to meet in person and in some cases do not even live on the same continent.

The Letterer

After the comic is penciled and inked, the pages are turned over to the letterer. The letterer draws all word/thought balloons and caption boxes (see Exhibit 1-1) and puts the scripted words into them. The placement of the balloons and boxes is important since the letterer must not block any important art and must also make sure that the reader will know the proper reading order of the dialogue (as you'll learn in Chapter 3, this was one of the reasons that manga was delayed in coming to America). The letterer also adds the sound effects and words on signs or printed material. In recent years, lettering has been done with the use of a computer.

The Colorist

The final artistic component, when needed, since many titles are in black and white, is the colorist. As with the lettering, much of the colorist's work these days is done with a computer. This allows for much more variety in color than was possible in the early days.

The Cover

The interior art team will often also take care of the cover, but this is not always the case. Sometimes the artists may be wonderful storytellers but might not be the best at creating eye-catching covers. Comic books are occasionally published with different covers known as "variants." These are often done by different artists, or even with a "photo cover." Sometimes the quantity of issues produced for a book with cover "A" is the same as the number of issues for cover "B," but other times cover "B" (or "C," "D," etc.) is on a smaller percentage of comics, which makes them more appealing to collectors. On some occasions the variant is used to indicate a new printing of the issue.

Exhibit 1-1. Word Balloons and Captions

Word balloons are used to convey dialogue. The pointer on the balloon that indicates the speaker is called the tail. Thought balloons show what a character is thinking and are connected to the character by a series of small circles. Sometimes the shape of the balloon is changed. For example, if a person is speaking in a "cold" tone of voice, the letterer may put icicles on the balloon. If a person is "under the influence" and speaking, then the balloon would demonstrate this state as well by looking "shaky." In some comics, especially books in the superhero genre, the main character's "interior monologue" may be displayed in a caption box at the top of the panel. Besides first-person narration and "off-camera" dialogue, captions are also used to establish location or for third-person narration (see the end of this chapter for more on reading a graphic novel).

An example of speech balloons in a conversation.

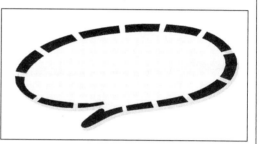

Dotted lines indicate whispering.

An example of a "thought balloon."

In "wordless comics," a question mark may be used to indicate that a character is asking a question, without actually having dialogue. An exclamation point, or symbols such as "$" may be used to further convey what the character is "saying."

Although today all of the contributors to a comic book story receive credit, this has not always been the case. For decades, the writer and/or artist might or might not be credited, and the others rarely (if ever) would. Carl Barks, who worked for decades on the *Donald Duck* comics and created the character of Scrooge McDuck, was not allowed to sign his name to his work until Walt Disney's death in 1966. For years, many fans simply knew him as "The Good Duck Artist" (Goulart, 2004: 32-33).

Formats

As covered in Chapter 2, comic books come in all genres. They are also published in several styles and formats.

Series

A comic book series can best be described as an open-ended run of a comic book title. Issues in a series generally come out on a monthly, bimonthly, or quarterly basis, or on some other steady schedule. Occasionally, they are also produced biweekly or even weekly, though this is usually only temporary. Some series, especially those by smaller companies or self-publishers may come out on a more infrequent basis. Like a television series, when a comic book series begins, there is no limit regarding how long it will last. A show with high ratings can last for years, whereas one that nobody is watching can be cancelled after only a few episodes. With comics, good sales can mean a title runs for decades, and poor sales can lead to the comic's cancellation in a few months.

The oldest comic book series still being published is *Detective Comics*, a Batman title from DC Comics that has been published continuously since 1937. However, during a more frequent publishing schedule and a brief weekly run in the 1980s, DC's Superman book, *Action Comics* (1938–), has produced more issues (862 by December 2007 to *Detective's* 841). However, the American comic book with the largest number of issues is the Dell Comics anthology series *Four Color Comics* (1939–1962). Multiple issues were published each month, each about a different character, with no continued stories, and most featured licensed characters such as Donald Duck. Due to irregular numbering, it is unclear exactly how many issues were published, but estimates put it at more than 1,300 issues.

Poor sales are not the only reason to end a series. Other reasons include the creators or publishers deciding they've told all the stories that they wanted to tell (similar to television shows ending on a "high note"), the publishers deciding that they want to restart the book at issue #1, and, in the most extreme case, the publisher going out of business (see Chapter 6).

Limited Series

A limited series (LS) is the equivalent to a television miniseries. It is known from the beginning how many issues will be published, with the covers often proclaiming something along the lines of "issue X of Y." Limited series have the same publication schedule possibilities as ongoing series. They are also known as "mini-" or "maxi-" series, depending on the number of issues, though the number of issues in which a "mini" becomes a "maxi" is unclear. Although technically no highest number is set, most limited series do not exceed 12 issues (a number considered a maxiseries).

Although many short-lived titles have been published, the first one considered to be a limited series, even though it was not billed as such, was DC's

World of Krypton (1979).[1] The first title to actually call itself a limited series was *Marvel Superheroes Contest of Champions*[2] in 1982, and also in 1982 the 12-issue *Camelot 3000*[3] became the first maxiseries.

There are several different reasons to create a limited series. The publisher may want to tell a story with a character such as Batman or Spider-Man, but not put it in one of its regular titles. A supporting character in a title or a minor character might be the featured character in a limited series, possibly with an eye toward creating a regular series if sales are good. Batman's teen partner Robin was the star of three limited series before getting his own title, which has since run for more than 150 issues. On the other hand, a limited series might feature new characters altogether or just tell a new story, without having to create a new, ongoing series. The limited series might even be an anthology, with each issue having one or more distinct stories that are not continued in the following issue. Some of the smaller comic book companies produce primarily limited series and have no ongoing titles.

In most cases, by its last issue the limited series will have told at least one complete story, with a beginning, an ending, and a plot resolution. Some limited series have sequels, and in some cases there are even "series" of limited series in which, instead of being in an ongoing series, the characters will simply appear in limited series after limited series after limited series. The *Courtney Crumrin*[4] and *Allison Dare*[5] titles are examples of this. Starting with *Marvel Superheroes Secret Wars*[6] in 1984 and DC's *Crisis on Infinite Earths*[7] in 1985, the "event" limited series, in which the story line would cross over into the various series, became a regular event for these two publishers. The stories in these "event" titles can have an effect on the ongoing titles, and this can affect your decision when deciding whether or not to purchase the collected volume (see the following sections and Chapters 5 and 6 for more information).

Annual

As the word implies, an annual is a comic book that comes out on an annual basis. They tend to be at least twice as long as an issue of a series, and are almost always tied into an existing series (e.g., *Batman Annual, X-Men Annual*, etc.). They have been around since the 1940s, and similar to series and limited series titles, they can contain more than one story. The stories may tie into a story going on in the regular series, and just as there have been "event" limited series, there have also been "event" annuals, in which the story line continues from annual to annual, or years during which all of a publisher's annuals shared the same theme (e.g., DC's 1995 "Year One" theme, which told of the character's early adventures).

Specials

The term "special" can be applied to a number of kinds of comics. The most obvious have the word "special" in the title. Sometimes they are similar in size to an annual, but unlike annuals they come out on a more irregular basis. Other times they have the same page count as the regular series and LS comics. An example of a special is DC's various *Secret Files* books, which have both stories and background information on characters. Many specials have more than one issue, but not all. However, a one-issue special is not necessarily the same as a "one-shot," which is discussed in the following section.

One-Shot

A one-shot comic book is usually, but not always, a 32-pager for which only one issue of the title is intended to be made. It is often related to an existing comic or character. On some occasions several one-shots with a similar theme will come out over several weeks, such as *Marvel Monsters* (2005), which consisted of five one-shots by various creators dealing with some of the monsters of the Marvel Universe. DC Comics has had stories told in a series of one-shots, sometimes with a two-issue limited series providing "bookends."

Reprints

Reprints are comics that reprint other comic book stories. Sometimes an issue of an ongoing series will contain a reprinted story in addition to or in place of a new one. Reprints have also been published as one-shots and limited series, and there have even been long-running, ongoing series in which older material is reprinted, including the Spider-Man title *Marvel Tales* (1966–1992) and *Classic X-Men* (also called *X-Men Classic*, 1986–1995). Reprints are also published as a tie-in to an ongoing story in other titles, as a way to collect recent issues that were sold out (this is different from a second printing and will be published under a new title, such as *Marvel Must-Haves*), or for a special occasion, such as when DC put out 52 *Millennium Editions* in 2000, reprinting classic stories from the previous 60-plus years.

Reprints also can clean up mistakes, such fixing the story in *Amazing Spider-Man #3* (1963) in which Dr. Octopus calls Spider-Man "Superman." All subsequent reprints of this issue have had Spider-Man called by his proper name. *Classic X-Men* even occasionally added additional pages to the story to tie it into later story lines. Trade editions, covered later in this chapter, are another form of reprint title.

Other Formats and Sizes

Some comic books have different formats and layouts than the standard sort, or have different paper or stronger covers. Although most are still in the "floppy" format, a few are occasionally produced in "bookshelf" format. Also called "prestige format," comics published in bookshelf format are printed with glossy paper, more durable card-stock covers, and spines similar to books. Therefore, unlike regular comic books, they can stand up on a bookshelf. One-shots produced in a bookshelf format can be and have been purchased for libraries and put on the shelves with other books. Limited series in this format (there are no series produced this way) could also be purchased by libraries, but if any one issue is lost, damaged, or stolen, the story will remain incomplete. Technically speaking, some of the one-shot comics in bookshelf format can be considered to be an original graphic novel.

Sometimes comics will be in a different size from the standard comic book. Digests, for example, are small, square-bound books (referred to as digest-sized), often with reprinted material. Perhaps the most familiar of these are the digests put out by Archie Comics, which are often sold in the checkout lines of supermarkets, near the tabloids and *TV Guide*s. Some trade editions are also published in digest size, and some digests are larger (in both height and width) than others. Speaking of tabloids, many tabloid-sized comics are much bigger than the *National Enquirer* and contain no gossip. Besides the early examples of comics, many tabloids were produced in the 1970s, including reprints such as DC's *Famous First Editions*, and new stories that included *Superman vs. Shazam!*, *Superman vs. Wonder Woman*, and even *Superman vs. Muhammad Ali*. More recently, writer Paul Dini and artist Alex Ross put out a series of tabloids in which superheroes dealt with social issues (see *The World's Greatest Superheroes* in Appendix A). Since these were similar to bookshelf format books, including having a hard spine, these books were able to be purchased for libraries.

Types of Graphic Novels

Now that you know more about comics, graphic novels can be discussed. What, then, is a graphic novel? Author Gail de Vos, who teaches a library school course on the subject, defines them as "bound books, fiction and non-fiction which are created in the comic book format and are issued an ISBN" (de Vos, 2005). Other sources will give a slightly different answer, but in this book de Vos's definition will be the one followed here. There is some controversy among both creators and readers over what constitutes a graphic novel. Some do not like the term at all, and others feel that the term tends to be applied too broadly. Writer Alan Moore, whose well-known works include *Watchmen* and *V For Vendetta*, feels that it is just a marketing term (Kavanagh, 2000), and that it has been used to get away from the "stigma" of the term "comic book." Other creators have used terms such as "comic-strip novel" or "picture novella." For this book, the term "graphic novel" (or GN) will be used as an umbrella term for both original graphic novels—the "true" graphic novels—and trade editions, as well as for manga, which will be covered in Chapter 3.

Disagreement over what constitutes a graphic novel also means disagreement over what does not. For this book, with very few exceptions, books that reprint comic strips are not considered graphic novels, even if they are produced by comic book publishers such as the multivolume *Complete Peanuts* from Fantagraphics. Neither—again with a few exceptions—are "easy reader" children's books, even if they use word balloons or other comics techniques (Mo Willems's *Pigeon* books, for example), since in most picture books the illustrations are part of the "full-page narrative," whereas the illustrations in graphic novels "correspond directly to the text" (Jones, Gorman, and Suellentrop, 2004: 134).

Books about comics, comic book creators, or comic book characters are not graphic novels, even if they may be cataloged in the same area, and the same goes for books on drawing comic characters.

Original Graphic Novels

Original graphic novels (OGNs) are referred to as such because the material they contain has not previously appeared in comic book form. Original graphic novels come in both hard and softcover, are in color or black and white, may contain more than one story, and come in various sizes, shapes, and page lengths. Some OGNs are very short (which makes them more like "graphic novellas"), while others are longer than many "regular" novels. For example, Craig Thompson's "older reader" GN, *Blankets* (Top Shelf, 2003), is 592 pages long.

As with the term itself, *when* exactly graphic novels began has been a matter of debate. Prototypes included *He Done Her Wrong* (1930), a hardcover, wordless comic by Milt Gross. Perhaps the first graphic novel as we know it today was the digest-sized *It Rhymes with Lust* published by St. John Publishing Company in 1950. Billed as "An Original Picture Novel," the book, written by Drake Waller (a pseudonym for Leslie Walker and Arnold Drake) and drawn by Matt Baker (one of the first African Americans in mainstream comics) and Ray Osrin has panels, word balloons, captions, and everything else associated with comic books and graphic novels. Both *He Done Her Wrong* and *It Rhymes with Lust* have recently been reprinted.

According to comic historian R.C. Harvey, the term was first used by Richard Kyle in 1964 in an article for *Capa-Alpha*, a comics-themed amateur press association publication (Arnold, 2003). *Blackmark*, a sword and sorcery/science fiction story created by Archie Goodwin and Gil Kane and published in 1971 in paperback by Bantam, is another early example and was called a "paperback comics novel" when it was given an award by The Academy of Comic Arts. In 1975, three books, Richard Corben's *Bloodstar*, George Metzger's *Beyond Time and Again* (which, since it reprinted comic book stories, was technically a trade edition), and Jim Sterenko's *Chandler: Red Tide* all had the words "graphic novel" either on the cover or on one of the interior pages (Arnold, 2003).

In 1978, the book that many sources have given as the first graphic novel came out, Will Eisner's classic *A Contract with God, and Other Tenement Stories*. After completing the book, which he did in an attempt "to take a serious subject matter and create it in [the comic] medium" (Read, 1990), Eisner looked for a publisher. At the 2002 University of Florida Conference on Comics and Graphic Novels, he recounted his pitch to an editor at Bantam Books:

> So I called him and said, "There's something I want to show you, something I think is very interesting."
>
> He said, "Yeah, well what is it?"
>
> A little man in my head popped up and said, "For Christ's sake stupid, don't tell him it's a comic. He'll hang up on you." So I said, "It's a graphic novel."
>
> He said, "Wow! That sounds interesting. Come on up."
>
> Well I did bring it up and he looked at it and looked at me through his reading glasses and said, "This is a comic book, bring it to a smaller publisher." (Eisner, 2004)

Eisner brought it to Baronet Books, who published it. Although the words "graphic novel" did not appear on the original hardcover version, which did not have a dust jacket, it was on the paperback version, and the term eventually moved into common usage. The book has changed publishers over the years, and was most recently reprinted by W.W. Norton and Company. Eisner later said that he was unaware at the time of the term's previous usage, and he knew that he was not the first to produce a book in that format, but he had felt that he was "in a position to change the direction of comics" (Arnold, 2003). Interestingly, *A Contract with God* is actually four short stories/novellas, including the title story. Eisner would write 16 additional graphic novels before his death in 2005 (not counting new comic book stories or the children's books that he did for NBM).

In the 1980s, mainstream comic book companies began to publish their own graphic novels. Between 1982 and 1988 Marvel published a series of numbered graphic novels in a 10" × 7" paperback format (as well as a few hardcover and/or unnumbered graphic novels), and DC put out hard- and softcover graphic novels beginning in 1983. Other companies also began to create their own GNs, and this continues to this day. Although comic companies were the main producer of OGNs for many years, in the 2000s, more and more noncomics publishers are publishing, and even commissioning, their own graphic novels.

Trade Editions

Trade editions, also called trade paperbacks (TPBs) when they are in softcover (which the majority of them are), are comic books stories that have been collected into book form. A literary equivalent of this is a novel that is first serialized in a periodical before appearing in book form. Another example would be a collection of short stories, whether it is an anthology or a work by a single author, in which the stories were originally printed in various places but are now all collected in a single book. As with books, trades have ISBN numbers and a spine and come in a variety of sizes. In some cases, the pages of the trade are larger or smaller than they were in the original comic book. This is especially true with the digest-size TPBs, which are growing in popularity. Despite the shrinking of the images, these digests are helpful for libraries that purchase graphic novels since they are much cheaper than the full-sized books.

The color in trade editions is usually the same as what was in the original comic book, though some color comics have been reprinted in black and white to save on costs, most notably DC Comics' *Showcase*[8] books and Marvel Comics' *Essential*[9] line, and in some older comics the color has been improved. They may be fewer than 100 pages or, like the *Showcase* and *Essential* books, more than 500 pages (and in the case of the *Bone: One Volume Edition*, more than 1,300 pages, though this is technically an omnibus edition). Again, these are not graphic novels in the truest sense, since GNs are mainly original work and trades are reprints. However, for simplicity's sake, they will be referred to as trades, trade editions (TEs), or TPBs when discussing them in the specific, but as graphic novels when discussing them in general terms.

Trades have proliferated, with hundreds of titles coming out each year. The practice of collecting comic stories into books had been popular in Europe for a long time, the *Tintin* collections being one of the best examples (see Chapter 3). The earliest American collections came out in the 1960s but, as with the early OGNs, were generally not put out by comic book publishers. One of the first was *The Great Comic Book Heroes*, an anthology of reprints put together by Jules Feiffer in 1965. Feiffer, who had worked in comics in the 1940s, including working as Will Eisner's assistant, and who at the time had a strip in *The Village Voice* (and whose future work included children's books such as *Bark George*), was given the idea for the book by his editor at Dial Press, E.L. Doctorow. Besides essays by Feiffer, this hardcover anthology included reprints of stories from the 1940s, including early appearances by Superman, Batman, and Captain America. The book sold well, and the essay portions were later reprinted by Fantagraphic Books in 2003.

Soon afterward, Ballantine Books put out two paperback books, *Autumn People* (1965) and *Tomorrow Midnight* (1966), which reprinted the Ray Bradbury adaptations from *Tales from the Crypt*, *Weird Science*, *Vault of Horror*, and other comics that EC Comics published in 1952 and 1953. The reprints were in black and white and were reprinted vertically, with two panels per page, so that the reader had to turn the book onto its side in order to read it.

DC Comics characters appeared in several collections in the 1970s, starting with the primarily black-and-white *Superman from the Thirties to the Seventies* and *Batman from the Thirties to the Seventies* put out by Crown Publishing in

1971 and *Wonder Woman* from Holt, Rinehart and Winston in 1972. Reprint collections with Marvel characters were put out by Simon & Schuster starting with *Origins of Marvel Comics* (1974), *Son of Origins of Marvel Comics* (1975), and *Bring on the Bad Guys* (1976).[10]

Other notable trades of the period included *A Smithsonian Book of Comic-Book Comics* (copublished by Smithsonian Institution Press and Harry N. Abrams, Inc, 1981),[11] the 53-volume *Complete EC Library*[12] (Cochran 1979–1989), the 30-volume *Carl Barks Library*[13] (Another Rainbow 1984–1990), and the 18-volume *Little Lulu Library* (Another Rainbow 1985–1992). More trades were produced in the 1980s and were coming from comic publishers, but trades did not begin coming out on a regular basis until the 1990s. At first it was the most popular stories that were being collected, but more and more comic book stories are now being put into a trade, sometimes less than two months after the "newest" issue is sold. And, as covered in Chapter 6, not only recent material but a great deal of older material is finally being collected into trades.

The majority of trade editions fall into at least one of four categories: limited series, chronological, story line, and theme.

Collected Limited Series

The collected limited series trade is just what it sounds like, a comic book limited series collected together in (usually) one volume. Some of the earliest trades that were published by the originating comic book company were of this sort of trade. Given that the majority of limited series are written as a complete story, the collected editions allow the reader to get the entire story, with (again, usually) no subplots that will be resolved in future issues/volumes. In rare cases, due to the length of the limited series, the story is broken up into more than one volume, and in other cases, the limited series has a story that is continued in a new limited series. For example, the issues of the 12-issue limited series *Justice*[14] (2006–2007) were collected into three separate volumes of four issues each. Marvel's *The Ultimate Galactus Trilogy*[15] is an example of a limited series with sequels. The three four-issue limited series *Ultimate Nightmare*, *Ultimate Secret*, and *Ultimate Extinction* were then collected in three volumes: *Ultimate Galactus*, Volume 1: *Nightmare*; *Ultimate Galactus*, Volume 2: *Secret*; and *Ultimate Galactus*, Volume 3: *Extinction*.

Chronological Collections

In most examples, a chronological trade simply collects issues "A" through "B" of a comic book series. The next volume produced in the series will then begin with the issue after "B." For example, the first trade edition collection of the ongoing series Ultimate Spider-Man[16] collects issues #1–#7, the second collects issues #8–#13, the third #14–#21, and so forth. In some cases, such as

Ultimate Spider-Man, nearly every issue has been collected, and new readers can easily catch up to the most recent issues. In other cases, especially with books that have been around for a long time, only a portion of the series has been collected. Only a fraction of the stories that appeared in *Superman* and *Batman* since their 1940 debuts have been collected. Many books with a shorter lifespan have not been collected at all, and some have been only partially collected. Although the 1996 *Supergirl* series from DC lasted about 80 issues, only the first six and the last six issues have so far been collected. Even when most of the series have been collected, there might be the occasional omission. In *Showcase Presents: Shazam!* (DC, 2007), the entire run of the series is collected except for three issues that contained reprints, and the final issue which featured a character that DC had licensed but no longer had the rights to (see Chapter 2 for more on licensed characters).

The second type of chronological collections occurs when the reprinted stories are still in chronological order of a character's appearance but are not necessarily from the same title. These are usually seen in reprints of older material such as in the Showcase and *Essential* books, and their color, hardcover counterparts *Archive Editions*[17] and *Marvel Masterworks*.[18] For example, the volumes of DC's *Archive Editions* collect the adventures of the futuristic superhero team the Legion of Super-Heroes (LSH) and follow their adventures in order from occasional appearances in *Adventure Comics*, *Action Comics*, and *Superman* to their regular spot in *Adventure Comics*, to their backup feature in *Action Comics*, and finally to their own title. The LSH stories also are an example of how even if one story in a comic book is reprinted, every story in that issue is not necessarily reprinted along with it. The Legion story from their debut in *Adventure Comics* #247 is included, but the Green Arrow and Aquaman stories are not. For that matter, Superman's first appearance in *Action Comics* #1 has often been reprinted, but the other stories have appeared much less frequently. Thanks to the *Showcase* and *Essential* books, many older and short-lived series have finally been collected.

In addition, at times an annual, limited series, special, or one-shot will be included along with the issues of a series that came out at the time. *Ultimate Spider-Man*, Volume 15: *Silver Sable* (2006) includes *Ultimate Spider-Man Annual* #1 (2005) along with issues #86 through #90. On some occasions, a collected limited series is counted as one of the volumes in a series of chronological collections, such as the seven-issue *Ultimate Six* limited series, which was collected and published as *Ultimate Spider-Man*, Volume 9.

Collected Story Lines

The collected story line type of trade collects a multipart comic book story in one or more volumes. When the reprinted issues are all from the same comic book, the volume is also a chronological collection, though some chronological collections will also contain both a multipart story along with one-shot or shorter "two-part" stories. Some story lines cross over into other comics. Sometimes these are titles in the same "family" (the various Batman titles, X-Men titles, etc.), and other times they are in the same publisher "universe." For example, "War Games," a 2004 story line that ran through most of the Batman family of books and dealt with a gang war that raged through Gotham City, ran through several issues of the ongoing series *Batman, Detective Comics, Batgirl, Robin, Nightwing, Batman: Legends of the Dark Knight, Batman: Gotham Knights*, and *Catwoman*. "War Games" is also an example of a collected story line that continues into additional volumes. The three collections, which came out in 2005 and include the previously listed comic books, had the subtitles of *Act 1: Outbreak, Act 2: Tides*, and *Act 3: Endgame*.

Another sort of multivolume, story line collection includes those books which reprinted the stories related to Marvel's "event" limited series *House of M*, in which the history of the Marvel Universe is changed so that mutants, not humans, are dominant. These nine volumes collected stories from six ongoing series, five limited series (including the titular one), and a one-shot titled *Secrets of the House of M*—a total of 43 comic book stories.

Crossovers can cause problems. Some writers do not like having their ongoing story lines interrupted or changed in order to fit into the crossover. Writer Peter David has told of how a story arc in Supergirl that was supposed to run for less than a year took two years to complete due to all of the publisher-imposed crossovers, while the delay of some of the issues of the event LS *Civil War*[19] caused delays in several of the monthly titles that the story line affected so that plot twists would not be "spoiled."

There has been much discussion among comic book readers as to if they should continue buying the monthly comic book if the stories are just going to appear soon after in a trade. After all, the trade will fit on a bookshelf; have no ads or text or letters pages; and the reader will not have to wait months for the story line to be resolved. Plus, if it turns out to be a bad story, they will not have wasted their time and money. This is the equivalent of not watching a new television series but instead waiting for the collected DVD to come out so that you can watch the show without commercials or any other onscreen ads and you don't have to wait nine months for the season-long mystery to be resolved (and also, like the graphic novel, you might be able to get it for free at the library). The downside to this is that if sales are poor, the issues might not be collected.

There has also been some feeling among readers that in some cases, the writer, under orders from the publishers, will pad the story so that it extends into more issues than should be required to tell the story, just so that it will be put into a "collected story line" type of trade (Byrne, 2004; M., 2006). The biggest downside in creators "writing for the trade" is that some of the individual issues do not "hold up" on their own, and the reader, who has paid $2.50 to $5.00 for the comic, feels cheated and disappointed. If this happens too often the reader may end up dropping the book altogether and may not even bother with the trade.

Others will not purchase the trade since they've already purchased the original comic book issues. To counter this, trades will sometimes include extras to entice the buyer, much as special edition DVDs are made to entice those who had already purchased a copy of a particular film. Trade extras include scripts, additional artwork, covers (including all of the variants), essays and "behind the scenes" information, extra stories (such as a related one-shot), and even deleted scenes (the 1997 collection of the DC limited series *Kingdom Come*[20] included not only a deleted scene, but a new epilogue). Perhaps the most unusual "extra" was in the 1997 collection of Marvel's 1985–1986 *Squadron Supreme*[21] maxiseries. When writer Mark Gruenwald died in 1996, his will stipulated that he wanted to be cremated with his ashes mixed in with printer's ink and used in a comic book. Since *Squadron Supreme* was considered by many to be his best work, it was decided that the TPB would be the perfect place for the ashes. This resulted in many examples of black humor on the comic-related Usenet groups along the lines of "I've heard of an author throwing himself into his work but this is ridiculous" and "Who do we use if there's a second printing?"

Theme Trades

Theme trades are usually anthologies. The comic books reprinted in theme trades are often from several different titles and may span decades. Some of the early trades of the 1970s were of this type. Theme trades can contain reprints of comics from a particular period (*Archie Americana: Best of the Forties*, *Superman in the Seventies*), comics dealing with a particular character (*The Greatest Batman Stories Ever Told*, *The Best of the Fantastic Four*), stories with a common theme (*A DC Universe Christmas*, *Marvel Weddings*), the work of a particular writer or artist (*Marvel Visionaries: Chris Claremont*, *Hulk Visionaries: Peter David*), and more. Some of these trades will have multiple volumes and, such as in the case of David's *Hulk* collections, which have been collecting his 1987–1998 run, can also be chronological.

There are, of course, a few trades that will not fall into any of these categories, as well as new volumes of previously released trades that are redone in new formats. Hardcover volumes are usually released in paperback form within a year of the original release. DC Comics has produced various

"Absolute" editions, which have reprinted stories in an oversized format. There are also "collections of collections," omnibuses in which a newly released book collects stories that have already been collected in two or more "series" volumes. For example, 2006's *Marvel Adventures Spider-Man*, Volume 1,[22] collects the stories that already had been printed in the first two collections of *Marvel Adventures Spider-Man: The Sinister Six* (2005) and *Power Struggle* (2006). The 1,332-page *Bone: One Volume Edition*[23] collects the stories that had previously been reprinted in the nine individual trades. These are helpful for libraries that want to collect the older volumes, especially when those volumes are unavailable.

Trade editions have also been helpful to comic book publishers. By putting comics in book form, they have been able to get them into libraries, bookstores, and other places where they will be seen by people who don't go into comic book shops (see Chapter 5 for more on comic shops). In fact, in some cases, such as the *Spider-Man/Doctor Octopus: Out of Reach*,[24] the trade has sold better than the original five-issue limited series (Macdonald, 2004). The collections of the older issues of Marvel's *Spider-Girl*[25] comic have also been credited with saving the title from cancellation (Hinze, 2005).

Hybrids

One last type of comic/graphic novel is one that is on the border between comic and book: the hybrid. Hybrids have elements of both, with several pages in comic-book format followed by several pages of text (or vice versa). Whether these are truly comics and graphic novels is another debatable subject, but a handful will be included in the Appendix A book list. These include the *Thieves and Kings* series, Barron's Graphic Classics, the *Black Belt Club* series, *Mercer Mayer's Critter Kids Adventures*, and Stone Arch's Graphic Flash line. Books that may have only a few pages of comics but are almost all text should not be considered hybrids, even if the text has illustrations, as in the case of the *Captain Underpants* series. However, there have been some recent notable juvenile fiction titles that can be considered hybrid graphic novels, including the popular *Diary of a Wimpy Kid* and the Caldecott-winning *The Invention of Hugo Cabret*.

How to Read a Graphic Novel

"Words, pictures, and other icons are the vocabulary of the language called comics," says Scott McCloud, author of *Understanding Comics*, *Reinventing Comics*, and *Making Comics*, three instructional books that are also themselves graphic novels (McCloud, 1994: 47). Children who may have been reading comics for years may find it easier to do so than teachers and librarians who read their last comics decades ago, if at all, and may find comics

---

Exhibit 1-2. Types of Panels

In his books, McCloud lists six categories of panel-to-panel transition:

1. Moment-to-moment
2. A single subject in action-to-action progression
3. Subject-to-subject while staying within a scene or idea (sitting on couch, cut to door)
4. Scene-to-scene: change in time or space
5. Aspect-to-aspect, which sets a "wandering eye on different aspects of a place idea or mood"
6. Nonsequitur, which has no apparent relation between panels

The second category is by far the most common in a multitude of genres (McCloud, 1994: 70–73).

"incomprehensible" now. Part of it is reading—captions, dialogue, and so forth, but then the reader must "take in" the artwork since it, too, is telling part of the story. It can show the setting, the action, the characters, and so much more in just one small picture. Continuity exists from panel to panel (see Exhibit 1-2); the reader must figure out what action has occurred between them. Sometimes it is obvious, while on other occasions it takes some intuition.

Imagine, for example, a comic book script that reads as follows:

> At two o'clock, Joe was sitting on his couch watching television when there was a knock on the door. He walked over to the door, opened it, and greeted his friend Jerry.

In a book, readers would imagine this occurring. In a television show or movie, they could see and hear it happening. In a comic book, seeing a picture and imagining the action are combined. So let's say in this case the writer has asked the artist to make a standard six-panel page, but has not given panel-by-panel directions. They artist might do it like so:

PANEL ONE

Joe on his couch looking at the television, which is seen from the rear. The artist can choose to have a sound effect coming out of the television to show that is on, or a word balloon with the noise from the television. The tails of such balloons are usually shaped like a lightning bolt. The artist can also choose to show Joe and the couch from the rear, so that the reader can see what's on the television. In either case, a clock on the wall can show the time or even a clock on a VCR or DVD player. Another choice is a caption balloon that says "2:00 p.m." This would be used if that sort of "caption clock" was used throughout the whole story to show, for example, what Joe's day was like.

PANEL TWO

A picture of the door. "Knock Knock" sound effect (subject to subject panel).

PANEL THREE

Close-up on Joe, whose head is turned toward the door (subject in action for panels three through six).

PANEL FOUR

Joe is walking toward the door.

PANEL FIVE

Joe is at the door with his hand on the knob.

PANEL SIX

The door is open, and the reader sees Jerry. If at this point the reader has not been told the character's names, dialogue balloons ("Hi, Jerry" and "Hi, Joe") might be used.

Readers do not see Joe standing up, opening the door, or other interpanel actions but can figure it out by what they see in the next panel.

Now say the writer wants to have more on the page after this, and asks the artist to keep a six-panel page, but to show the previous scene in only four panels, or wants only a four-panel page. In this case, it might go like this:

PANEL ONE

Joe on his couch looking at the television, which is seen from the rear. Television sound effects if needed. Clock or caption telling the time. However, this time the picture shows more of the room, including the front door, from which there is a "Knock Knock" sound effect.

PANEL TWO

Joe is walking toward the door. This panel can be smaller than the first panel if the artist wishes to show more detail in panel one.

PANEL THREE

Joe is at the door with his hand on the knob.

PANEL FOUR

The door is open, and the reader sees Jerry. Dialogue if needed.

In this scenario, by combining two panels and eliminating another, the artist has been able to show basically the same action, and the reader has only to imagine what he or she had to in the six-panel page. It is all subject in action.

But what if the page itself has only a top and bottom panel, or if the writer wants the action to be shown in only two panels, with the other four on the page used to continue the story? The artist then might do something like this:

PANEL ONE

Joe on his couch looking at the television, which is seen from the rear. Television sound effects if needed. Clock or caption telling the time. However, this time the picture shows more of the room, including the front door, from which there is a "Knock Knock" sound effect.

PANEL TWO

The door is open, and the reader sees Jerry. Dialogue if needed.

The panel-to-panel transition is subject to subject. It's the same location, but panel one is Joe on the couch and the next panel is Jerry at the open door. The reader comprehends that in between the two panels, Joe got up, walked to the door, and opened it. The amount of space on the page can also affect how much information is shown. If it is only two panels on the entire page, much detail can be given in the first panel, and both characters can be seen in the second. If it is reduced to only one-third of the page, some details might be left out. If the time or the fact that Joe is watching television is not important, then it could be cut out. The room's design in panel one can also be changed so that, unless it contradicts what has previously been shown, the door can be seen behind where Joe is sitting. Panel two can also be changed so that only Jerry is seen, and if Joe has any dialogue it is coming from "offstage." The fact that readers have to use their imagination to understand what happens between panels can be used as a classroom activity.

In *Understanding Comics* (1994) and especially in *Making Comics* (2006), McCloud shows how artists use their drawings to convey information. For example, facial expressions can show the character's feelings. When, for example, we see Joe and Jerry in the last panel the expressions on their faces can tell a lot. Are they both looking happy? Does one look sad or mad? If so, why? This can be part of the story. What about Joe? Is he unhappy that Jerry is there? The look on his face might show this.

Of course being a comic book or graphic novel, it is not just the picture. How words are used also adds to the understanding of the story. McCloud lists several ways in which words and pictures can be combined:

- Word specific: "pictures illustrate, but don't significantly add to a largely complete text."
- Picture specific: words just add a "soundtrack."
- Duo specific: words and pictures say the same thing.
- Additive or intersecting: "words amplify or elaborate on an image or vice versa."
- Parallel combinations: words and pictures follow different courses without intersecting (dialogue in boxes has nothing to do with action; conversation from something else).
- Montage: words are treated as part of the picture.

- Interdependent: this is the most common kind, in which words and pictures go hand in hand and wouldn't work alone; however, the two are not always equally balanced. (McCloud, 1994: 152–155)[26]

Now you know what comics and graphic novels are, how they are created, and how to read them. In Chapter 2 you will learn more about their contents.

Notes

1. A look at Superman's home planet.
2. Superheroes from around the world must compete against one another.
3. King Arthur, Merlin, and the reincarnated Knights of the Round Table save earth from aliens in the year 3000.
4. See Appendix A.
5. See Appendix A.
6. An omnipotent being takes heroes and villains to another world and has them fight one another.
7. This 12-issue limited series changed the face of the DC Universe.
8. See Appendix A, under DC Archive Editions and Showcase Presents titles.
9. See Appendix A under Marvel Masterworks and Essential Marvel.
10. The origins and first appearances of Marvel Comics' heroes and villains, interspersed with newer stories.
11. A collection of comics from the 1940s and early 1950s.
12. All of the comics published by EC in the 1950s from the famous (*Tales from the Crypt*) to the lesser known (*Psychoanalysis*).
13. A large collection of the stories Barks did for Disney.
14. The Justice League fights supervillains in this limited series "painted" by Alex Ross.
15. The heroes of Marvel's *Ultimate* line (see Chapter 6) must stop an alien race from destroying the earth.
16. See Appendix A under Spider-Man.
17. See Appendix A under DC Archive Editions and Showcase Presents titles.
18. See Appendix A under Marvel Masterworks and Essential Marvel.
19. Following a disaster, the government wants all superheroes to register and work for them. This leads to a conflict between two groups of heroes—one led by Iron Man (for) and the other by Captain America (against). It and the series that it crossed over into (see Chapter 6) have all been collected.
20. In the near future, superhumans are out of control, and it is up to Superman, Batman, Wonder Woman, and the other "Old Guard" heroes to stop them.
21. When the world is thrown into chaos, the superheroes must set it right, even if it means taking over.
22. See Appendix A under Spider-Man.
23. See Appendix A.
24. Spider-Man battles one of his oldest foes.
25. See Appendix A under Spider-Man.
26. This is expanded on page 130 of *Writing Comics*.

References

Arnold, Andrew D. "A Graphic Literature Library." Time.com (November 21, 2003). Available: www.time.com/time/columnist/arnold/article/0,9565,547796,00.html. Accessed: June 27, 2006.

Byrne, John. "Tricks of the Trade" (January 7, 2004). Available: www.ugo.com/channels/comics/features/johnbyrne_imo/archive_01_07_04.asp.

de Vos, Gail. 2005. "ABCs of Graphic Novels." *Resource Links* 10, no. 3 (February). Available: www.resourcelinks.ca/features/feb05.htm.

Eisner, Will. 1985. *Comics & Sequential Art.* Tamarac, FL: Poorhouse Press.

Eisner, Will. 2004. "Keynote Address from the 2002 'Will Eisner Symposium.'" *ImageTexT: Interdisciplinary Comics Studies* 1, no. 1. Available: www.english.ufl/edu/imagetext/archives/v1_1/eisner/index.shtml. Accessed: July 25, 2006.

Gertler, Nat, and Steve Lieber. 2004. *The Complete Idiot's Guide to Creating a Graphic Novel.* New York: Alpha Books.

Goulart, Ron. 2004. *Comic Book Encyclopedia: The Ultimate Guide to Characters, Graphic Novels, Writers, and Artists in the Comic Book Universe.* New York: HarperCollins.

Hinze, Scott. "The Lowe-Down With Nick Lowe." Comic-Con International (November 6, 2005). Available: www.comicon.com/cgi-bin/ultimatebb.cgi?ubb=get_topic;f=36;t=004386.

Inge, M. Thomas. 1990. *Comics As Culture.* Jackson, MS: University Press of Mississippi.

Jones, Patrick, Michele Gorman, and Tricia Suellentrop. 2004. *Connecting Young Adults and Libraries*, 3rd ed. New York: Neal-Schuman.

Jones, Seth. 2006. "A Gallon of Gas or a Comic? How Rising Oil Prices Affect the Comic Industry." *The Comic Wire*, May 13. Available: www.comicbookresources.com/news/newsitem.cgi?id=7434.

Kavanagh, Barry. "The Alan Moore Interview." Blather.net (October 17, 2000). Available: www.blather.net/articles/amoore/northampton.html. Accessed: August 16, 2006.

M., Chris. "The Ebb and Flow of Traditional Superhero Serial Comics." Howling Curmudgeons. Available: www.whiterose.org/howlingcurmudgeons/archives/009843.html. Accessed: August 16, 2006.

MacDonald, Heidi. 2004. "Marvel Classics Coming in '05." *Publisher's Weekly*, December 20. Available: www.publishersweekly.com/article/CA488207.html. Accessed: July 11, 2006.

McCloud, Scott. 1994. *Understanding Comics.* New York: HarperPerennial.

McCloud, Scott. 2006. *Making Comics.* New York. HarperCollins.

Read, Calvin. 1990. "Picture This: Batman, Popular Syndicated Cartoons and Sophisticated Graphic Novels Have Paved the Way for the Comic's Success in All Markets." *Publisher's Weekly*, October 12, p. 17.

Russell, Michael. "History of Comic Books Part II." *Ezine Articles* (December 17, 2005). Available: http://ezinearticles.com/?History-of-Comic-Books—Part-II&id=114701. Accessed: July 28, 2007.

Chapter 2

Superheroes and Other Genres

As stated in the preface, if you take one thing away from reading this book, let it be that graphic novels are a format, not a genre. As with any other form of fiction, graphic novels come in all genres. Some of these genres are straightforward, while other titles are a combination of genres. After all, a book about a detective solving a crime is called a mystery, but what if that story takes place in the 1600s, the 2600s, or if the detective has magical powers? It would still be a mystery book, but it would also be in the genres of historical fiction, science fiction, or fantasy. For this chapter, the basic genre heading will do, starting with the best known.

Superheroes

Say the words "comic book" to anyone, and the odds are good that the image that comes to mind is of a superhero[1]—Superman, Batman, Spider-Man, or any of the others whose adventures have been thrilling readers for decades. They have been on television, in movie theaters, on posters, on toys, on postage stamps, and even on underwear. What defines a superhero? Wears a costume? Fights crime? Has a "secret identity"? Has powers "beyond those of mortal men?" Perhaps, though not all of those are necessary, especially the last one. Batman, who just has his brains, brawn, and gadgets, is a perfect example of this.

Who was the first superhero? That's also something that has been debated for years. Hercules from mythology and Samson from the Bible had super strength, Robin Hood had a secret identity of sorts, and Zorro, who first appeared in 1919, had a secret identity, a distinctive costume, a secret head-quarters, and fought injustice. Zorro was even one of the inspirations for Batman. The "dilettante" act that Don Diego De la Vega puts on when not Zorro, or for that matter the one put on by Sir Percy Blakeney aka the Scarlet Pimpernel (created in 1905), is similar to the one Bruce Wayne puts on when not Batman. The Zorro connection has been followed up in the Batman stories, as several versions of his origin have his parents killed by a mugger after the family was walking back from seeing a *Zorro* movie.

The earliest original (not from a literary or film source) masked hero was Centaur publication's The Clock, who debuted in 1936, either in *Funny Pages* #6 or *Funny Picture Stories* #1, both of which came out the same month. He had no powers, and former district attorney Brian O'Brien wore a three-piece suit and fedora instead of a colorful costume, but he did wear a black full-faced mask as well. Less than two years later a super-powered costume character made his debut, one who in the past 70 years has been the star of thousands of comic book stories, a number of books, a radio program, more than a dozen movies and television shows, and even a Broadway musical—Superman!

Created by Jerry Siegel and Joe Shuster, the Man of Steel was not exactly as he is today. He couldn't fly but instead could only leap one-eighth of a mile, and he wasn't as indestructible as he would later become. But his popularity quickly grew and the imitators soon came. Other costumed heroes soon popped up from different companies in the next two years, some with powers and some without—Batman, Green Lantern, Hawkman, Sub-Mariner, the Spirit, the Human Torch (who was actually an android), Amazing-Man, Blue Beetle, Doll Man, Sandman, Black Hood, Flash, and many more.

This era also saw the introduction of several "mainstays" in superhero comics. The first teen sidekick, Batman's partner Robin, debuted in 1940 and was soon followed by others, including the Sandman's partner Sandy, Green Arrow's sidekick Speedy, and Captain America's partner Bucky. In a reversal of circumstances, the adult Stripesy was the sidekick of the teenaged Star-Spangled Kid. The first superhero team, the Justice Society of America (JSA), also first appeared in 1940. Members included the original versions of the Flash, Green Lantern, the Atom, Dr. Fate, Hourman, and others, including part-time members Superman and Batman. The JSA is still around today with a mixture of old and new members, some the children of the originals. *Pep Comics* #17 in 1941 featured the death of the Comet, the first superhero to be killed. Twenty-five years later, the Comet returned from the grave, something else that has become common in superhero comics (see Exhibit 2-1).

The superhero craze ended by the late 1940s, with many superhero titles being cancelled or changed to non-superhero features. But with the start of the "Silver Age" in 1956 they once again became popular, with both new versions of old characters as well as brand new ones. Today, 50 years after the start of the Silver Age, they are still popular. Many characters from the Golden and Silver Ages are still around, and new heroes, some with the same names as older ones, are still being introduced.

Many superheroes, especially those in DC and Marvel Comics, live in a "shared universe." Superman may face one of Batman's villains, the Fantastic

---

Exhibit 2-1. Death and Superheroes

When he returned in the 1960s, The Comet revealed that he was not killed, but actually transported to another planet. This is an example of a basic rule in superhero comics, one that has been seen in everything from Sherlock Holmes to Soap Operas—if there's no body, then they are not dead. If there is a body, then there is only a 50-50 chance that they are permanently dead. It's been joked that Superhero Heaven has a revolving door in place of the pearly gates. Superman, Hawkeye, and Green Lantern, are among the many heroes who have come back to life. Even in the superhero world this is a given. When the girlfriend of Marvel character Rick Jones, sidekick to the Hulk and other heroes, was murdered, he went to magical superhero Dr. Strange for help, and when Dr. Strange said that he couldn't help, this conversation occurred:

> DR. STRANGE: Rick . . . I don't know how to break this to you, but if she's dead . . . then she's dead.
>
> RICK: Don't gimme that. People come back to the dead all the time. I mean . . . I've come back from the dead. I bet you have too! Admit it!
>
> STRANGE: Well . . . yes I have. But I am a professional.
>
> RICK (to Dr. Strange's assistant, Wong): How about you Wong? You ever die and come back?
>
> WONG: To be honest . . . yes.
>
> RICK: There! Three out of three people surveyed came back from the dead! So Marlo should be able to come back too!" (David, 1992: 11)

Although Dr. Strange still was unable to help her, Marlo later did come back from the dead and married Rick.

Four and the X-Men may team up, and so forth. This of course comes into play when you have story lines that continue in different titles and the "event" limited series mentioned in Chapter 1. When it comes to the passage of time, the actual calendar date does not matter. An Avengers adventure that was published in 1963 happened only a handful of years ago as far as the Team of 2008 is concerned. Of course this is not restricted to only superhero comics. Archie and his friends have gone from listening to Benny Goodman on a "78" to listening to Kelly Clarkson on iPods and have remained teenagers the whole time. For that matter, certain book series and television shows, such as *The Simpsons*, do something similar. No matter how many birthdays, holidays, etc., are shown, not much time has passed. This has also been referred to as a "sliding-scale timeline."

Comic book universes also tend to share a similar continuity. However, due to new stories or occurrences such as the passage of time, continuity has to be changed, and this is known among comics fans as a "retcon." Short for "retroactive continuity," a "retcon" (the term can be used as a verb—to "retcon" an event—and as an adjective—the story/character that was "retconned") can be done in several different ways. The most basic is the filling in of past information, such as a new story that took place early in an established character's career. Another is changing minor details of past stories to better fit modern times. In 1964 it was Lyndon Johnson who asked the Avengers for help, but if they are recounting that adventure in 2007, it was George W. Bush who contacted them. This has been done with other Marvel characters whose origins are linked to the Cold War, such as the Fantastic Four, who gained their powers when they went into space in order to "beat the Russians to the stars"; Bruce Banner, who became the Hulk when a Soviet double agent did not stop the "gamma bomb" from exploding when Banner was near it; and Tony Stark, who became Iron Man after being wounded by communists in Southeast Asia.

The most extreme sort of retcon is when a character is totally revamped, revised, or "reimagined." A major example of this happened in 1986 with DC's *Man of Steel*. Written and penciled by John Byrne, this limited series made many changes in Superman's history, powers, and supporting cast, with additional changes introduced in the regular *Superman* titles (see Exhibit 2-2). Of course, since the DC Universe shares continuity, changes in one character's history can then affect another's. The changes in Superman's history affected that of the Justice League and the Legion of Super-Heroes, and new stories had to be written to explain these new discrepancies.

Sometimes a retcon will undergo a retcon, with new changes superseding the old. The origin and history of the Legion has undergone several changes since the 1980s. Sometimes a writer will simply ignore a retcon and go back to an earlier continuity. Comic book writer Peter David calls this a "stetcon" (David, 2006: 112). For example, some of the pre–*Man of Steel* elements of Superman's history have returned in recent years. With the recent increase in collections of older stories, two books with contradictory continuities may be next to each other on the shelf. For that matter, in a "theme" trade that spans decades, not all of the stories in that volume will be part of the same exact continuity.

Superheroes also have a place in popular culture, especially when it comes to children. On Halloween many Supermen, Batmen, Spider-Men, and other heroes roam the streets. They are featured on children's T-shirts, sneakers, and backpacks. Besides movies based on comic book superheroes (discussed later in the book), the genre has created such films for children as *Sky High* (2005), *Zoom* (2006), *The Adventures of Shark Boy and Lava Girl* (2005), and *The Incredibles* (2004), and original television shows including *Mighty Morphin Power Rangers* and *The Powerpuff Girls*.

Many children's books also use the superhero theme. Probably the best-known chapter books are the *Captain Underpants* series by Dav Pilkey. Others include Greg Trine's *Melvin Beederman, Superhero* series, and Dan Danko's *Sidekicks* books. Some of the books for younger readers are *Superhero* by Marc Tauss, *Superdog: The Heart of a Hero* by Caralyn Buehner, *Noodle Man: The Pasta Superhero* by April Pulley Sayre, *SuperHero ABC* by comic artist Bob McLeod, and *Atomic Ace: (He's Just My Dad)* by Jeff Weigel.

Exhibit 2-2. Changes in Superman		
	Silver Age Superman	After *Man of Steel*
Home planet of Krypton	Amazing world of fantastic technology, Jewel Mountains and other natural wonders, and animals such as "Thought-Beasts."	Amazing technology, but cold and sterile.
Foster parents Ma and Pa Kent	Died when he was a teenager.	Still alive, and there to offer good advice.
Early life	Powers developed early. Fought crime as Superboy.	Powers gradually developed. Became Superman as an adult.
Powers	Extremely powerful. Could fly faster than light, did not need to eat, drink, or breathe. Had odd abilities such as "super-ventriloquism."	Still powerful, but his abilities were less "cosmic." No super-ventriloquism.
Relationship with other heroes	Best friends with Batman. Founding member of the Justice League.	Uneasy relationship with Batman. Did not join the League until later (this has been changed to how it once was).
Clark Kent	As Clark, he pretended to be weak and wimpy.	As Clark, he his hid abilities, but acted more "normal."
Lex Luthor	Criminal scientist who had hated Superman since they were teens.	Genius billionaire who used respectability to hide evil deeds. Hated Superman because he became more popular. Other villains also had their origins changed.

Something important that must be pointed out is that although many super-hero books are appropriate for children, this is not always the case. As will be discussed in Chapter 6, even books that feature Superman, Batman, and Spider-Man may have elements in their story lines that some parents would not want their younger children to read.

Even though superheroes are the best-known genre in American comics, they are far from the only ones. The following sections offer a brief look at some of the other genres of graphic novels.

Science Fiction and Fantasy

These genres have long been a part of comics. Notable historical titles include *Weird Science* and *Weird Fantasy* from EC Comics. *Amazing Adult Fantasy*, the last issue of which, as *Amazing Fantasy*, introduced Spider-Man; *Magnus Robot*

Fighter, which was set in the year 4000; *Elfquest*; the limited series *Camelot 3000*, which mixed both genres; and various comics based on Flash Gordon and Buck Rodgers. The latter two have previously appeared in books, comic strips, and movies, and other science fiction comic book series based on non-comics sources include the comics based on *Star Trek* and *Star Wars*. Super-hero comics have also incorporated science fiction and fantasy, with alien heroes (including Superman and the Martian Manhunter) and villains (the alien shape-changing Skrulls of Marvel Comics), magical heroes (Dr. Strange), and comics set in the future, most notably the *Legion of Super-Heroes*, which takes place 1,000 years in the future. Besides the *Star Wars* titles, other notable science fiction and fantasy titles listed in Appendix A include *Bone*; *The Dreamland Chronicles*; *Adventures in Oz*; *Jason and the Argobots*; *Lullaby*; *The Courageous Princess*; *Akiko*; *Castle Waiting*; *Once in a Blue Moon*; *Lions, Tigers, and Bears*; *Zapt!*; *Thieves and Kings*; *Vögelein*; and *Grease Monkey*.

Horror

Horror comics have been making a comeback, but unfortunately not many of them are child friendly. After the comics code helped get rid of such classics as *Tales from the Crypt* in the 1950s (see Chapter 9), horror comics didn't become big again until the 1970s. Perhaps reflecting a trend in movies, "zombie" comics have become popular recently, including the mature audience comic *Walking Dead*. Besides licensed works such as *Buffy, The Vampire Slayer*, books with vampires, again mainly for mature audiences, are also becoming popular. Some of Marvel's horror and superhero/horror books from the 1970s, including *Tomb of Dracula*, *Ghost Rider*, *Man-Thing*, and *Werewolf by Night*, have recently been collected in Essential editions, and *Tales from the Crypt* returned both as a new collection of the 1950s material, and as a new series from NBM/Paper-cutz. Also for younger ages are the *Goosebumps* graphic novels, based on the popular children's series, and the *Courtney Crumrin* series. Some of the titles with horror elements also fall in the "humor" category. Others include *Leave It to Chance*, and adaptations of classic horror stories by Mary Shelley, Bram Stoker, H.P. Lovecraft, Edgar Allan Poe, and other notable authors.

Juvenile

Some comics are definitely for kids, and many of these titles also fall into the humor genre. Over the years, children have read the adventures of Casper the Friendly Ghost, Richie Rich, and especially Archie Andrews and his friends from Riverdale, whose adventures are still being published. Archie first appeared in MLJ's *Pep Comics* #22 (May 1941). He got his own self-titled book the following year, and became such a popular character that in 1946 MLJ changed its name to Archie Comics Publications. Over the years many spin-offs have been published with both Archie and with the solo adventures of his friends, and some of the older stories can be found in the *Archie Americana* series of trades. Dark Horse Comics has also been putting out collections of *Little Lulu*, *Richie Rich*, *Casper*, and other classic children's comics. More recent comics and graphic novels aimed at younger ages are *Owly*, *Amelia Rules*, *Babymouse*, *Patrick the Wolf Boy*, and *Fashion Kitty*. Then there are, of course, the Disney comics. These will be discussed in the following section.

Licensed Properties and Adaptations

Although not exactly a genre, licensed properties have allowed comic books and graphic novels based on popular television, film, literary characters, characters from toys, and even real people to be published for decades. Even though many of these have been in the science fiction/fantasy/horror genre (*Buffy, The Vampire Slayer*; *Star Trek*; *Star Wars*), action, mystery, Westerns, animated series, and even sitcoms have been made into comic books. These are generally not considered to be part of the official continuity of the shows/movies, but these comic book stories can outlive the source material.

Since they are basically rented, licensed properties can jump from publisher to publisher. Comics based the on the various *Star Trek* series, for example, been published by several companies including Gold Key, DC, Marvel, and IDW, and even Tokyopop has put out a version drawn in a manga style. Sometimes shows with spin-offs will have one show licensed by one publisher, while comics based on the spin-off are produced by another. For example, in 2007, Dark Horse was producing a *Buffy* comic book, while IDW was simultaneously publishing limited series based on its spin-off, *Angel*. Licensed characters can even interact with established characters from the licensee as well as other companies. The X-Men have met the crew of the Starship Enterprise, and, long before they fought each other in the movies, the Aliens and the Predators battled Superman and Batman.

Many popular animated characters have found their way into comic books. Animated television programs ranging from *The Flintstones* to *The Simpsons* have been turned into comics, and, in an interesting situation, animated series based on comic books have in turn inspired comic books based on the animated program (these include the recent *Batman, Teen Titans, Legion*, and *Justice League* cartoons). While comic strip reprints had appeared in magazines as early as 1933, Disney characters first appeared in comic book form in *Four Color* #4 (Dell, February 1940), with reprints of the *Donald Duck* comic strip, and later that year *Walt Disney's Comics and Stories* began, first with more comic strip reprints, but eventually with original stories and spin-off comics, including *Mickey Mouse, Donald Duck*, and *Uncle Scrooge*. In recent years, Gemstone Publishing has been producing comics with Disney characters. This includes *Walt Disney's Comics and Stories*, which has changed publishers over the years but has still kept its original numbering, is available in prestige format. The Disney Press collects comics published in the *Disney Adventures* magazine as well as Junior Graphic Novels, with books based on *Finding Nemo* and other Disney works.

At the same time that Dell was publishing the adventures of Mickey and Donald, they were also publishing comic books with Bugs Bunny, Daffy Duck, and the rest of Warner Brothers' classic characters, starting in 1941 with *Looney Tunes and Merrie Melodies Comics* #1. As with the Disney characters, the Warner's characters also had their own books published by Dell and its successors. Since Warner Brothers and DC Comics are currently both part of Time-Warner, comic books and graphic novels featuring the Looney Tunes characters are now published by DC as part of their Johnny DC kids line (and Bugs Bunny has even teamed up with Superman). This line also puts out *Batman Strikes!* and the other books based on DC character cartoons, as well as *Scooby Doo* and characters featured on the Cartoon Network.

Literary adaptations have long been a part of comics, both with classic works in the public domain and with newer books. The best known of these was *Classics Illustrated*. Originally called *Classic Comics*, it was created in 1941 by Albert Kanter in response to complaints in editorials and by parent-teacher groups that comics, especially the horror and "blood and thunder" types, were having a "terrible effect" on juvenile minds. The first adaptation was of *The Three Musketeers*, which had an initial print run of 200,000 copies, less than most other titles at the time. The early art and writing weren't the best, but they soon caught on. Comics historian Ron Goulart credits the comic's popularity in part to children who used them in order to write their book reports. The book's quality soon improved once more professional comic writers and artists began to work on it, and, since, unlike other publishers, it constantly kept its issues in print, sales were very good, with its first 28 issues selling more than 100 million copies by 1946. The title changed to *Classics Illustrated* in 1947 and stayed that way until its cancellation in 1962. It had its competitors and imitators, and many attempts to revive it have been made, including a period from 1989–1991 when a new series was created in bookshelf/prestige format and was sold in both comic shops and bookstores (Goulart, 2004: 89-90). Due to their format, issues of this series found their way into libraries. In 2007, a new version of *Classics Illustrated* was begun by NBM/Papercutz, starting with an adaptation of *The Wind in the Willows*.

Many more literary adaptations are being produced, and in the case of titles in the public domain, some graphic novel versions are being put out by more than one publisher. For example, several adaptations of *The Wizard of Oz* came out between 2005 and 2006. A new "graphic classics" publisher has been putting out graphic novels that adapt both short stories and novellas from writers such as Edgar Allan Poe, Robert Louis Stevenson, H.P. Lovecraft, and Mark Twain, though some of these are intended for older readers. Penguin's Puffin children's line has produced a series of Puffin Graphics, adapting classic stories, and another Penguin imprint has adapted Anthony Horowitz's *Stormbreaker*. Scholastic's Graphix line is publishing books adapting the *Baby-sitter's Club* and *Goosebumps* series, while Hyperion Press has adapted Eoin Colfer's *Artemis Fowl*. Marvel Comics also has several limited series (later collected) that adapt both classic stories (*Treasure Island, Last of the Mohicans*) and modern novels by "adult" writers. Several publishers of nonfiction graphic novels are also including publishing book series with very condensed versions of classic stories. Original stories with literary characters are also being done by publishers such as Papercutz, which produces graphic novels featuring the Hardy Boys and Nancy Drew.

Many other fiction genres have a long tradition in comics, but many of the modern titles in those genres are not fully appropriate for children and tweens. Other genres, such as humor, can also be placed in one of the previous genres (see Exhibit 2-3). Particular graphic novels in the action/adventures, war, Western, mystery, romance, religious, and other genres will be discussed elsewhere in this book, and are listed in Appendix A. Some of the genres that are found in manga and in foreign publications will be discussed in the next chapter.

Nonfiction

Nonfiction comic books have been around for more than 60 years, with 1940s titles that included *Picture Stories from American History*, *Picture Stories from Science*, and *True Comics*. These comics covered both historical and contemporary biographies, history, science, and current events. In recent years there has been a rise in nonfiction graphic novels, often from non–comic book publishers.

Graphic novels that are autobiographical, or at least semiautobiographical, have become very popular, though they have mainly been for teen and adult audiences. Many of Will Eisner's stories have some element of biography in them, especially *The Dreamer*, and other notable mature titles that are either

---

Exhibit 2-3. Examples of the Humor Genre

Humor/Superhero: *Plastic Man, Showcase Presents Captain Carrot*
Humor/Science Fiction & Fantasy: *Bone, Pinky and Stinky, Sardine in Outer Space*
Humor/Horror: *Death Jr., Grumpy Old Monsters*
Humor/Juvenile: *Babymouse, Fashion Kitty*
Humor/Adapted or Licensed Work: *Harvey Comics Presents, Simpsons*
Note: See the listing in Appendix A for more information.

autobiographical or have a autobiographical feel to them include *Perseoplis*, *Blankets*, Harvey Pekar's *American Splendor* stories, *Pedro and Me*, and *Fun Home*. At the moment, very few graphic novel autobiographies are aimed at children. One of the few is *To Dance: A Memoir* by Siena Cherson Siegel, in which she tells how she became a ballet dancer.

Although most autobiographies are for adults, the vast majority of "graphic biographies" are aimed at elementary-school-aged children. Capstone, Abdo, Rosen, and Gareth Stevens are among the publishers to create graphic biography lines in their graphic nonfiction series. Digital Manga Publishing has brought from Japan a series of "edu-manga" biographies, and Tokyopop has a series of "cine-manga" about NBA players. Several other "mainstream" publishers have published the occasional graphic biography, including Papercutz's *The Life of Pope John Paul II . . . In Comics* (2006). This was actually the late Pope's second graphic biography, the first being a comic book put out by Marvel comics in 1982.

Along with the graphic biographies, new series of graphic nonfiction are being produced, and more and more publishers of nonfiction are creating their own graphic nonfiction lines. These books are aimed for an elementary school/early middle school age, and are sometimes written or drawn by people in the comics industry. History, mythology, and science are among the graphic nonfiction subjects available (see Exhibit 2-4 for more information). Some nonfiction works have come out from comic book companies as well. Writer/artist Jay Hosler has written about bees (*Clan Apis*) and evolution (*The Sandwalk Adventures*), while Jim Ottaviani writes graphic novels about science and scientists (*Dignifying Science*, *Two Fisted Science*).

Diversity in Comic Books

Although the majority of the well-known comic book characters are white males, many notable exceptions exist.

Female Characters in Comics

Many significant female comic book characters have been created over the past 70 years. Some have been main characters, while others were, at least early on, only supporting characters and crime-fighting partners. Some were created for "boys' comics," some for "girls' comics," and some were enjoyed by both. Some were drawn "cute," while others were drawn in a more "cheesecake" style (depending on the type, it has been called "good girl" or "bad girl" art).

In the world of superhero comics, they have had to put up with some degree of sexism. The adult sidekicks of Hawkman and Bulletman were called Hawkgirl and Bulletgirl (Supergirl and Batgirl were, at least, teenagers when they started). In the 1940s, Wonder Woman, despite being able to defeat half of

Exhibit 2-4. Graphic Nonfiction

The following are some of the graphic nonfiction published and their series. See Appendix A for more information.

Abdo Publishing Magic Wagon Graphic Planet
    Bio-Graphics
    Graphic History

Capstone Graphic Library
    Disasters in History
    Graphic Biographies
    Graphic History
    Graphic Science
    Inventions and Discovery

Gareth Stevens Publishing Graphic Nonfiction
    Graphic Biographies
    Graphic Histories
    Graphic Greek Myths
      and Legends

Lerner Graphic Universe
    Myths and Legends

Osprey Graphic History
    Civil War and WWII Battles*

Rosen Publishing
    Graphic Battles of World War II
    Graphic Biographies
    Graphic Civil War Battles*
    Graphic Mysteries
    Graphic Mythology
    Graphic Natural Disasters
    Graphic Nonfiction Biographies
    Jr. Graphic Biographies
    Jr. Graphic Mysteries
    Jr. Graphic Mythologies

School Specialty Publishing
    Stories from History

* Through an agreement between the publishers, Osprey's books on the Civil War and World War II have the same content as those by Rosen.

Justice Society single-handedly, was the team's secretary. Feminism had not yet reached the thirtieth century in a Legion of Super-Heroes story in *Adventure Comics* #309 (June 1963), in which alien supergenius Brainiac 5, while choosing members for a mission, said, "We'll draw lots for the job . . . excluding Saturn Girl because it's too risky a mission for a girl." However, the following year, in issue #319 (April 1964), Saturn Girl, who was a founding member of the team and in both issues the team's *leader*, stood up for herself, saying, "I was selected by fair chance and I claim my right to go" (Hamilton 1963, 1964).

The portrayal of women in comics today is an issue that has been discussed among readers and comic scholars. Some feel that too many female characters in superhero comics are drawn with overdeveloped bodies and sometimes scantily clad costumes. There has also been some controversy over whether or not a disproportionate amount of bad things happen to female characters in superhero comics compared to their male counterparts. Information on some of the female characters in comics today—not just in superhero genre—is listed in Exhibit 2-5.

Exhibit 2-5. Popular Female Characters

Amelia McBride
Fourth-grader Amelia Louise McBride lives with her recently divorced mother and her aunt, and has adventures with her friends in the wonderful independent comic *Amelia Rules*.

Barbara Gordon
As a teenager, Barbara Gordon became Batgirl, helping the dynamic duo fight crime. She continued as Batgirl into adulthood, and even became a librarian. Shortly after retiring, she was crippled by the Joker. However, she used her great intelligence and library research skills to become Oracle, provider of information to the Justice League and other heroes. She also became the leader of the female crime fighters known as the Birds of Prey.

Betty and Veronica
Both introduced in the early 1940s, wholesome Betty Cooper and wealthy Veronica Lodge have long been rivals for the affections of Archie Andrews. Besides sharing Archie's book, they have shared a title and starred in comic books of their own.

Black Canary
Following in the footsteps of her mother, The Golden Age Black Canary, Dinah Drake Lance has used her detective skills, martial arts skills, and "sonic scream" to battle evil solo, as a member of the Justice League, as partner (and girlfriend) of Green Arrow, and as, with Oracle, a founder of the Birds of Prey.

The Invisible Woman
When she first got her powers in Fantastic Four #1, Susan Storm, the Invisible Girl, could only turn invisible. Soon her powers grew and she became the equal, if not superior, of her teammates. Over the past 45 years, she's been a wife, a mother, and one of the preeminent superheroes—male or female—in the Marvel Universe. A younger version of the Invisible Woman also appears in Marvel's "Ultimate" line, in which, besides being powerful, she is also a genius.

Jean Grey
A founding member of the X-Men, Jean, who has been known as Marvel Girl and Phoenix, has used her mental abilities to save the world. Although she is currently dead in the X-Men comics, it is not the first time. Jean is also a character in the Ultimate Universe and has appeared in both the animated television series and the feature films.

Kitty Pride
Also known as Shadowcat, this mutant with the power of intangibility joined the X-Men at the age of 13½. She is also a character in the Ultimate Universe, where she is the girlfriend of Spider-Man.

Lois Lane
Introduced in the same comic book issue as Superman, the *Daily Planet*'s star reporter has long been a part of his life, both as someone to rescue, someone trying to figure out his secret identity, and as a girlfriend (and was the star of her own comic book, *Superman's Girlfriend Lois Lane*). The revised version of Lois ended up falling in love with Clark Kent, and became engaged to him before she ever knew that he was Superman. The pair has now been married for years.

Raven
Introduced as one of the "new" Teen Titans in 1980, this mystical empath has been a member (and an occasional villain and also dead) on-and-off for many years. She is also a major character on the Teen Titans animated series and its comic book version *Teen Titans Go!*

(Cont'd.)

Exhibit 2-5. Popular Female Characters *(Continued)*

She-Hulk

When attorney Jennifer Walters was seriously injured, her only hope was a blood transfusion from her cousin Bruce Banner, aka the Incredible Hulk. Although the transfusion allowed her to become large and green with super-strength, She-Hulk, unlike her cousin, retains her intelligence. Often preferring to stay in her super-powered form, She-Hulk has starred in her own title several times, has been a member of the Fantastic Four and the Avengers, and has worked in the "only in the comics" field of "Superhuman Law."

Spider-Girl

In a possible future of the Marvel Universe, May "Mayday" Parker is the teenage daughter of Peter Parker, the retired Spider-Man, and his wife Mary Jane. When powers similar to that of her father began to develop, May decided to follow in her father's footsteps. Popular with the fans, Spider-Girl's comic book was saved from cancellation several times, and when it finally ended at issue #100, to restart again a few months later, it was the highest numbered Marvel comic book with a female lead.

Starfire

Introduced in the same comic book story as Raven, Starfire is an alien warrior princess who has been a member of several incarnations of the Teen Titans, and also appears in the cartoon and related comic.

Supergirl

The "classic" version of Supergirl, introduced in 1959, was Kara Zor-El, Superman's younger cousin who had lived on a piece of Krypton that had survived the planet's destruction but now was also doomed. At first she acted as Superman's secret weapon while he trained her, but her existence was eventually revealed, and she fought evil solo, with her cousin, and even with the Legion of Super-Heroes in the future. This version was killed in 1985, and "retconned" out of existence the next year. Other versions were introduced, and one had her own title, but they too have been retconned away. The newest version of Supergirl was introduced in 2004, with a history very similar to the original.

Wonder Woman

The archetypical female superhero, Wonder Woman, aka Princess Diana of the Amazons, has been around in several incarnations since 1941. Though elements of her history, abilities, and paraphernalia have changed over the years, she is still the biggest female hero in the DC Universe, and has starred in her own book (though in three different series) since 1942. The current version appears both in her own book and in *Justice League* of America.

Non-Caucasian characters have not always been portrayed properly in comics. Unfortunately, racial stereotypes were once prevalent. This can be seen in some of the reprints of 1940s comic books. In several of the *DC Archive Editions* that reprint stories from the 1930s and 1940s, there is a note on the table of contents that reads: "The comics reprinted in this volume were produced in a time when racism played a larger role in society both consciously and unconsciously. They are reprinted without alteration for historical reference." The situation has improved over the years, but non-Caucasian characters are still underrepresented in comics (DC Comics, 2005).

Black Characters in Comics

Early black characters were stereotypical, with physical characteristics that were common in drawings of the time and the speech patterns often heard in radio programs and films. Some of these characters had their own strips in anthology titles, such as Sam the Porter, who was introduced in 1936. Others were sidekicks or supporting characters, including the Spirit's sidekick Ebony White and Whitewash Jones of the Young Allies, who, while helping heroes, were also used as comic relief.

In 1947, a one-shot comic called *All-Negro Comics* came out and introduced what was technically the first black superhero—Lion Man. Lion Man was a young African scientist sent by the United Nations to oversee a massive uranium deposit at the African Gold Coast. Along with Bubba, a young war orphan, he fights the evil Doctor Blut Sangro (List of Black Superheroes, 2008). Other African-American themed comics at the time included *Negro Heroes* (1947–1948), which spotlighted people such as Jackie Robinson, and *Negro Romance* (1950).

Things had improved by the 1960s. Despite that the United States Army was segregated during World War II, both DC and Marvel have had war books set in that period with African-American soldiers who were not stereotypes (Jackie Johnson in DC's Sgt. Rock and Easy Company stories and Gabe Jones in Marvel's Sgt. Fury and his Howling Commandos). In 1965, the first issue of *Lobo*, a Western comic book with an African-American protagonist, was published by Dell. Although his comic lasted for only one more issue, Lobo was the first African-American character to star in his own, self-titled book.

Marvel introduced the first modern-day black superhero, the Black Panther, in 1966, and the first African-American superhero, the Falcon, in 1969. Both heroes eventually joined the superhero team the Avengers. In 1972, Marvel's Luke Cage, who later took the name Power Man and was in part inspired by the blaxploitation films of the time, became the first African-American hero with his own comic book, and in 1975, Storm of the X-Men became the first black heroine.

DC's first African-American hero was, at the time, only a temporary hero. John Stewart was introduced in 1971 as a "backup" for the "regular" Green Lantern, Hal Jordan. In 1977, Black Lightning became their first African-American hero with his own title. More characters have been introduced over the years from many comic companies (see Exhibit 2-6), a few who have had their own titles, and others who have been in the forefront of team books, occasionally even as team leader. Between 1993–1997, DC published books from Milestone Media, which featured many African-American and other minority characters.

Asian Characters

Asian characters in American comics also have had to escape stereotypes, both visual and cultural. During World War II, Japanese characters sometimes took

Exhibit 2-6. Black Characters in Comics

The following are some of the more significant black comic book characters still seen in comics.

Black Lightning
Olympic gold medalist turned teacher Jefferson Pierce first put became Black Lightning to help those in the "Suicide Slum" area of Metropolis, but later battled global threats as a member of the Outsiders and the Justice League. His daughters are the superheroines Thunder and Lightning.

Black Panther
Introduced in 1966, he is T'Challa, ruler of the African Country of Wakanda, a country that mixes ancient tradition with advanced technology. The Black Panther is a master fighter and athlete and has enhanced senses along with his scientific knowledge and gadgets. Besides being the first black member of the Avengers, he has starred in several incarnations of his own title. In 2006 he married Storm of the X-Men. The Black Panther was created before the organization of the same name, and for a brief time he went by the name "Black Leopard" to avoid confusion.

Chuck Clayton
The son of Riverdale High School's Coach Clayton, Chuck, who was introduced in 1974, hangs out with Archie Andrews and his friends and has dreams of becoming a comic book artist.

Cyborg
Half man, half machine, Victor Stone brought both strength and technical knowledge to the Teen Titans when he joined them in 1980. Today he serves as mentor to the next generation of teen heroes. Cyborg is also one of the main characters on the animated Teen Titans series and its comic book counterpart *Teen Titans Go!*

The Falcon
The first African-American superhero, Sam Wilson was first recruited by the villainous Red Skull to use against Captain America, but he instead helped to defeat the Skull, and soon became Captain America's partner. The Falcon was briefly brought onto the Avengers (as a result of a government-ordered quota), and although he soon left, he still occasionally aids the team. Many of the Falcon's 1970s adventures with Captain America have been reprinted.

John Stewart
When he first appeared in 1971, architect John Stewart was chosen to be a "backup" for regular Green Lantern, Hal Jordan, filling in for him every now and then. When Jordan quit for a while in the 1980s, Stewart became a fulltime Green Lantern, and has continued in that role even after Jordan's return. When the Justice League cartoon began in 2001, it was the Stewart Green Lantern who they chose to use.

Joseph "Robbie" Robertson
"Robbie" Robertson was introduced as a supporting character in the Spider-Man titles in 1967. As editor in chief of the Daily Bugle, he is a friend to Peter Parker, and is much friendlier to Peter's alter-ego Spider-Man than is the paper's publisher, J. Jonah Jameson. His son, Randy, is a friend of Peter's as well.

Luke Cage
Wrongly convicted and sent to prison, an experiment gave Cage super-strength and titanium-hard skin. He set up an office in Times Square and became a "Hero For Hire." He later took the name Power Man, and later teamed up with martial arts hero Iron Fist.

(Cont'd.)

Exhibit 2-6. Black Characters in Comics *(Continued)*

Luke Cage *(Cont'd.)*
Recently, he married superhero-turned-private-investigator Jessica Jones, had a child, and became a member of the Avengers.

Mr. Terrific
Taking his name from a Golden Age superhero, Michael Holt has used his incredible intelligence and skills to fight crime as a member of both the Justice Society (of which he was chairman) and the spy agency Checkmate. He is considered to be the third smartest person in the DC Universe.

Spawn
Before he came back from hell as an undead HellSpawn, Al Simmons, introduced in 1992 as one of the earliest, and now one of the oldest, Image Comics characters, was an African-American CIA agent killed while trying to expose corruption. Spawn is one of the most popular characters to come out of Image, and was the star of both and animated series and a 1997 feature film, as well as a series of action figures. The first issue of *Spawn* holds the record for bestselling independent comic books issue.

Static
Perhaps the best known of the Milestone characters, teenager Virgil Ovid Hawkins was given electrical powers after being exposed to an experimental chemical, and must balance the life of a teenager with the life of a superhero. Static was the star of animated Saturday morning cartoon *Static Shock* (2000–2004, WB).

Steel
After Superman "died" in 1993, scientist John Henry Irons created an armored suit to help him carry the fight in Superman's name. After Superman's return, he aided the Man of Steel, joined the Justice League, and continued his solo adventures. He has appeared both in animated form and in a 1997 film in which he was played by basketball star Shaquille O'Neal.

Storm
Ororo Munroe was introduced in 1975 as part of a new X-Men team that included a Russian, a German, and a Native American. Storm was born in Harlem to an American father and a Kenyan mother and was orphaned at a young age. First becoming a street thief in Cairo, she later went into the Serengeti, where her mutant weather-controlling powers led to the natives worshiping her as a goddess. Storm later became one of the X-Men's leaders and best known characters. She married the Black Panther in 2006, and the story of a childhood meeting between the two was told in a limited series by author Eric Jerome Dickey.

Vixen
African-born Mari Jiwe McCabe uses the Tantu Totem to give her animal-like powers. She is the first full-time black member of the Justice League, and made several appearances in the animated series.

Additional information on black characters in comics can be found at the Museum of Black Superheroes Web site at www.blacksuperhero.com.

---

on an almost demonic appearance. Even heroic characters, such as the Crimson Avenger's sidekick Wing or "Chop-Chop" of the paramilitary World War II group the Blackhawks (both of whom were Chinese), were shown with exaggerated features and speaking in "pidgin" English, with "r" being substituted for "I" (see Exhibit 2-7). Although they are not stereotyped in the manner today, many Asian characters' powers, gimmicks, or abilities are based on being a ninja, wielding a sword, or being proficient in martial arts. Some of the more notable recent Asian characters in American comics include new Batgirl, Cassandra Cain, Jubilee of the X-Men, Katana of the Outsiders, and Ryan Choi the newest version of the Atom.

Other Ethnicities

Characters in comic books, especially superhero comics, are becoming more diverse, and are also moving toward escaping the stereotypes of the past. Hispanic characters in recent comics include Fire, the new Blue Beetle, Arana, the new White Tiger, Rictor, and a future version of Spider-Man. Many of the major Native American characters in comics have come from Marvel's *X-Men* and its spin-offs, including Warpath (Apache), Mirage (Cheyenne), Shaman (Sacree), and Forge (Cheyenne). Some stereotyping still exists in that many of these characters, as well as other Native American characters, have ties to "Indian Mysticism." The X-Books also feature one of the more prominent Middle-Eastern characters in comics, Dust. Part of the "New X-Men," the X-Men in training, Dust is a Sunni Muslim teen from Afghanistan, who, even when fighting evil, chooses to cover her hair and face with a *niqub*.

Religious Diversity

Besides Dust, there is some religious diversity in comics. Although a large number of characters are assumed to be Christians, they generally tend to to show it only around the holidays. Characters whose religion has been part of their characterization includes Kitty Pryde, who often wears a Star of David;

Exhibit 2-7. Chop-Chop

While the other members of the Blackhawks were from foreign countries, their ethnicities were at best shown only in their dialogue. In the comics of the 1940s, Chop-Chop was drawn as having yellow skin, big ears, a pigtail, large teeth, odd clothes (the others wore uniforms), and a generally comical appearance, all befitting his actions, which were mainly comic relief. His dialogue, when he was not cursing or speaking Chinese, went something like this:

> You oughta be ashlame! Amelica . . . only countly in world were man can live like hooman-Being-is thleatened!! Okey-Dokey . . . you talk! Me ploud to help Amelica!! Chop-Chop go to fight!! Goom-bye!!! (French, 1942: 133)

Chop-Chop was eventually portrayed in a "normal" manner and was shown as an equal to other team members. In the first issue of the 1989 *Blackhawk* comic book, which took place after the war, Chop-Chop, going by his real name of Weng Chan, sees a comic book version of the Blackhawk adventures (which is of course the actual comic of the time) and is understandably upset about his portrayal.

Nightcrawler, also of the X-Men teams, who, despite looking like a demon, is a fervent Catholic who at one point was attempting to join the priesthood; and Connor Hawke, the second Green Arrow and son of the original, who is Buddhist. Religion is also featured in nonsuperhero comics, including the Christian-themed series *Serenity*. Even the gang from Archie Comics appeared in a series of Christian-themed comics from Spire Publishing, though these have not been collected.[2]

Sexuality

In 1992, Northstar, a member of Marvel's Canadian superhero team Alpha Flight, revealed that he was homosexual. He was the first mainstream comics character to do so, and this garnered some publicity in the mainstream press. Other gay, lesbian, and bisexual characters in comics read by tweens and teens include Hulkling and Wiccan, members of the Young Avengers who are in a relationship together; Karolina Dean, a character in *Runaways*; and the new Batwoman, whose introduction also garnered media attention.

This chapter has shown that fiction graphic novels come in as many genres as any other works of fiction in a library, and that the nonfiction fiction titles can be spread throughout the section. Ideas on selecting, cataloging, shelving, and using both graphic fiction and nonfiction titles are found later in the book.

Notes

1. This term can be written as "super-hero" or "superhero." DC Comics and Marvel Comics jointly own the trademark for the term, at least as it applies to the title of any publications or merchandising.

2. Information on other Christian-themed comics can be found at www.christian comicsinternational.org.

References

David, Peter. 1992. "A Convocation of Politic Worms." *Incredible Hulk* 399 (November): 11.

David, Peter. 2006. *Writing Comics with Peter David*. Cincinnati, OH: Impact Books.

DC Comics. 2005. *The Seven Soldiers of Victory Archives*. New York: DC Comics.

Goulart, Ron. 2004. *Comic Book Encyclopedia: The Ultimate Guide to Characters, Graphic Novels, Writers, and Artists in the Comic Book Universe*. New York : HarperCollins.

Hamilton, Edmond. 1963. "The Legion of Super-Monsters!" *Adventure Comics* 309, June 1963. Reprinted 2007 in *Showcase Presents: Legion of Superheroes* 1: 309.

Hamilton, Edmond. 1964. "The Legion's Suicide Squad." *Adventure Comics* 319, April. Reprinted in *Showcase Presents: Legion of Superheroes* 1: 494.

List of Black Superheroes. Answers.com (January 12, 2008). Available: www.answers .com/topic/list-of-black-superheroes.

Chapter 3

Manga and
Other Foreign Works

The United States is not the only place where comic books and graphic novels are popular. In fact, in many countries comics have long had the respectability that they are only now beginning to receive in America. Foreign comic books and graphic novels have also appeared in America for decades both in their original language and, when applicable, translated.

Manga

The type of foreign comic that has gained the most popularity in the United States is manga, which not only generates high levels of sales but has also influenced American comic art styles as well. In other chapters of this book, manga titles will fall under the umbrella term of "graphic novel," as do original graphic novels and trade editions. In addition, although "true" manga is from Japan, the word "manga" will be used to describe not only Japanese comics but also similar books from China, South Korea, and the non-Asian countries discussed later in this chapter.

The word "manga" (pronounced mahn-gagh) comes from the Chinese ideograms "man" meaning involuntary and "ga" meaning picture (Gravett, 2004: 9) (though other sources translate manga as "crazy drawings," "irresponsible pictures," and "whimsical pictures") and can refer to caricatures, cartoons, comic strips, or comic books.

History

As in other parts of the world, the use of art to tell stories in Japan dates back untold centuries. During the Edo period (1600–1867), there was an increase in comic pictures, though the government did restrict some satirical works. It was in 1814 when Hokusai published the first of the 15-volume *Hokusai Manga*, a collection of drawings of various, and often unrelated, subjects. The opening of Japan to the West in the 1800s also brought with it

Western-style cartooning, which influenced native artists. But it was in the post–World War II era, when Japan was rebuilding, that manga as we know it today began.

One of the first superstars in this field was a 19-year-old medical student named Osamu Tezuka, who in 1947 created *Shin Takarajima (New Treasure Island)*. Inspired by the classic Robert Lewis Stevenson work, this was actually Tezuka's second work, but it was the one that made him famous, selling more than 400,000 copies. Over the next five years, Tezuka's other manga creations included *Metropolis*, *Tetsuwan ATOM (Astro Boy)*, and *Jungle Taitei (Jungle Emperor)*, better known in America as *Kimba, the White Lion*. All three of these have appeared as anime (animated films or television series), a field in which Tezuka was also a pioneer. He has been referred to as "the father of manga," the "god of manga," and for his anime work, "the Walt Disney of Japan." Other creators soon joined Tezuka, and manga grew in popularity. At first it was created primarily for children, but it soon attracted an older audience. To further attract these readers, a darker style of stories (known as gekiga or "dramatic pictures") began to appear.

Manga's popularity grew even more over the next several decades, and in Japan manga is currently a multibillon dollar industry. In 2006, sales were roughly $3.9 billion ("2006 Japanese Manga Market Drops," 2007), and sales of individual titles—about 300 different titles each month—are roughly equivalent to those of such major American magazines as *Time* and *Newsweek*. Close to 40 percent of all material printed in Japan are manga magazines and books, and manga magazines account for one-sixth of the Japanese magazine industry (Brenner, 2007: 13).

Manga is popular with both sexes and all ages. It is estimated that in Japan, two-thirds of all boys and more than one-sixth of girls ages five to eighteen read manga (Aoyama and Izushi, 2004: 121). It is not uncommon to see adult businessmen reading manga as thick as phonebooks on the train. Many of these "phonebook" magazines, such as *Shonen Jump* and *Shojo Beat*, have squared, glued backs, have between 250 and 400 pages, can contain up to 15 serialized stories, are usually in black and white, and come out on a monthly or weekly basis. In the same way that issues of a comic book are collected in a trade edition, chapters of a serialized story are collected in a book called a "tankōbon." Whereas the stories in the magazines are printed on cheap paper, the paper quality in the tankōbon is much sturdier. Some manga are sold in vending machines, and in cafés called "manga kissa," people pay (usually around 400 yen [$3.00] per hour) to sit and read titles from a manga library. Some cafés also offer food, drink, video games, Internet access, and even a place to sleep.

Genres

Manga comes in many different genres (see Exhibit 3.1), though the superhero genre does not dominate as it does in America, and is in fact relatively rare. The age level for manga runs from all ages to adults only. Although many titles fall into the science fiction and fantasy genres, many popular titles are similar to sitcoms, dramas (including teen dramas), or elements of everyday life. Plotlines of some well-known titles—appropriate for a variety of ages—include the following:

- After falling into a cursed spring, a boy turns into a girl whenever splashed with cold water (*Ranma 1/2*)

Exhibit 3-1. Manga Terms

Shōnen (or shounen): Manga aimed at six- to eighteen-year-old boys. Plots include fighting for justice, winning the girl, or achieving a goal despite problems. Examples include *Dragon Ball Z, Ranma 1/2, Eyeshield 21, Hikaru no Go, Naruto, Whistle!*, and *Zach Bell*. Around 39 percent of the manga magazines in Japan are shōnen.

Shōjo (or Shoujo): Manga written for girls, especially for girls under twelve. Characteristics include a focus on relationships (though not always romantic ones), and the stories are often more complex with more character interaction. They do, however, also often have stories containing action. Shōjo titles, such as *Marmalade Boy* and *Peach Girl* are very popular in the United States. Many boys read shōjo titles, just as many girls read shōnen manga. It is shōnen and shōjo titles that you will be purchasing for your library. Shōjo accounts for about 9 percent of Japanese manga magazines.

Terms for books that you should not buy for a children or tween audience:

Seinen and Josei: These types of manga are aimed at a late teen or adult audience. The violence is more explicit, there is more sensual content, and the women have a more "sexualized" appearance. The stories often have adults dealing with adult concerns. These manga make up about 44 percent of the magazines.

Shōnen-ai and Yaoi: Both deal with love between two male characters. In shōnen-ai ("boys love" or "BL") the attraction is more romantic, while yaoi is more sexually explicit. These titles have a strong following among female readers. Shōjo-ai and yuri are the female equivalent.

Hentai: Manga with explicitly sexual and/or pornographic imagery. Definitely on the "do not buy for a juvenile collection" list (and probably on the "do not buy for the adult collection" list as well).

Other terms:

Manga-ka: A creator of manga. Some manga titles are credited not to an individual writer or artist but to artistic teams. The most popular of these is Clamp, a female artistic group (currently at four members). Their better known titles include *Angelic Layer, RG Veda*, and the award-winning *Cardcaptor Sakura*.

Fanservice: Elements in manga that are put in only to pander to fans, and do not further the plot or develop characterization. This can include a close-up shot of a female character's cleavage or underwear.

- The lives of a group of high school girls (*Azumanga Daioh*)
- High school students are sent to an island where it is kill or be killed (*Battle Royale*)
- A young martial artist seeks to gain power by finding the Dragon Balls (*Dragonball, Dragonball Z*)
- A Japanese-American senator runs for president of the United States (*Eagle: The Making of an Asian-American President*)
- Teens play football (*Eyeshield 21*), soccer (*Whistle*), tennis (*Prince of Tennis*), basketball (*Harlem Beat* and *Rebound*), and the Japanese board game Go (*Hikaru No Go*) (Sports manga is very popular and influential in Japan. The protagonist in these stories can be male or female and is often an underdog who wants to make the team or joins in order to impress someone [Cha, 2005]).
- A magic notebook causes the death of anyone whose name is written in it (*Death Note*)
- A 12-year-old girl finds out that she is a goddess (*Kamichama Karin*)
- Characters from the video game Final Fantasy team up with Disney characters (*Kingdom Hearts*)
- Froglike aliens who are supposed to be part of an invasion but end up living with a human family (*Sgt. Frog*)
- The adventures of a cat, both acting "naturally" and in an anthropomorphic style (*What's Michael*)

Nonfiction manga is also published. Digital Manga Publishing has published translations of a series called "edu-manga," which are biographies of such notable people as Anne Frank, Mother Teresa, and Albert Einstein. Their "Project X" line tells of the history of such modern innovators as Momofuku Ando, inventor of Cup Noodles. For adults in Japan, technical manuals, government reports, and even legal case histories have been released in a manga format.

Many manga titles tie in to anime. Many manga titles have been adapted in anime form and vice versa (including many of the previously discussed titles). Some such as *Battle Royale* are based on books, and some manga series also have animated and live-action counterparts. Also, some Western works have been adapted into manga form in Japan, including the *Star Wars* movies and new, Japan-based adventures of Spider-Man.

The artistic style of manga is different from that of American comics in several ways. One way is facial enhancements in which the eyes of heroes often are drawn in a larger, Western style (and the villains tend to have smaller eyes). Another difference is that the pacing of the stories tends to be slower, with many more "silent" panels. There is also the use of "speed lines" to demonstrate movement, along with other artistic techniques.

Japanese books aren't the only Asian comics translated for American readers. Many of the same companies that publish manga in America also publish Chinese "manhua" and Korean "manhwa" (also spelled "manwha"). Translated manhua tends to come from Hong Kong or Taiwan, while manhwa comes from South Korea. Manga tends to more character-led, whereas manhua and manwha are more story-led (Pilcher and Brooks, 2005: 135).

Manga in America

Given that it is much easier to dub dialogue than to re-letter comics, anime appeared in America decades before manga, though it was commonly referred to as "Japanimation." The first dubbed anime was Tezuka's *Tetsuwan Atomu* (*The Mighty Atom*), which appeared in United States in 1964 as *Astro Boy*. Some of the other well-known anime television programs shown in America in the 1960s, 1970s, and 1980s were *Kimba, the White Lion*; *Gigantor*; *Battle of the Planets*; *Star Blazers Robotech*; and *Speed Racer*. Translation into English wasn't the only change made to some shows. Other edits were made to make them more "suitable" to younger audiences. For example, in the 1970s program *Battle of the Planets* (known in Japan as *Kagaku ninja tai Gatchaman*) violent scenes were altered by either cutting them or having a robot character (created especially for the new version) explain that, unlike in the original version, the destroyed cities had been evacuated, and that the destroyed armies consisted solely of robot troops. Character names were also changed to make the characters more Western, with, for example, the team leader's name changing from "Ken Washio" to "Mark" (later redubbed incarnations of the series called the same character "Ace Goodheart" and "Hunter Harris").

One of the first anime films to be big in America was the manga-based (and R-rated) *Akira* (1988), which debuted in America in 1991. Since then the popularity of anime has increased thanks in part to television shows such as *Pokemon*, *Sailor Moon*, and the various programs shown on the Cartoon Network; feature films such as *Princess Mononoke* and the Academy Award–winning *Spirited Away*; and the large number of animated films and television series available on video and DVD. DVD versions have become even more popular, since the viewer has the option of watching them subtitled instead of dubbed, something that many fans prefer. Many school and libraries even have anime clubs.

Anime may have been the driving force behind manga's popularity, but manga is now standing on its own. Manga titles tend to be on the top of the graphic novel sales charts, and if you go to a bookstore such as Barnes & Noble or Borders you will see that they have considerably more volumes of manga than of "Western" comics.

One of the earliest translated manga was Keiji Nakazawa's *Barefoot Gen*, a multivolume, semiautobiographical story about a young boy living in Hiroshima at the time the atomic bomb was dropped. Other English translations were done in the mid-1970s, and during the 1980s various manga titles appeared in the United States, though these were often reprinted in comic book form. These included *Lone Wolf and Cub*, *Akira*, and *Mai the Psychic Girl*. One of the first introductions of manga to American readers was actually through a noncomic book, *Manga! Manga! The World of Japanese Comics*, which Frederick Schodt wrote in 1983. By the mid-1990s, companies such as Viz and Tokyopop (originally called Mixx), both of which are incorporated in Japan, began publishing translated volumes and, along with companies such as Dark Horse, eventually produced them in the general sizes and formats that readers are familiar with today.

With its increasing popularity, more and more manga is being translated and reprinted for the American market (the translations are usually done by a native English speaker). The top American manga publishers put out more than 1,400 volumes in 2007, a 16 percent increase from the previous year ("Manga Releases Up," 2007; see Exhibit 3-2). This has some downsides. One concern is that manga titles are taking too much shelf space and crowding out other books. This occurs both because books in manga series come out with much greater frequency than their Western counterparts (often up to six times a year), and because many manga titles have an ongoing story line in which knowledge of the events in previous volumes is helpful if not necessary to fully understand the story. Therefore bookstores, and for that matter libraries, need to keep a complete set of the previous volumes in order to help new readers. Thankfully, the high manga circulation can help to keep the shelves from being too overcrowded. Another downside is that although a few years ago it was the "cream of the crop" that the publishers were reprinting, in an attempt to fulfill reader demand more titles are now being reprinted, and not all of them are of the same high quality.

Translating and re-lettering wasn't the only problem that American publishers had to deal with in reprinting manga. Even little details must be changed for American audiences, such as symbols for sound effects ("knock," "ring," and so forth), which differ between countries, and signs in the background

---

Exhibit 3-2. American Publishers of Manga

The following is a list of manga publishers in the United States. Some also publish nonmanga as well as original English language manga titles. See Chapter 6 for more information.

ADV	Go! Comi
CPM Manga	Seven Seas
Dark Horse	Tokyopop
DC Comics (CMX Line)	Vertical
Del Rey	Viz
Digital Media	Yen Press (an imprint of Hachette)

(which, if not altered, must at least have the translation somewhere on the page). In addition, in Japan the order of the pages, the panels, and even reading of the word balloons is right to left, so for American publication they had to be "flopped," so that they would appear in the manner that American readers were used to (though manhwa is already read left to right and does not need any changes). However, "unflopped" books, printed in the "proper" way have published more frequently in recent years. Besides being cheaper for the publishers (who have passed some of the savings on to their customers in the form of cheaper books), "authentic" manga has proved very popular among readers. Several publishers have tried to help readers of "unflopped" books in several ways, including putting "read this way" arrows on the pages, diagrams that explain the "proper" way to read the page, and even warnings with additional illustrations such as the one found on some Tokyopop titles:

> Stop! This is the back of the book. You wouldn't want to spoil a great ending! This book is printed "manga-style," in the authentic Japanese right-to-left format. Since none of the artwork has been flopped or altered, readers get to experience the story as the creator intended.

Although unflopped titles are gaining acceptance among readers, library workers are still getting used to them, and issues such as which sides to consider the front and back for processing are still being decided (see Chapter 7 for more on this). Another problem that librarians might encounter is due to cultural differences between the United States and Japan. For example, nudity, especially in a casual, nonsexual way, is not as big a deal in Japan as it is here. In the popular series *Ranma 1/2*, by Rumiko Takahashi, one of the world's most popular female comic artists, a teenage boy turns into a busty, redheaded girl when splashed with cold water, and in the stories nudity is sometimes used for comic relief, such as when Ranma finds himself in a public bath with other boys when he changes, or with girls when he changes back. Scenes such as this or ones in which a character of one sex accidentally seeing someone of the opposite sex changing clothes or coming out of the shower are meant for entertainment, not titillation. However, in America, reactions might be different, and even problematic.

An interesting case of "what's appropriate in one country may not be appropriate in another" occurred in 2007, when publisher Seven Seas Entertainment decided not to publish *Nymphet*, a translation of *Kodomo no Jikan* (*A Child's Time*), a sienan about a third-grade teacher who discovers that one of his students has a crush on him. Given the ages of the characters, and that the young girl's crush is sexual in nature, there was controversy, and Seven Seas, facing concerns from both readers and, more important, vendors, ended up pulling the title. Other publishers have made their own decisions in these cases, for example, when CMX, an imprint of DC Comics, released the first translated volume of the popular manga *Tenjo Tenge*, it was heavily edited, with more than 30 examples of nudity and "panty shots" covered up, and a tightly cropped rape scene. CMX did this because the Japanese edition was marketed to older teens and adults, while CMX was aiming for the younger teen market. Many fans were unhappy with this, since CMX advertises its manga as "100 percent the way the original Japanese creators want you to see it." Later editions were released with an older rating, though there was still some editing done with the author's approval (Harris, 2005).

English Language Manga

Manga's popularity has influenced comics in America, as seen in the rise of original English language (OEL) manga. Formerly referred to as "Amerimanga," OEL manga are comics and graphic novels (mainly graphic novel series) written and drawn by American creators. These books are usually printed in the "Western" (left-to-right) style. Several American publishers of Asian manga also publish OEL titles, including Tokyopop, who holds a Rising Stars of Manga competition. Titles that have come out of the competition include *Mail Order Ninja* and *Peach Fuzz*. Tokyopop also produces manga-style versions of juvenile and young adult novels from HarperCollins, including books by Meg Cabot and Erin Hunter. Many of the titles from publisher Antarctic Press are described as manga, including manga-style versions of *The Wizard of Oz* and *Alice in Wonderland*, and unlike most manga, many of Antarctic's titles are in color. Some of these first appear as comic books, but others are original graphic novels (though a few, such as *Peach Fuzz*, have been serialized in newspapers). Original manga is also produced in other countries. Tokyopop has a line of manga in Germany, and some of the original German language manga has also been translated into English.

Although not calling themselves OEL manga or Amerimanga, other mainstream comics attempt to copy the manga style or at least show an influence. These include Marvel's "Mangaverse" and "Tsunami" titles, and DC's *Teen Titans Go!*, which is based on the anime-like Teen Titans cartoon. There is some debate among the hard-core fans as to whether a comic should be referred to as manga if it didn't originate in Japan (or at least from Asia), but whether you call it "manga," "trade edition," or "original graphic novel," it is something popular, and something that should be on the shelves of your library.

Animanga

Another age-appropriate type of graphic novel that contains the word manga is known at Tokyopop as "cine-manga" and elsewhere as animanga. These are not really manga, and frankly stretch the definition of graphic novels. With cine-manga, frames from animated and live-action television shows and movies are reprinted in the books, with captions and word balloons used to tell the story and convey dialogue. The majority of these are aimed at children and tweens, and cine-manga series include *That's So Raven*, *Lizzie McGuire*, and *SpongeBob SquarePants*, as well as adaptations of such films as *Bambi*, *Finding Nemo*, and *The Incredibles*. A "junior cine-manga" line includes *My Little Pony*, and *Sesame Street*'s Elmo. Animanga books are similar, but generally take frames from anime films and television shows, including *Kiki's Delivery Service*, *Sailor Moon*, *Inu-Yasha*, and the *Pokemon* films.

As in Japan, manga is popular in America among all ages and both sexes, and some readers who are not into Western comics devour manga. So what is the appeal of anime and manga among children, tweens, and teens? According to librarian Gilles Poitras, the creator of "The Librarian's Guide to Anime and Manga" Web page (Poitras, 2007) and writer of books on anime, it's because "given the sameness of entertainment for children in America, anime and manga are developing audiences by being different," with some of those differences including having one story spread out over a series of episodes, more complex characters who are capable of maturing during the series, and story lines that require paying attention and thinking rather than having everything clearly explained for the audience.

More on manga, including cataloging, selection, and other collection development issues, can be found in the later chapters, and for additional information see the list of books and Web sites in Appendixes B and C (see also Exhibit 3-3).

Other Foreign Comics

Comics are also popular in other parts of the world, though only some foreign titles have been brought to America (even when translation is not necessary), and only a small part of those are suitable for children and tweens. Perhaps the best known of these is *The Adventures of Tintin* (see Exhibit 3-4) from Belgium and *Asterix* from France. American comics are sold around the world, and there are a number of writers and artists of American comics who come from, or for that matter still live, in different parts of the world.

British comics have a history dating back centuries. The earliest example of British sequential art was the Bayeux Tapestry, a 230-foot long needlework embroidery that was commissioned by William the Conqueror's brother Odo of Bayeux to tell the story of his conquest, and is a "flow of sequential images and text" (Talbot, 2007: 87–88) that tells a story. Centuries later, artist William Hogarth told stories in a single illustration or over a series of prints and referred to himself as the author of the work. Early series of prints include *The Rake's Progress*, *The Harlot's Progress*, and *Marriage à la mode*, and the contrasting twin engravings *Gin Lane* and *Beer Street*.

Exhibit 3-3. Selected Manga Titles Discussed in This Book

See Appendix A for more information.

Asian manga:
Angelic Layer
Beet the Vandel Buster
Beyblade
Edu-manga series
Hikaru No Go
Kamichama Karin
Kingdom Hearts series/*Kilala Princess*
Legendz
A Little Snow Fairy Sugar
Megaman NT Warrior
Pixie Pop: Gokkun Pucho
Pokemon
President Dad
Project X
Prince of Tennis
Swan
Tokyo Mew Mew
What's Michael
Whistle!
Yotsuba&!

OEL manga:
Biker Girl
Kat and Mouse
Mail Order Ninja
Neotopia
New Alice in Wonderland
Once in a Blue Moon
Oz: The Manga
Peach Fuzz
Rock and Roll Love
Sea Princess Azuri
Warriors
Zapt!

Animanga:
Castle in the Sky
Cine-manga books
Howl's Moving Castle
Kiki's Delivery Service
My Neighbor Totoro
Spirited Away

Of these, some of the best tiles to start with are *Kingdom Hearts* series, *Kilala Princess*, *Whistle*, *Prince of Tennis*, *Kat and Mouse*, *Mail Order Ninja*, and *Zapt!*. The books in the edu-manga series are also very good, but since they are nonfiction, they may not be as popular. These books are all rated "A" for all ages.

Shortly after *The Adventures of Mr. Obadiah Oldbuck* appeared in America, the British humor publication *Punch* published a series of five drawings that satirized the government. These drawings were called "Mr. Punch's Cartoons." Prior to this, the term "cartoon" meant a rough drawing used as a sample of a planned work. This came from the Italian word "cartone" (card), which has its origin with the Italian fresco painters and tapestry designers who would do a full scale "rough draft" on cardboard before beginning the main, and harder to change, work. Since a competitive exhibition featuring similar "roughs" was being held at the time in London, the artists at *Punch* were inspired to create their own. At first, *Punch* called these pictures "pencilings," but soon applied the term "cartoon" to any humorous drawing, be it political satire or just regular humor. The American imitators of *Punch*—*Puck* (1871), *Judge* (1881), and *Life* (1883, no relation to the later publication)—were sometimes referred to as "comic weeklies" (Harvey, 2001: 77–78).

Despite not having to worry about translations, the majority of British comics have not been reprinted for the American market, a smaller amount have been collected, and an even smaller amount are suitable for children and tweens, such as the *Wallace and Gromit* titles. Some of the better known British titles for older audiences include *Judge Dredd* and *V for Vendetta*, the latter of which began its story in the British comic magazine *Warrior* and finished in a DC Comics limited series. Many writers and artists of British comics have gained fame in the United States, including Alan Moore, Grant Morrison, Mike Carey, and Dave Gibbons.

In France and Belgium (many of the major French-language creators were Belgian), comics are known as "bandé dessinée" or BD (pronounced bay-day), which means "drawn strip." It is considered to be a legitimate and respected art form on par with painting, music, poetry, and film (and is also called "the ninth art"). One of the largest comic book conventions in the world is in France, the Angoulême International Comics Festival (Festival International de la Bande Dessinée d'Angoulême). Besides *Tintin* and *Asterix*, much of translated BD has been for adults. Recently, works for younger ages from creators including Joann Sfar (*Sardine, Little Vampire*) and Lewis Trondheim (*A.L.I.E.E.N., Mr. O*) are being translated by American publishers including, NBM and First Second. Many other European Countries have a long history of comics, including in Spain, Italy, Germany, and the Scandinavian countries.

Exhibit 3-4. Tintin

Tintin was created by Georges Remi aka Hergé (1907–1983). A young adventurer and reporter, he was first seen in 1929 in a weekly kids supplement to a Belgian Catholic newspaper called *Le Vingtieme Siecle*. Tintin and his dog Snowy (or Milou in French) traveled around the world, starting with places such as the Soviet Union and the Belgian Congo. Often with him was the sailor Captain Haddock and Thompson and Thompson, a pair of nearly identical detectives. In the 1940s Hergé revised his earlier works, improving the artwork and adding color. In total, 24 of Tintin's adventures have been translated into English (1 of 30 languages into which the books have been translated), from *Tintin in the Land of the Soviets* to *Tintin and the Picaros* and *Tintin and Alph-Art*, unfinished at the time of Hergé's death and published posthumously. Little, Brown, and Company is the current American publisher of the Tintin books.

Although he has never been as popular in America as he has been in Europe, where among other things he has appeared on postage stamps, commemorative coins, and has a chain of stores selling Tintin merchandise, Tintin has appeared in the United States in two animated series and a feature film. Some of the earlier *Tintin* editions have been criticized for Hergé's portrayal of non-Europeans, most notably his depiction of the Africans in *Tintin in the Congo*, and Hergé did make changes in later printings to satisfy some of the objections. Still, that portrayal in *Tintin in the Congo* caused controversy in the United Kingdom in 2007, causing bookstores there and elsewhere to either remove the book or move it away from the children's section and to either the adult or graphic novel sections of the store. Interestingly, the controversy caused sales of the book to increase almost 4,000 percent. Although the controversy did not spread to the United States, Little, Brown has pulled it from its catalog and will not be including it in a planned "complete" set of Tintin books.

Many Canadian writers and artists, including Seth, Chester Brown, and Michel Rabagliati have had their work published in the United States, often via the publisher Drawn and Quarterly. Elsewhere in the world, including India, Australia, the Middle East, the Philippines, Mexico, and parts of South America and Africa, comics are being created. Again, only a small amount of these books are being translated or are appropriate for younger readers. However, who knows what the future might hold?

In general, graphic novels that originated outside the United States, especially those in English, whether translated or OEL, should be treated the same as American titles, with the possible exception of cataloging choices and the shelving options associated with them. This will be explored further in Chapters 7 and 8.

References

"2006 Japanese Manga Market Drops Below 500 Billion Yen." Comipress.com (March 10, 2007). Available: http://comipress.com/news/2007/03/10/1622.

Aoyama, Yuko and Hiro Izushi. 2004. "Creative Resources of the Japanese Video Game Industry." In *Cultural Industries and the Production of Culture*, edited by Dominic Power and Allen John Scott. New York: Routledge, p. 121.

Brenner, Robin. 2007. *Understanding Manga and Anime*. Westport CT: Libraries Unlimited.

Cha, Kai-Ming. 2005. "Sports Manga Gets in the Game." *Publishers Weekly*, April 18. Available: www.publishersweekly.com/article/CA525098.html. Accessed: September 11, 2006.

Gravett, Paul. 2004. *Manga Sixty Years of Japanese Comics*. London: Laurence King.

Harris, Franklin. 2005. "Censored Book Not a Good Start." *The Decatur Daily*, February 10.

Harvey, Robert C. 2001. "Comedy at the Juncture of Word and Image: The Emergence of the Modern Magazine Gag Cartoon Reveals the Vital Blend." In *The Language of Comics: Word and Image*, edited by Robin Varnum and Christina T. Gibbons. Jackson, MS: University Press of Mississippi, pp. 77–78.

"Manga Releases Up 16% in 2007 According to ICv2 Guide." ICv2.com (February 7, 2007). Available: www.icv2.com/articles/news/10034.html.

Pilcher, Tim and Brad Brooks. 2005. *The Essential Guide to World Comics*. London: Collins and Brown.

Poitras, Gille. "The Librarian's Guide to Anime and Manga." Gilles' Service to Fans Page (April 24, 2007). Available: www.koyogi.com/Libguide.html.

Talbot, Bryan. 2007. *Alice in Sunderland: An Entertainment*. Milwaukee, OR: Dark Horse.

PART II

Building a Graphic Novel Collection

Chapter 4

Why Should I Offer Graphic Novels in My Library?

At the turn of the century, this would have been the most important chapter in this book. At the time, "Why should I have graphic novels in my library?" was the big question. Over the past decade graphic novels have gained in popularity to such a degree that the question has been changed to "Okay, since I know that I need to have graphic novels in my library, how do I go about doing it?" This question will be answered in the next few chapters.

However, despite their growing acceptance and popularity, some still question why their library's resources should be spent on graphic novels. It may be the higher-ups in the library system, a school principal or school board member, or even a patron who wonders why his or her tax dollars are being spent on this sort of material. Since school libraries are one of the newer homes to graphic novels, the first and probably most important reason is the educational benefits of having graphic novels in your library.

> There have always been books that have unfairly been given the stigma of "junk literature," or "lowbrow works." Librarians were encouraged not to buy them, and children were encouraged to read them only until they were ready for "a real book." Graphic novels are just getting over this stigma, but before them were the *Goosebumps* and *Baby-sitter's Club* books, and before these came the *Hardy Boys* and *Nancy Drew* titles. Interestingly, all four have recently come out in graphic novel form.

Classroom Use

The use of comics—and later graphic novels—in the classroom is a topic that has been discussed for almost as long as comic books have been around. Between 1935 and 1944 more than 100 critical articles about comics were published in both educational and nonprofessional periodicals, and in 1944 an entire volume of *The Journal of Educational Sociology* was dedicated to the topic (Yang, 2003). In this chapter the educational reasons for having graphic novels in the library, especially in the school media center and even in the classroom, will be discussed. Some of the practical applications, including what teachers have done in the past, will be covered in Chapter 8.

Reluctant Readers

> If educators ever find out what constitutes the fantastic motivating power of comic books, I hope they bottle it and sprinkle it around classrooms. (Haugaard, 1973: 54)

Comic books, and by extension graphic novels, have long been considered as a way to attract the interest of reluctant readers. Many school librarians have reported "outstanding success" in getting children to read by using graphic novels (Buchanan, 2006). Since some reluctant readers can find themselves intimidated when they see a full page of text, having the pictures on the page makes the book a little friendlier. Also, they may not consider the graphic novel to be a "real book," and this will put them more at ease, and the format, which often will contain familiar characters, makes it that much easier for the child to comprehend the themes, plots, and characterization, something that in the past may have just added to their frustration when reading a "text" book ("How Comic Can Reach Reluctant Readers," accessed 2008). There is also the "fun factor." A survey of 1,000 parents and children for the Kids and Family Reading Report found that 92 percent of kids enjoy reading for fun, but they don't read as much as they could because they cannot find books that they like (Allen, 2007). That comics are "fun to read" is often the main reason cited in surveys as to why kids like comics. Robert Sylvester in his book *A Celebration of Neurons: An Educator's Guide to the Human Brain* points out that emotion drives attention and attention drives learning. The more emotionally connected that students feel to a piece of material, the more concepts and skills they are able to learn (Cary, 2004: 19).

A survey in the late 1990s of 419 sixth-graders in three schools in a socio-economically and ethnically diverse district in Texas found that comic books were the second most preferred reading material (right behind juvenile horror books) regardless of the student's income, reading achievement, attitude toward reading, or gender (Worthy, Moorman, and Turner, 1999: 12–27). Graphic novels and comics can make reluctant readers want to read and in fact can encourage them to read for pleasure (Lyga and Lyga, 2004: 7). And, as it turns out, they can end up reading more than they thought they were reading. In his *Read Aloud Handbook*, Jim Trelease points out that when, for example, a child is reading a *Tintin* graphic novel that contains 8,000 words, he or she is unaware that they are reading 8,000 words (Trelease, 2001: 135). Also, just one comic book a day would mean more than 500,000 words in a year, half of the average reading volume of most middle-class children (Krashen, 2004: 97). Since the average original graphic novel, manga, or trade edition is at the bare minimum two to four times larger than a comic book and, depending on the book, can be many times larger, children who regularly read graphic novels, especially along with other books, can find themselves reading at well above the average rate.

It is not just the reluctant readers who benefit from graphic novels. Teachers and school librarians have used them not only because they "enable the struggling reader" and "motivate the reluctant ones," but also because they "challenge the high-level" readers as well (McTaggart, accessed 2008: 4). Although some think that comics are appropriate only for poor readers, surveys and research on the subject have proven otherwise. Many studies have shown that those who regularly read comics and graphic novels will often continue to read not only graphic novels, but other books as well. One such study showed that six- to eighteen-year-olds who did "a significant amount of light reading, developed a habit of reading into adulthood and a mastery of more difficult reading" (Serchay, 2004: 29). Other studies have found that those who read comics read just as much, if not more, than those who do not. In addition, these readers are also at the very least equal to noncomics readers in terms of reading, language development, and overall school achievement (Krashen, 2004: 103).

Stephen Krashen in *Every Person a Reader* (1996) observed, "Middle school boys who read comic books also read more in general, read more books, and reported that they liked reading better than those who did less comic book reading" (Hill, 2002: 5). In a survey conducted in the 1970s, when interest was again growing regarding comics in the classroom, it was found that students who earned good grades and those who earned bad grades were both comic book readers, but in general a higher number had good grades, and 91 percent of the "good grade" kids and 79 percent of the "bad" also read other books (Swain, 1983: 73). Another study, published in *Reading Research Quarterly*, looked at 155 fifth graders and found a small but significant positive relationship between the amount of book reading and the amount of comic book reading. Again, those students who normally read more books also read more comic books (Anderson, Wilson, and Fielding, 1988: 285-303).

Increased Vocabulary

A study published in the *Journal of Child Language* found that comic books introduced children to slightly more "rare" words—words not among the most common 10,000—than the average children's book, and also contained more than five times as many rare words as the average conversation between an adult and a child (Krashen, 2004: 104). Comic book writer Jim Shooter, who had his first comic book story published at the age 13 and later was editor in chief of

Marvel Comics and founder of several other comic companies, has told the story of how in first grade he impressed his teacher by not only knowing what bouillabaisse was, but also how to correctly spell it, something that he had learned from a *Donald Duck* comic book (Krashen, 2004: 91-92). How many children over the past 60 years have learned the word "invulnerable" from reading Superman comics? (For more examples of words that children are exposed to when they read comics and graphic novels, see Exhibit 4-1). Some studies have suggested that comics introduce more new words than even adult-level books (McTaggart, accessed 2008: 8). Similar to many adult bestsellers, as well as popular young adult titles, and magazines such as *Time*, comic books and graphic novels tend to be written on a fourth- or fifth-grade level (Crawford, 2004: 26).

Improved reading through comics is not just something found in the United States. For example Finland, which has the highest literary and library usage rates (McTaggart, accessed 2008: 8), also has the children with the highest reading score according to International Association for the Evaluation of Educational Achievement (IEA) assessment of 32 countries. Of Finnish children

Exhibit 4-1. Examples of Words Found in Graphic Novels		
Title	Format	Words included
Prince of Tennis, Volume 8	Nine-chapter manga 170 pages	Calculated, strategically, critical, crucial, designated
Tommysaurus Rex	Original graphic novel 112 pages	Melodrama, prehistoric, obedience, socially, excruciating
Zorro, Volume 2: *Drownings*	From three comic book issues 90 pages	Beau, appalled, sarcasm, chasm, scoundrel, hoodwinked, dysentery, snob, precipice, ambush, inadequacy, disciplinarian
Lullaby	From four comic book issues 96 pages	Pining, indulge, lingering, clarity, encroach, paranoid, vigorously, codger
Isis & Osiris	Original nonfiction graphic novel 48 pages	Sarcophagus, unseemly, pilgrimages
Marvel Adventures Spider-Man, Volume 1: *The Sinister Six*	From four comic book issues 96 pages	Implications, technology, appetizer, responsibility, insufferable, imbeciles, pestilent, plagued, exclusive, suspicions, punctual, preposterous, decency, triumphs, carcass, arrogant, arachnid, blithering, cahoots, rue, polymer, whelp

surveyed, 59 percent reported that they read a comic book almost every single day (Trelease, 2001: 133).

Why do children like graphic novels, and why does it help them educationally? Besides some of the obvious reasons, it could also be that children are much more used to visual elements in conjunction with their text. This has been true for several decades, and is even truer today. Modern children are surrounded by videos, television programs with "crawls" and pop-ups, online games in which they have to read along while looking at images, chatting online while looking at pictures, and more.

Publisher Ian Ballantine once said that "the young today . . . have an immense inventory of visual images. Their visual literacy is the important thing. It doesn't inhibit literary literacy. It encourages it" (McCloud, 1993: 51). San Francisco Young Adult librarian Francisca Goldsmith, author of *Graphic Novels Now: Building, Managing, and Marketing a Dynamic Collection*, has pointed out:

> Graphic Novel readers have learned to understand not only print, but can also decode facial and body expressions, the symbolic meanings of certain images and postures, metaphors and similes, and other social and literary nuances teenagers are mastering as they move from childhood to maturity. (Lyga and Lyga, 2004: 9)

Even if a child has not yet learned to read, comic books can still be educational. In her book *Keeping Kids Reading: How to Raise Avid Readers in the Video Age*, Mary Leonhardt recommends that instead of putting your child down in front of a Donald Duck video, sit with the child and read aloud a Donald Duck comic. "Comics," she says, "usually have plot lines of much greater interest to children than most picture books. They motivate children to try to figure out what happens next from pictures [and] keep [their] interest" (Leonhardt, 1996: 41).

In 1993, when the graphical Internet was still in its infancy, Scott McCloud predicted that "children raised on comic books and computers will be quite comfortable with the written word. They will see literacy as a means to an end [and] they will be visually literate as well" (McCloud, 1993: 51), and at the 2006 ICV2 Graphic Novel conference, Pantheon Books editorial director Dan Brown compared the comic panel to the computer screen:

> You're looking at the same interplay or word and image within this little white rectangle. And the generations that have been brought up on computers know how to look at that screen and read it immediately. For them, comics are natural. It's what they've been looking at. It becomes a conduit if information that they're completely familiar with. I have a feeling that call it a medium or call it a language, it's a universal language. Comics have a power that very few other media have. ("'Manga Is a Problem,'" 2006)

Besides reluctant readers, comics and graphic novels can also be helpful in teaching children for whom English is not their first language, mainly for the same reasons. Once again, since comics provide visual clues that "increase the amount of comprehensible input and [boost] reading comprehension," the anxiety and frustration some students may feel with regular text—this time because the text is in an unfamiliar language—is lessened, and the "fun factor" of the material is helpful as well (Cary, 2004: 13).

In addition, comic books and graphic novels will introduce these children who have recently come to the United States to "nonstandard" words and phrases that are often not found in textbooks. Comics often contain American slang, idioms, abbreviations, and even onomatopoeia that are different from what they are used to (such as a dog going "guau guau" in Spanish and "bow wow" in English). In addition, if the graphic novel is in a "normal setting" such as in a school, the reader can even get some cultural knowledge, even if the schools in the books aren't exactly similar to the school he or she is attending (Chow, accessed 2008). Since some English language comics are available in Spanish (and occasionally French or other languages), purchasing editions in each language could also help. Additional information can be found in Stephen Cary's book *Going Graphic: Comics at Work in the Multilingual Classroom*.

Of course no one recommends using *only* comics and graphic novels as a reading aid. After all, not all children will enjoy reading them. They should supplement the other readings, not supplant them. Nor should they be treated only as a "stepping-stone" to other forms of literacy ("Zoiks!" 2007). But there is no doubt that they can be a reading aid. Fifth-grade teacher Brenda Pennella sums it up well:

> . . . with graphic novels the scaffolding necessary to build solid readers is in the architecture of the genre. The illustrations not only support the text they are a part of the text. Students are given context clues within the subtle and sometime not so subtle expressions, symbols, and actions of the characters with in the story. Vocabulary is also supported within the illustrations and text. The framework or grid layout of this art form lends itself perfectly to the predicting strategies needed to reach higher-level understanding in reading comprehension. (Pennella, accessed 2008)

Graphic Nonfiction

Improving reading skills is not the only reason to have graphic novels in schools. As seen in Chapter 2, there is a surge in the amount of juvenile nonfiction graphic novels being produced, mainly by non–comic book publishers. Biography and history are the two largest subjects, but graphic novels dealing with science, mythology, and other areas are also published. Some are basically straightforward, while others have more of a story format, a sort of "nonfiction

fiction." For example, *Clan Apis* by Jay Hosler (2000) ostensibly tells the story of a bee named Nyuki (Swahili for "bee"), but also continuously provides the reader with facts about bees, as shown in this scene:

> Nyuki: The new hive is depending on us girls. If this [the honeycomb] doesn't get built there will be no place to store the honey and pollen and no place for us to raise brood. And are we awesome architects or what?! Each Comb is precisely 0.95 centimeters from the next and each cell is 5.2 millimeters in diameter. Or 6.6 millimeters to raise our husky drone brothers. Ha ha! (Hosler, 2000: 94)

Although most of the nonfiction graphic novels—"straightforward" and otherwise—are informative, for the most part they should not be used as a primary source if a child has to do a school report on a person or subject. They can be helpful if a second or third source is required or if no "nongraphic" books are available, and they are also good if the child is simply reading for fun.

Harkening back to the days of the "classic comic books," there are also many literary adaptations. Some, such as *The Wizard of Oz* and *Black Beauty*, are adapted by multiple publishers. Some are heavily abridged, and others make other changes. Antarctic Press's version of *The Wizard of Oz* is drawn in a manga style, while Puffin Graphic's version of *Macbeth* retains the Shakespearean dialogue, but puts it in a science fiction setting (much in the way that certain film adaptations of Shakespeare have put the classic tales in other eras and circumstances). Many of the nonfiction titles are also on the Accelerated Reader List, providing another reason to have graphic novels in the library (see Exhibit 4-2).

Librarians can also use graphic novels in connection with other books in the collection, either along with the GN or in a "if you liked X then you might like Y" situation. Even those who back in the 1940s were opposed to comic books used them as a way to get children to read books (more on this in Chapter 9) (Kunitz, 1941: 846-847). First there are the works of fiction based on comic book characters or themes. This goes at least as far back as the "Big Little Books" and the 1942 novel *Superman* by George Lowther. These books have been aimed at juvenile (on the easy reader, beginning reader, and chapter book levels), young adult, and, in some cases, even adult audiences. Some have been written by comic book writers, and others have been novelizations of comic book story lines (such as the death of Superman, which became Roger Stern's *The Death and Life of Superman*) and limited series (including Elliot S. Maggin's adaptation of *Kingdom Come*), and similar to film novelizations, book versions of comic stories tend to add on to the original work.

It is not just the superhero titles that have found themselves turned into books. Mark Criley's *Akiko* series has appeared in both adapted and original

---

Exhibit 4-2. The Accelerated Reader List

Produced by Renaissance Learning, Accelerated Reader (AR) is "a daily progress monitoring software assessment in wide use by primary and secondary schools for monitoring the practice of reading" ("Accelerated Reader," 2008). Children read books on the AR list, and each book is given a reading level and "point" level. Only a very small percentage of the available AR titles are graphic novels, but they are available for elementary, middle, and high schools, and their being on the list at all shows the inroads that graphic novels have made in schools. Besides the nonfiction titles, a keyword search for graphic novels at Renaissance's Web site for quizzes (www.renlearn.com/store/quiz_advanced.asp) produces a list of such children and tween titles as the *Babymouse*, *Bone*, and *Little Vampire* series, *Jackie and the Shadow Snatcher*, *Queen Bee*, titles from Stone Arch Books, and various Marvel Comics issues that have been converted to hardcover books by Abdo Publishing.

The Abdo books take a single comic book and reprint it in hardcover—minus ads, letter pages, backup stories, etc.—and in a slightly larger size. It should be noted that many of the Abdo Marvel titles are also available in digest form from Marvel Comics, with each digest collecting four comic book issues. However, although they are more expensive, the Abdo titles are sturdier, and if you are buying from the AR list it is easier to know what books to get as opposed to the digests for which you would have to look inside the book to get the title. For example Abdo's *Spider-Man: Kraven the Hunter*, which was originally published in *Marvel Age Spider-Man* #14 (December 2004), is also one of the stories reprinted in the digest *Marvel Age Spider-Man*, Volume 4: *The Goblin Strikes*. More information on Abdo's Marvel Comics titles can be found in Appendix A.

---

works, and prior to being brought to America in graphic novel form, the *W.I.T.C.H.* series was produced as a series of novels. Besides including the various graphic novel adaptations of literary works in their collections, libraries can place Papercutz's original *Hardy Boys* and *Nancy Drew* graphic novels alongside the hardcover and paperback text versions that they have in the collection.

In addition to the original books and series with superhero themes mentioned in Chapter 2—*Captain Underpants*, *Melvin Beederman*, *Superhero Sidekicks*, *SuperHero ABC*, and so forth—graphic novels with science fiction, fantasy, horror, or even real-life themes can be used to point children to books with similar themes. The reverse can also be true. A child reading a book in Beverly Cleary's *Ramona* series can be recommended an *Amelia Rules* graphic novel and vice versa.

Graphic novels can also lead children to read works of nonfiction, some of which tie in with fictional works. DK has a series of books, the JLA Readers, which feature DC Comics' superheroes with ties to various nonfiction topics. They include *Wonder Woman's Book of Myths* (Wonder Woman has ties to Greek Mythology), *The Flash's Book of Speed*, and *Aquaman's Guide to the Ocean*. Reading these, as well as many of the nonfiction graphic novels, can lead young readers to reading other works on the subject. *Clan Apis*, for example, can lead to other books on bees or other insects.

Enjoying graphic novels can also lead children to read nonfiction books about graphic novels. DK has published books about comic book characters, their creators, and their history. There are even books on how to write and draw comics. If libraries have these in the collection, they may be checked out along with the graphic novels. See Appendix B for a list of many of these books.

Comics Become Respectable

Comics and graphic novels have also become more respectable in recent years. They have been regularly reviewed in many mainstream publications, not only in library periodicals such as *VOYA* and *Library Journal* (see Chapter 6), but in periodicals including *Time, Entertainment Weekly*, and *Publisher's Weekly*. They are also regularly discussed, both by themselves and in comics-related events, in newspapers all around the country. In almost all of these, the subject is treated with respect, instead of portraying it as "junk literature" that is fit to be read only by little kids, illiterates, and "geeks."

Still, even some of the respectable coverage has had its drawbacks. Headlines and stories still continue to include the "Pow" and "Bam" sound effects from the campy 1960s Batman television show, even when it's telling how comics are now "serious." For example, an Associated Press story on a new line of comics featuring Middle Eastern characters was published in one paper as "Comics Introduce Middle East Superheroes," and in another as "Mideast Conflicts—Pow! Zap! Blam!—Resolved" (Rogers, 2006a, 2006b). Newspapers have also been including comic book stories. In 2006–2007, many Sunday newspapers included a supplement containing a reprint of 1960s Spider-Man stories, and serialized and abridged versions of the comic books *Lions, Tigers, and Bears* and *Hopeless Savages*, and the original English language manga's *Mail Order Ninja* and *Peach Fuzz* have also appeared.

Of course comic books and graphic novels have long been a topic for discussion in library publications, dating back to the 1940s and 1950s, when there were both positive and negative (though more negative) articles dealing with the topic of having comics in libraries. Articles over the next three decades took on a more positive note, though not in all occasions, and some even looked at comics from an academic point of view, ranging from use in elementary schools all the way up to usage, collections, and research at the college level (Ellis and Highsmith, 2000: 21-43). One notable article was written by Will Eisner for *School Library Journal* in which he argued that it was time that comic books were placed in the school library (Eisner, 1974: 270). The 1990s saw many positive articles in library literature, and as more graphic novels and trade editions began to appear, so did reviews in library publications. Having graphic novels reviewed, and generally favorably, in these publications helped to show that it was okay to have them in libraries.

Exhibit 4-3. 2002 YALSA Graphic Novel Preconference

On the day before the 2002 American Library Association Annual Conference in Atlanta, Georgia, an all-day preconference on graphic novels was held by YALSA, the young adult wing of ALA. The preconference, which was the best attended that year, including talks by Neil Gaiman, Colleen Doran, Jeff Smith, and Art Spiegelman. Representatives from various comic book companies also attended, and additional discussions dealt with issues of having graphic novels in the library. The following year, Gaiman mentioned the event while giving the keynote address at the Eisner Awards:

> Last summer, at the American Library Association, a number of comics people were invited to talk to Librarians. I was one of them. I went along, expecting to be talking to the 250 comics fans who had grown up to be librarians. I couldn't have been more wrong: the librarians were getting pressure from their readers. The librarians knew that graphic novels—whatever they are—were popular, and they wanted to know what they were. So they got me, and Jeff Smith, and Colleen Doran, and Art Spiegelman, and several other people in to tell them what we thought they should know. And the libraries have started ordering the books. (Gaiman, 2003)

Other signs that graphic novels have gained respectability in the library and publishing worlds include graphic novel programming in library conventions (and in reverse comic conventions have had programming about libraries), library associations creating recommended lists (such as YALSA's "Great Graphic Novels for Teens List"), and giving space to graphic novel publishers at the ALA main and midwinter conventions (where they can be found in the "graphic novel alley") as well as Book Expo America. More non–comic book publishers are beginning to publish graphic novels, and it is not just those who produce juvenile nonfiction titles who are doing this, as many major fiction publishers have been putting out their original graphic novels for children, teen, and even adult audiences (see Exhibit 4-3).

Mainstream Awards

Although comics and graphic novels have had their own awards for decades (see Chapter 6), they have also started to compete with "regular" books. In the past it has primarily been titles for mature or at least older readers that have won mainstream awards, including *Watchman* (Hugo Award), *Maus* (Pulitzer Prize), and *Sandman* (World Fantasy Award), but the 2006 graphic novel *American Born Chinese* is a graphic novel for a younger audience that has made headlines. Gene Luen Yang's book was a 2006 finalist for the National Book Award's Young People's Literature Category and the winner of the 2007 Michael L. Printz award, which is for young adult literature, the first graphic novel ever to do so. Unfortunately there were some who didn't feel that a "comic book" should be nominated for a book award along with "real" books (Long, 2007), so it seems that graphic novels still have a way to go in order to be accepted by everyone.[1] However, that Brian Selznick's 2007 book *The Invention of Hugo Cabret*, which has elements of a hybrid graphic novel, won the Caldecott award is another promising sign.

Some literary awards also have a special graphic novel category. Some recent examples include the Cybil Awards—Children and YA literary awards chosen by bloggers—which named *Amelia Rules: Superheroes* and *American Born Chinese* the year's best graphic novels for ages 12 and under and 13 and up, respectively, and the Independent Book Publishers Association's Franklin Award, which awarded best graphic novel honors to *The Demon of River Heights*, the first book in Papercutz's *Nancy Drew* series.

Besides their use in elementary, middle, and high schools, colleges have also been incorporating graphic novels. In addition to classes on the topic, as electives in high schools, library schools have also begun to include classes on graphic novels in libraries, including one at the University of Alberta taught by author Gail de Vos, and others are including graphic novels as a part of their regular classes. In addition, this book and others similar to it, show that graphic novels have gained respect in the academic world.

Comics and Graphic Novels in Entertainment

As discussed in Chapter 2, many movies and television shows have been made into comic books, and the reverse is also true. Comics have been the basis of radio programs, live-action and animated television series, and feature films. As seen in Exhibit 4-4, many of them have been based on superhero comics, and many well-known actors have taken part in them, including a number of Academy Award and Emmy winners.

When a book is made into a film or becomes the basis for a television program, then there is often renewed interest in the book. Sometimes new editions will come out with a "blurb" on the cover mentioning that this was the source material of the movie/show. Libraries may find that, at least for a time, the circulation of these books—either the original or the re-released editions—will go up. The same can occur with graphic novels that serve as the source of a film/show or at least feature the same characters that viewers have seen.

Just as with "nongraphic" adaptations, changes are made when the printed work is put on screen. The appearances, backgrounds, ages, and even the names of major and minor characters can be altered. A popular, though possibly untrue story says that the first name of Bill Bixby's character on *The Incredible Hulk* television show was changed from "Bruce" to "David" because "Bruce" was considered to be an "unmanly" name.[2] On the animated *X-Men: Evolution*, several characters were younger than they were in the comics, and in the *Spider-Man* films, the character's "web-shooters" were organic, whereas in the comics, at least at the time of the first film, he used a mechanical device. The comic book version soon got organic "web-shooters" as well, possibly due to the influence of the films.

Even though the adaptations are not in the official continuity, they can affect the original books. Prior to appearing in the comics, Superman's weakness

---

Exhibit 4-4. Comic Book Adaptations in Film and Television

These are many of the film and television adaptations of comic books over the past 60-plus years. Comic book tie-ins refer to those comic books created specifically to tie in to the continuity and characters in the films or on the programs. Many of these comic book stories have been collected in trade editions, and the majority of the films and many of the television programs are available on DVD. This list does not include adapted manga, and a small number of the films on this list are rated PG-13.

Superman (and Related)

Films: Fleisher *Superman* Cartoons (1941–1943), *Superman* (1948 serial), *Atom Man vs. Superman* (1950 serial), *Superman* (1978), *Superman II* (1980), *Superman III* (1983), *Supergirl* (1984), *Superman IV: The Quest for Peace* (1987), *Superman Returns* (2006).

Television (live action): *Adventures of Superman* (1952–1958), *Superboy* (1988–1992), *Lois and Clark: The New Adventures of Superman* (1993–1997), *Smallville* (2001–).

Television (animated): *The New Adventures of Superman* (1966–1969), *Superman* (1988–1989), *Superman: The Animated Series* (1996–2000), *Krypto, the Superdog* (2005–), *Legion of Super-Heroes* (2006–).

Direct to video/DVD: *Superman: Braniac Attacks* (2006), *Superman: Doomsday* (2007).

Other: *It's a Bird . . . It's a Plane . . . It's Superman* (1975 television production of the 1966 Broadway play). Also *The Adventures of Superman* radio show (1940–1949).

Collected comic book tie-ins: *Superman Adventures* (1996–2002), *Smallville* (2003–2005); also adaptations of films.

Batman (and Related)

Films: *The Batman* (1943 serial), *Batman and Robin* (1949), *Batman* (1966), *Batman* (1989), *Batman Returns* (1992), *Batman: Mask of the Phantasm* (animated 1993), *Batman Forever* (1995), *Batman & Robin* (1997), *Batman Begins* (2005), *The Dark Knight* (2008).

Television (live action): *Batman* (1966–1968), *Birds of Prey* (2002–2003).

Television (animated): *The Batman/Superman Hour* (1968–1970), *The New Adventures of Batman* (1977–1981), *Batman: The Animated Series* (1992–1999), *Batman Beyond* (1999–2001), *The Batman* (2004–).

Direct to video/DVD: *Batman: SubZero* (animated 1998), *Batman Beyond: Return of the Joker* (animated 2000), *Batman: Mystery of the Batwoman* (animated 2003), *The Batman vs. Dracula* (animated 2005).

Collected comic book tie-ins: *The Batman Adventures* (1992–1995), *The Batman Adventures: Mad Love* (1994), *The Batman and Robin Adventures* (1995–1997), *The Batman Adventures: The Lost Years* (1998), *Batman: Gotham Adventures* (1998–2003), *Batman Beyond* (1999–2001), *Batman Adventures* (2003–2004), *The Batman Strikes* (2004–); film adaptations.

Fantastic Four

Films: *Fantastic Four* (2005), *Fantastic Four: Rise of the Silver Surfer* (2007).

Television (animated): *Fantastic Four* (1967–1969), *Fantastic Four* (1978–1979), *Fred and Barney Meet the Thing* (1979), *Fantastic Four* (1994–1996), *Fantastic Four* (2006–).

Spider-Man

Films: *Spider-Man* (2002), *Spider-Man 2* (2004), *Spider-Man 3* (2007).

Television (live action): *The Amazing Spider-Man* (Pilot 1977, series 1978–1979).

(Cont'd.)

Exhibit 4-4. Comic Book Adaptations in Film and Television *(Continued)*

Spider-Man (Cont'd.)

Television (animated): *Spider-Man* (1967–1970), *Spider-Man* (1981–1982), *Spider-Man and His Amazing Friends* (1981–1983), *Spider-Man* (1994–1998), *Spider-Man Unlimited* (1999–2000), *Spider-Man: The New Animated Series* (2003), *The Spectacular Spider-Man* (2008–).

Archie (and Related)

Films: *Josie and the Pussycats* (2001).

Television (live action): *Sabrina, the Teenage Witch* (1996–2003).

Television (animated): *The Archie Show* (1968), *The Archie Comedy Hour* (1969), *Archie Funhouse* (1970), *Josie and the Pussycats* (1970–1971), *Sabrina and the Groovie Goolies* (1970), *Archie's TV Funnies* (1971), *Sabrina, the Teenage Witch* (1971–1974), *Josie and the Pussycats in Outer Space* (1972–1974), *Everything's Archie* (1973), *U.S. of Archie* (1974), *The New Archie-Sabrina Hour* (1977), *Sabrina, Superwitch* (1977), *Archie's Bang-Shang Lalapalooza Show* (1978), *The New Archies* (1997–1989), *Archie's Weird Mysteries* (1999– 2000), *Sabrina: The Animated Series* (1999–2000), *Sabrina's Secret Life* (2003–2004).

Television movies: *Archie: To Riverdale and Back Again* (1990), *Sabrina Goes to Rome* (1998), *Sabrina Down Under* (1999).

The Hulk

Film: *Hulk* (2003), *The Incredible Hulk* (2008).

Television (live action): *The Incredible Hulk* (1977–1982); also three made-for-television sequels.

Television (animated): *The Incredible Hulk* (1982–1983), *The Incredible Hulk* (1996–1997).

Other: The Hulk along with Captain America, Iron Man, Thor, and Namor, the Sub-Mariner were all featured in the 1966 animated series *The Marvel Superheroes*. The Hulk has also guest starred on other cartoons.

The X-Men

Film: *X-Men* (2000), *X2: X-Men United* (2003), *X-Men: The Last Stand* (2006).

Television (animated): *X-Men: The Animated Series* (1992–1997), *X-Men: Evolution* (2000–2003).

Television movies: *Generation X* (1996).

Other: *Pryde of the X-Men* was a 1989 animated pilot. The X-Men had also appeared on *Spider-Man and His Amazing Friends*, which featured former X-Man Iceman.

Teenage Mutant Ninja Turtles

Film: *Teenage Mutant Ninja Turtles* (1990), *Teenage Mutant Ninja Turtles II: Secret of the Ooze* (1991), *Teenage Mutant Ninja Turtles III* (1993), *TMNT* (2007).

Television (animated): *Teenage Mutant Ninja Turtles* (1987–1996), *Ninja Turtles: The Next Mutation* (1997–1998), *Teenage Mutant Ninja Turtles* (2003–).

Notable Others

Film: *Swamp Thing* (1982), *Richie Rich* (1994), *Casper* (1995), *Men in Black* (1997, sequel in 2002), *Blade* (1998, sequels in 2002, 2004), *Daredevil* (2003), *Ghost Rider* (2007), *Iron Man* (2008).

(Cont'd.)

Exhibit 4-4. Comic Book Adaptations in Film and Television *(Continued)*

Notable Others (Cont'd.)

Television (live action): *Shazam* (aka *The Shazam/Isis Hour*, 1974–1977), *Wonder Woman* (1976–1978).

Television (animated): *Super Friends* (the name changed several times) (1973–1986), *Iron Man* (1994–1996), *Men in Black: The Series* (1997–2001), *Static Shock* (2000–2004), *Justice League* (aka *Justice League Unlimited*, 2001–2006), *Teen Titans* (2004–).

Direct to video/DVD: *Ultimate Avengers* (2006), *Ultimate Avengers 2* (2006), *Invincible Iron Man* (2007); all animated.

Collected comic book tie-ins: *Super Friends* (1976–1981), *Justice League Adventures* (2002–2004), *Justice League Unlimited* (2004–), *Teen Titans Go!* (2003–).

---

kryptonite was introduced on the radio show, reportedly so voice actor "Bud" Collier could take some time off during the episodes in which Superman was incapacitated. The radio show also introduced the well-known phrase "Up, up, and away," since the radio audience obviously could not see Superman "taking off." Characters from the adaptations also find their way into comics, including the Marvel Comics heroine Firestar, introduced on *Spider-Man and His Amazing Friends*, and the Batman villain Harley Quinn, who first appeared on *Batman: The Animated Series*. Harley even ended up with her own comic book series.

The effect of these adaptations on comic book readership is debatable. When a new version comes out on film or television, it often raises the popularity of the character. Artist George Perez, who with writer Marv Wolfman worked on DC's *Teen Titans* titles in the 1980s has told at comic book conventions of how, since the introduction of the *Teen Titans* cartoon series, he has encountered children who have shown great excitement over meeting the man who helped to create Starfire, Raven, and Cyborg. However, if these children come to a comic book store, or see the collected editions in the library, they may find that the original versions of these characters are very different than what they are used to. For that matter, their favorite characters from the film/show might not even appear in the comic.

Some comic books are based on the adapted works (see Exhibit 4-4 for the titles that have been collected), but now the children can see the original material, including those stories that helped to create the stories that they have viewed (for example, the *Teen Titans* animated series has adapted many of the classic Wolfman/Perez stories). Unfortunately, as will be covered in Chapter 6, some of the comics/trades with characters from child-friendly cartoons may not be as child friendly as their animated counterparts. Another question is that even if children read the *Teen Titans* books, will they be interested in reading the other books in the graphic novel collection? Still, the publishers know how to take advantage of a film or show's popularity. For example, around the same time that *Spider-Man 3* came out—with Spider-Man fighting villains Sandman and Venom—

Marvel released the trade editions *Spider-Man: Saga of the Sandman* and *Spider-Man: Birth of Venom*, both featuring the characters' earlier appearances.

There are a number of novelists and film and television writers who have also worked in comics. Some work in comics before entering the area that they are better known for, others gain fame in one field before working in comics, and still others work in both at the same time. Those who have worked on comics recently are found in Exhibit 4-5. That writers of comic books also write novels can be used as an argument to get graphic novels, especially in a public library. After all, if the library will purchase a "regular" novel by Peter David, Neil Gaiman, Brad Meltzer, etc., why not also purchase a graphic novel? In 2006, a "first" occurred when Brad Meltzer simultaneously had both the number one bestselling novel (*The Book of Fate*) and the number one best-selling comic book (*Justice League of America*, Volume 2, #0), a comic book that included an except from the novel (MacDonald, 2006).

If all of the other things in this chapter cannot convince "The Powers That Be" that the library or media center's collection should include graphic novels then this one fact might: Having graphic novels in the library collection increases circulation.

Since the 1940s, surveys have shown that a great amount of children read comics. Additional surveys and articles in recent years have shown that when libraries and school media centers include graphic novels in their collections circulation rates have been "astronomical" (Bilton, 2004: 30). For example, in South Florida's Boynton Beach High School, the media specialist found that even though graphic novels made up only 1 percent of the collection, they accounted for 25 to 30 percent of the circulation, and this was with a four-book limit. This is actually down from when the collection was first introduced (Heckman, 2004: 3). The same situation has applied to other libraries all around the country—both school and public—with tales of books that are constantly flying off the shelves and readers clamoring for more.

It has also been found that in many of these cases, readers of graphic novels will then go on to check out other library materials, leading to an overall increase in circulation. Some libraries have doubled, tripled, and even quadrupled their young adult circulation when graphic novels were added to the collection (BWI Public Library Specialists, 2005). This has long been the case, even before graphic novels and trade editions were common items. In 1979, a Missouri junior high school put noncirculating comics in the library, and soon library traffic increased 54 percent, with a 30 percent increase in circulation. The comics even became an incentive for the kids to work hard so that they'd be allowed to go the library (Dorrell and Carroll, 1983: 41–43).

The last word on the topic of why libraries should carry graphic novels goes to author Scott McCloud:

Exhibit 4-5. Selected Comic Book, Novel, and/or Film and Television Scriptwriters

Creator	Comic Work Includes	Other Work Includes
Peter David	*The Incredible Hulk, Supergirl, X-Factor, Marvel Adventures Spider-Man*	*Star Trek* novels including the juvenile Starfleet Academy series. Creator of Nickelodeon television series *Space Cases*
Neil Gaiman	*Sandman, Marvel 1602, Eternals*	The juvenile novels *Coraline, M is for Magic, The Day I Swapped My Dad for Two Goldfish,* and *The Wolves in the Walls.*
Paui Dini	*Detective Comics, Jingle Belle*	Writer on the Batman and Superman animated series of the 1990s.
J. Michael Straczynski	*Amazing Spider-Man, Fantastic Four*	Creator and head writer of *Babylon 5*
Brad Meltzer	*Identity Crisis, Justice League of America*	*New York Times* Best Selling writer
Jeph Loeb	*Superman/Batman, Batman: The Long Halloween, Batman, Superman For All Seasons*	Writer on *Smallville, Lost,* and other shows
Joss Whedon	*Astonishing X-Men, Runaways, Buffy the Vampire Slayer*	Creator of *Buffy the Vampire Slayer* and *Angel*
Holly Black	Graphic novel *The Good Neighbors* (Scholastic)	Writer of the Spiderwick Chronicles and YA Fantasy books
Avi	*City of Light, City of Dark: A Comic Book Novel*	Many children's books including *Crispin: The Cross of Lead* and *The True Confessions of Charlotte Doyle*

. . . the benefits of libraries collecting comics are the same benefits as reading comics. For children, comics have often been a doorway into literacy. But to see comics as only that is a mistake. Comics are a valid medium and can hold their own against the great works of traditional literature and can provide the same enrichments as prose and poetry. (Weiner, 1996: 40)

Notes

1. A similar thing happened in 1991. Neil Gaiman's Sandman story "A Midsummer Night's Dream" (from *Sandman* #19 September 1990) won the World Fantasy Award. Shortly afterward, the rules were changed to prevent a comic book from winning again.

2. This story was repeated in the *Mad Magazine* parody of the show, and as David is speaking, a television in the background is saying how *Bruce* Jenner is the greatest athlete in the world.

References

"Accelerated Reader." Wikipedia (January 8, 2008). Available: http://en.wikipedia. org/wiki/Accelerated_Reader.

Allen, Erin. 2007. "Graphic Novels Growing Presence in Youth Services." *The Salisbury Post*, September 17. Available: www.salisburypost.com.

Anderson, R.C., P.T. Wilson, and L.G. Fielding. 1988. "Growth in Reading and How Children Spend Their Time Outside of School." *Reading Research Quarterly* 23 (Summer): 285–303.

Bilton, Karen. "Kids Love Comics, Too!" *School Library Journal* (July 2004). Available: www.schoollibraryjournal.com/article/CA429346.html.

Buchanan, Rachel. 2006. "A Case for Comics: Comic Books as an Educational Tool—Part Two." *Sequential Tart*, July 1. Available: www.sequentialtart.com/article. php?id=186.

BWI Public Library Specialists. 2005. *The Public Librarian's Guide to Graphic Novels*. Lexington, KY: BWI.

Cary, Stephen. 2004. *Going Graphic: Comics at Work in the Multilingual Classroom*. Portsmouth, NH: Heinemann.

Chow, Natsuko. "Comics: A Useful Tool for English as a Second Language (ESL)." Diamond Bookshelf. Available: http://bookshelf.diamondcomics.com/public/ default.asp?t=1&m=1&c=20&s=182&ai=37714&ssd=.

Crawford, Philip. 2004. "A Novel Approach: Using Graphic Novels to Attract Reluctant Readers." *Library Media Connection* 22, no. 5 (February): 26.

de Vos, Gail. 2005. "ABCs of Graphic Novels." *Resource Links* 10, no. 3 (February). Available: www.resourcelinks.ca/features/feb05.htm.

Dorrell, Larry and Ed Carroll. 1983. "Spider-Man at the Library." In *Cartoons and Comics in the Classroom*, edited by James L. Thomas. Littleton, CO: Libraries Unlimited.

Ellis, Allen and Doug Highsmith. 2000. "About Face: Comic Books in Library Literature." *Serials Review* 26, no. 2: 21–43.

Eisner, Will. 1974. "Comic Books in the Library" *School Library Journal* 21, no. 2 (October 15): 75–79.

Gaiman, Neil. "Not Waving but Drowning. Well Waving a Bit" (July 20, 2003). Available: www.neilgaiman.com/2003/07/not-waving-but-drowing-well-waving.asp.

Haugaard, Kay. 1973. "Comic Books: Conduits to Culture." *The Reading Teacher* 27, no. 1: 54–55.

Heckman, Will. 2004. "Reading Heroes for a New Generation." *Media Quarterly* (Spring): 3.

Hill, Robyn A., ed. 2002. *The Secret Origins of Good Readers: A Resource Book*. Comic-Con International. Available: www.night-flight.com/secretorigin/sogr 2002.pdf.

Hosler, Jay. 2000. *Clan Apis*. Columbus, OH : Active Synapse.

"How Comics Can Reach Reluctant Readers." Diamond Bookshelf. Available: http://bookshelf.diamondcomics.com/public/default.asp?t=1&m=1&c=20&s=182 &ai=37708&ssd=.

Krashen, Stephen D. 2004. *The Power of Reading*, 2nd ed. Westport, CT: Libraries Unlimited.

Kunitz, Stanley J. [As SJK]. 1941. "The Comics Menace." *Wilson Library Bulletin* 15: 846–847.

Leonhardt, Mary. 1996. *Keeping Kids Reading: How to Raise Avid Readers in the Video Age.* New York: Crown Publishers.

Long, Tony. 2006. "The Day the Music Died." *Wired*, October 26. Available: www.wired.com/news/columns/0,71997-0.html.

Lyga, Allyson A.W. and Barry Lyga. 2004. *Graphic Novels in Your Media Center: A Definitive Guide.* Westport, CT: Libraries Unlimited.

MacDonald, Heidi. 2006. "Meltzer: King of All Media." *The Beat*, September 18. Available: www.pwbeat.publishersweekly.com/blog/2006/09/18/Meltzer-king-of-all-media.

"'Manga Is a Problem' and Other Highlights from the ICv2 Graphic Novel Conference." ICv2.com (March 5, 2006). Available: www.icv2.com/articles/home/8313.html. Accessed July 5, 2006.

McCloud, Scott. 1993. "Comics and the Visual Revolution." *Publisher's Weekly*, October 11, pp. 47–56.

McTaggart, Jacquie. *The Graphic Novel: Everything You Ever Wanted to Know but Were Afraid to Ask* (handout). Available: www.theteachersdesk.com/. Accessed: January 2008.

Pennella, Brenda. "The POW!-er in the Classroom! A Teacher's Perspective." Brodart.com. Available: http://www.graphicnovels.brodart.com/teachers_perspective.htm. Accessed: January 12, 2008.

Rogers, John. 2006a. "Comics Introduce Middle East Superheroes." *The Cincinnati Enquirer*, May 13.

Rogers, John. 2006b. "Mideast Conflicts—Pow! Zap! Blam!—Resolved." *The New Journal*, May 13.

Serchay, David S. 2004. "But Those Aren't Really Books! Graphic Novels and Comic Books." In *Thinking Outside the Book: Alternatives for Today's Teen Library Collections*, edited by C. Allen Nichols. Westport, CT: Libraries Unlimited.

Swain, Emma. 1983. "Using Comic Books to Teach Reading and Language Arts." In *Cartoons and Comics in the Classroom*, edited by James L. Thomas. Littleton, CO: Libraries Unlimited

Trelease, Jim. 2001. *The Read Aloud Handbook*, 5th ed. New York: Penguin Books.

Weiner, Stephen. 1996. *100 Graphic Novels for Public Libraries*. Northampton, MA: Kitchen Sink Press.

Worthy, J., M. Moorman, and M. Turner. 1999. "What Johnny Likes to Read Is Hard to Find in School." *Reading Research Quarterly* 34 (Jan–Feb–Mar): 12–27.

Yang, Gene (uncredited). "History of Comics in Education." Comics in Education (2003). Available: www.humblecomics.com/comicsedu/history.html

"ZOIKS!" Comic Books Offer a Key to Literacy Says UOFW Prof." 2007. News Release. January 18. University of Windsor, Ontario, Canada.

Chapter 5

Purchasing Your Graphic Novel Collection

According to Milton Griepp, Chief Executive of ICv2,[1] which tracks pop culture retail, libraries add an estimated 5 to 10 percent to retail sales of graphic novels (Twiddy, 2007). There are many methods that libraries can use to purchase their graphic novels, ranging from going through the standard vendors to acquiring them through local merchants.

As with any other collection in your library, the first step is purchasing, and the first step in purchasing is deciding certain budget issues. Do you, for example, want graphic novels to be a separate area of your collection budget, or will they be part of the overall budget? With the former, you will have to decide what percentage of the budget is going to go to graphic novels. With the latter, it could simply be a matter of what you feel like buying ("Okay, let's get the new *Junie B. Jones* book, a book on Australia, and the latest *Amelia Rules* collection").

Library Vendors

In many cases, libraries use the same vendors to purchase their graphic novels as they do the other books in their collection. The discounts may be higher, a professional relationship is already established between the vendor and the library with all necessary paperwork already filled out, and, in many cases, the vendors are able to bind and process the materials before sending them to the library. Library vendors have been quick to recognize the growing interest in graphic novels and have spotlighted them with special catalogs and on their Web pages. They offer libraries both individual volumes and standing order plans that arrange a regular order for ongoing manga or trade series. The following are among the better-known vendors that you might use.

Book Wholesalers, Inc. (BWI)

Among its other publications, BWI puts out the *Public Librarian's Guide to Graphic Novels*. Besides listing books available through BWI, the guide also tells about graphic novels and discusses issues such as genres, mature content, cataloging, shelving, and dealing with challenges. They also publish another guide dealing with anime. Its online catalog, *Titletales* (www.bwibooks.com), has a special section on graphic novels that includes special lists of award winners, "kid safe" graphic novels, recommended titles, shōjo, and shōnen. Titles are in the catalog several months prior to the actual publication, and entries occasionally include descriptions and reviews from *Booklist*, *Publishers Weekly*, and other review sources, including an in-house reviewer.

Brodart

Brodart's public graphic novel Web page (www.graphicnovels.brodart.com/) provides a list of kid-safe graphic novels, core lists, and selection criteria. A number of articles, several written by librarians or from library publications, are also archived on the site. A site for subscribers, Bibz, contains monthly lists compiled by *VOYA* graphic novel reviewer Kat Kan. There are lists for public libraries (juvenile, young adult, and adult) and for schools (elementary, middle, and high), the latter of which generally contains "kid-safe" titles. The lists include some older backlist titles as well as upcoming titles. Also part of Brodart is McNaughton, which provides leased books, a service that allows libraries to purchase a large quantity of a title when it is "hot" (often books on the bestseller list), but return the majority of them when interest dies down. Graphic novels are among those books offered, though only a few are "kid-safe."

Baker & Taylor

Baker & Taylor has its own graphic novel publication called *Imagery*, which comes out twice a year and is available both through the mail and at their Web site (www.btol.com), which includes a list of recent and upcoming titles. In addition, they have a quarterly newsletter called *Panels & Ink* devoted to graphic novels.

Ingram

Similar to the others, Ingram also has a standing order program for its graphic novels. There is also a graphic novels section of their trade publication *Advance*, and a special graphic novels supplement comes out twice a year. More information can be found at www.ingrambook.com. Again as with the other companies, additional online information and services are available to those who subscribe to their program.

Comic Book Stores

Although they may or may not have discounts and definitely will not provide any cataloging or processing assistance, another method of purchasing graphic novels is in the local comic book store, also called comic book shops and comic specialty stores.

For several decades comic books were sold in newsstands, drugstores, supermarkets, and even in bookstores, but no stores sold comic books as their primary merchandise. Some bookstores would stock old comics the same way they would stock old magazines, and even back in the early 1940s, retailers such as still-existing Bonnet's books in Dayton, Ohio, and a Kansas store owned by Harvey "Pop" Hollinger would actively buy and sell "old" (which at the time was less than ten years) comic books. However, what is considered to be the first "true" comic book shop—one in which comic books were the main product sold—opened in San Diego, California, on April 1, 1968. Seven Sons Comic Books was owned by seven partners, the youngest of which was 16 years old. Soon after this, the still-existing San Francisco Comic Book Company started and became both a seller and publisher of Underground Comics. By the following year, comic book stores were opening up across the county.

At first comic shops got their books from the same periodical distributors as the newsstands, but the 1970s saw the rise of the direct market. It was created by Phil Seuling, who in 1972 formed Seagate Distribution, the first wholesaler created specifically to sell comic books to the comic book shops. One major difference for the store owners was that with the periodical distributors, unsold comics could be returned, whereas with the direct marketer they could not. However, since they were assuming this risk, the store owners were able to purchase the comics with a much larger discount. This also led to stores selling older issues (called back issues) of comic books.

Many additional distributors were set up, and thousands of stores opened up around the country, using the direct market to get their comics several weeks before drugstores, bookstores, and the other places that did not use the direct market. Publishers also began using the direct market to their advantage. Many independent publishers began to distribute their titles with only the direct market, while other publishers created certain direct-market-only titles. The first maxiseries, DC's *Camelot 3000* was one of these, and soon both DC and Marvel were publishing comics that were sold only via the direct market.

The late 1980s/early 1990s were a hot time for comic shops. Not only were regular comic book readers and collections coming in, but so were the speculators, people who were purchasing comics, sometime multiple copies of the same issues, simply for the investment value. At one point there were around 7,000 comic book shops around the country. By the mid-1990s the situation had changed. As with other "hot" investments, the bubble burst, the investors stopped buying, and many shops ended up going out of business. Currently there are, at best, half the number of stores than there were at the peak.

The direct market was also going through changes during this period. For a time there were many distributors, and they all offered comics from most if not all of the comic book publishers. In 1995 this all changed. First Marvel Comics purchased the distributor Heroes World and announced that they would be the exclusive distributor of all Marvel titles. Then DC signed an exclusive agreement with Diamond Distributors (see Exhibit 5-1). The major independents began to go with either Diamond or Capital City, though not always with an exclusive deal. The market was odd for a while, with comic stores having to go with several distributors to get the popular titles. Eventually many of the other distributors went out of business, Diamond bought Capital City, and Marvel shut down Heroes World and went back to Diamond.

In the decade that followed, Diamond became the main supplier for comic books shops. Other current distributors include Cold Cut Distribution, which calls itself "the industry's leading reorder distributor for quality independent comics" and specializes in getting new copies of comics and graphic novels from "independent" publishers quicker than Diamond,[2] and Last Gasp Books, which mainly distributes (and for more than 30 years occasionally publishes) "underground" comics for older readers.

The recent rise in graphic novels from "mainstream" publishers has also led to some changes in the way that comic shops purchase graphic novels. In order to get these books sooner, the shops have been using BWI, Baker & Taylor, and other sources familiar to librarians. Since these publishers are still

---

Exhibit 5-1. Diamond Distributors

Founded by Steve Geppi in 1982, Diamond Comic Distributors is the largest comics distributor in North America, sending the products of most of the comic book publishers to stores and even to libraries. Diamond published a catalog called *Previews*, which comic book stores and the store's subscribers use to order merchandise. Dark Horse, DC, Image, and Marvel have special places in *Previews* (Marvel has a separate insert), followed by the other independents. Although it is mainly upcoming titles that are listed, backlists of older graphic novels and trade editions are often listed as well. Besides comics and graphic novels, *Previews* also includes listings for books, statues, action figures, sports cards, clothing, toys, magazines, and more. The listings for comics and graphic novels tell about the work, but it is for sales purposes and is not a review. Since subscriptions are $150 a year, if you want to purchase a copy from your library, it is best to do so from a comic book store where you can buy one for $4.50.

Diamond has also made itself available in special ways to libraries. Its Web page, www.bookshelf.diamond.com, has sections for both libraries and schools. The site includes news and information, a list of print and online resources, reviews by Kat Kan, and special sections for schools and libraries. The school section includes lists of age-appropriate titles (divided into school levels) and lesson plans, while the library section includes a list of recommended titles (mainly for adults with a few YA titles) and information on setting up the collection and cataloging. Additional title listings for schools and libraries are found on the main page under "products," and are divided into age and genre. Similar to other vendors, Diamond does provide a discount, but they do not provide any binding or cataloging services. In 2006, Diamond also launched a division called Diamond Kids Group, which concentrates on juvenile titles.

learning to use the direct market, sometimes it is simply easier for stores to order from these companies. Besides possibly getting them sooner, using a book vendor also allows the shop to reorder titles from all graphic novel publishers without having to pay Diamond's reordering fee (Rosen, 2006).

Some areas have an abundance of comic book stores, while others have one or two or even none at all. To locate a store in your area, check the yellow pages (in print or online), often under the category "bookstores." You can also call Diamond's Comic Shop Locator at 1-800-Comic-Book, or go to www.comic shoplocator.com. Another online source is The Master List of Comic Book & Trading Card Stores, located at www.the-master-list.com. Besides comics and graphic novels, the stores might sell other merchandise as well, including sports cards, role-playing games, card games such as Pokemon, other related games, books, DVDs (especially anime, comic related, and "cult" films), toys, statues, posters, clothing, materials for the preservation of comic books (bags and boards), and so forth. Many of these stores also offer subscription services for their regular customers, in which comics and graphic novels are "pulled" from the weekly deliveries and held for them. Therefore, subscribers do not have to worry about a title being sold out, and they are often able to purchase their comics at a discount.

The stereotype about comic shops—that they are strange places, not female-friendly, and filled with "geeks" and people like "Comic Book Guy" from *The Simpsons*—is generally *not* the case. Some stores have multiple locations, and a few stores are even nationally known due to events they hold or because of mentions in the comics-related press. These include Midtown and Jim Haneley's Universe in New York City, Mile High Comics in Colorado, and Golden Apple Comics in Los Angeles. A branch of one Salt Lake City store, Night Flight Comics, is even located in the same building as a library.

Bookstores have also become a major source of graphic novels, especially the larger chain stores such as Barnes & Noble, Books-A-Million, and Borders, where you can find entire rows of bookshelves with graphic novels on them. Bookstores have stocked graphic novels for a long time, often placing them either in the same section as comic strip collections or in with the science fiction and fantasy books. They still tend to be found in or near those sections, but in 2003 the Book Industry Systems Advisory Committee of the Book Industry Study Group, Inc., gave graphic novels their own shelving classification (MacDonald, 2003). Not only did the group recommend shelving options for comic books, but on the back of some paperbacks the words "graphic novel" or "manga" appear beside such terms as "drama," "romance," "action," "fantasy," and so forth. Just as "mainstream" publishers are learning how to work with the direct market, comic book publishers are learning to work with bookstores. One thing that they are doing is teaming up with the "mainstream" publishers to help in distribution. Among others, Simon & Schuster distributes Viz, while HarperCollins distributes Tokyopop titles. Diamond has also created a separate book division to work with bookstores.

Like libraries, bookstores are learning how to deal with the graphic novel boom. Although graphic novels may have their own shelves, they are generally intermixed, except for manga, which is usually kept separate from (but next to) the nonmanga, and all-ages titles can be found right next a mature audience books. The abundance of titles, with manga taking up the majority of them, had caused some concern among fans that some titles, especially those by smaller publishers, could be "squeezed out" of shelf space. Bookstores can at times offer discounts or at least "clubs" in which purchases can lead to future credit or discounts.

Online sources are also a possibility. Sites such as Amazon.com, DeepDiscount. com, and the online stores of Barnes & Noble and other bookstores provide discounts and, if the amount of the purchase is high enough, free shipping. Some comic shops, including Mile High and Midtown have online stores and subscription services that ship around the country. Some publishers also have online stores so that you can purchase directly from them. Of course, as when purchasing from comic book shops of bookstores, any sort of processing will have to be done by your library. As they have for decades, certain comic companies offer subscriptions, but this is almost always for individual, ongoing comic book series, not graphic novels or trade editions.

So which method is the best? There is no one perfect source, as they all have their advantages and disadvantages. With the vendors, your library/school may already work with them, they usually provide a discount, they can process the books and improve their binding, and you can also order other types of books along with the graphic novels. An advantage in dealing with Diamond or going through your local comic book shop is that you can get the books much quicker, even on the day they first come out, and they may carry some titles that your regular library vendor does not. Since comic shops often carry a large supply of graphic novels, they can also be helpful if you need to replace a lost or damaged book in a hurry. The comic shop may even still stock books that are out of print, allowing you to get something that you could not get from a vendor. Some libraries use a combination of sources to get their graphic novels, to get the best value out of each one. Consider the needs of your library, as well as what is the most practical for you, in choosing how you purchase your books.

Notes

1. Short for Internal Correspondence version 2, ICv2 provides information on five areas of pop culture—anime/manga, comics/graphic novels, games, movies/television

licensed products, and toys—through its Web site (www.icv2.com) and through retailer guides. ICv2 has taken an interest in the area of graphic novels in libraries, sponsoring discussions, reporting on panels, and using librarian as reviewers.

    2. In 2008, Cold Cut was purchased by Rogue Wolf Entertainment. How this will affect Cold Cut's policies was not known at the time of publication.

References

MacDonald, Heidi. 2003. "Bookstore Revolution: Graphic Novels Get Their Own Category" *Pulse News*, January 20. Available: www.comicon.com/ubb/ultimatebb. php/ubb/forum/f/36.html.

Rosen, Judith. 2006. "Comic Shops Turn to Book Distributors for Graphic Novels." PW Comic Week. *Publisher's Weekly*, July 18.

Twiddy, David. 2007. "Pictures Causing Problems." *The Gazette* [Cedar Rapids–Iowa City, Iowa], January 14, p. 5L.

Chapter 6

So Much to Choose From: Deciding What to Purchase

Chapter 4 explained why you should purchase graphic novels, and Chapter 5 presented various ways of doing so. Now that you know why and how, the big question is *what*. With space and especially budget considerations, what should you buy for your library or library system?

This is another time that you should treat graphic novels exactly as you do the other items in your library. Of course you will want the books that are of superior quality both in terms of story and art, but you will also want books that will circulate. Hopefully these books will be one and the same, but as every librarian knows, this is not always the case. You might have a title of dubious quality that has a high rate of circulation, or you might have a highly praised book that is a "shelf-sitter." Since one of the library's duties is serving the needs of the public, it may very well own many more copies of the former than the latter.

Mainstream Comic Book and Graphic Novel Publishers

There are several dozen comic book publishers out there, some that publish comics, trades, manga collections, and original graphic novels, and a smaller number that publish only the latter. This section and the following one look at some of the publishers whose books you will most likely want to include in your collection.

DC and Marvel

With soft drinks it's Coke and Pepsi. With fast food it's Burger King and McDonald's. With comic books the "big two" are DC and Marvel. They put out dozens of comic books a month and hundreds of original graphic novels and trade editions each year, and their characters are known all around the world.

DC Comics, home of Superman, Batman, and Wonder Woman, has been around since 1935, when National Allied Publications, founded the previous year by Major Malcolm Wheeler-Nicholson, published *New Fun* #1, the first comic book with all original material.[1] This was soon followed by *New Comics*, which later became the long running *Adventure Comics* (1935–1983), and the still-published *Detective Comics* (1937–) and *Action Comics* (1938–). National Allied soon merged with others to become National Comics, but many of their titles had a logo with the words "A DC Publication" (DC for Detective Comics), and long before it became the company's official name, the company was being referred to as "DC Comics." Hyping its other popular character, several of the later logos also had Superman's name or image.

In 1956, DC published *Showcase* #4, which introduced a new version of the 1940s superhero the Flash, marking the beginning of the "Silver Age" of comics. Besides introducing new characters during this period, several other "Golden Age" characters were revised, often with a science-fiction-based origin. For example, while the old Green Lantern has a magic power ring, the new version got his ring from a dying alien, and whereas the original Atom was simply short, the new version could shrink to microscopic size. Some of this was due to editor Julius "Julie" Schwartz, a pioneer of science-fiction fandom and former literary agent whose clients included Ray Bradbury and H.P. Lovecraft. While the 1940s heroes formed the Justice Society, the new ones formed the Justice League, which has existed in one form or another since 1960.

Besides the "regular" DC line, there are also several imprints. The Johnny DC line, named after DC's cartoon mascot of the 1960s and also known as DC Kids, is geared especially for younger readers, and mainly has comic book versions of popular cartoons, both based on DC characters (*The Batman Strikes!*, *Teen Titans Go*, etc.), characters such as Scooby Doo and Bugs Bunny, and characters from the Cartoon Network, which, like DC, is owned by Time Warner. Collections of these titles are usually put out in a cheaper, digest form.

DC also has a mature audience line, Vertigo, whose notable titles have included *Sandman*, *Fables,* and *Hellblazer*. Although these and many other books in the Vertigo line contain well-written stories, these stories occasionally feature nudity, foul language, excessive images of gore or violence, and other elements to which you may feel younger children should not yet be exposed. If you are in a public library, your library (or library system) should purchase these books, but in almost every case they should not be read by children.

Another DC line is Wildstorm, a creator-owned line (many of the characters in DC and Marvel are owned by the company, not their creators), which was once part of Image (see the following section in this chapter, "The Independents"). Many Wildstorm titles (*Authority*, *League of Extraordinary Gentlemen*, etc.) are meant for mature audiences, so purchase accordingly. DC also published a line of manga under the CMX imprint, and in 2007 began Minx, a line aimed at teenage girls.

Marvel Comics publishes such popular characters as Spider-Man, the X-Men, and the Fantastic Four. Marvel's earliest incarnation was Timely Comics, which was begun in 1939 by pulp-magazine publisher Martin Goodman. Its first comic was *Marvel Comics* #1, which introduced the android version of the Human Torch, and the Sub-Mariner who, along with Captain America, who first appeared in 1941 (in *Captain America Comics* #1), is still a major character in the "Marvel Universe." After superhero books went out of fashion the company changed its name to Atlas and published a variety of other genres. By 1961, when it changed its name to Marvel Comics, the company had several existing titles, most notably *Strange Tales*, *Journey into Mystery*, and *Tales to Astonish*, all which would soon become superhero titles. Later that year *Fantastic Four* #1 was published, and this is considered to be the start of the "Marvel Universe," and the year that Marvel has cited in many anniversary celebrations.

What made Marvel's characters stand out was that they were not perfect and had problems beyond "Oh no, Lois Lane is trying to discover my secret identity again." Spider-Man may stop the bad guy, but at the end of the day his aunt is sick, he can't pay the bills, and, thanks to bad press, people don't like him, and the X-Men, who "defend a world that hates and fears them," have always been a metaphor for people who have to deal with prejudice.

Marvel also has several imprints, though the one most suited for this book is the Marvel Adventures line. Originally called Marvel Age, this line is geared toward younger ages and has adventures of Spider-Man, the Fantastic Four, the Avengers, Iron Man, and other characters. These series have a continuity that is separate from "mainstream" Marvel Universe, so, for example, the events in the other Spider-Man titles do not affect what is going on in *Marvel Adventures Spider-Man* and vice versa. As with the Johnny DC line, most of the trade editions for this line are in digest form. Comic books from these titles are also converted into hardcover books by Adbo Publishing's Spotlight Books.

Another line from Marvel features the titles set in the "Ultimate Universe." This universe, which was introduced in 1999 with the first issue of *Ultimate Spider-Man*, is similar to the mainstream Marvel Universe, though with some significant differences. In the mainstream Spider-Man books, Peter Parker (Spider-Man) is in his twenties, has graduated college, and has had several occupations, including freelance photographer for *The Daily Bugle*. In *Ultimate Spider-Man*, Peter is a teenager, is still in high school, and has a part-time job working on the *Bugle*'s Web page. Many of the characters in the "regular" universe have "Ultimate" counterparts, but in many cases their ages, personalities, histories, and even ethnicities are different. *Ultimate Spider-Man* is acceptable for older tweens, but the rest of the line is better for teens and older. Other Marvel lines include Marvel Knights, which is aimed at teenagers and older readers, and Marvel Max, the "mature audience" line, with stories that, as in DC's Vertigo, may contain language, nudity, and so forth.

The Independents

Where there is Burger King and McDonald's, there is also Wendy's, Checkers, Big Boy, Steak 'n Shake, Sonic, and other places, right down to the local diner down the street. The same goes for the comic book industry, where they are collectively known as "Independents." Although the independent companies may not equal the "big two" in terms of output, several of them match and occasionally surpass them in terms of influence, popularity, and, more important, sales. The following is a quick look at some of them.

Dark Horse

Founded in 1986, Dark Horse Comics is one of the major independents. Among their publications are a number of licensed properties, including *Buffy, the Vampire Slayer* and *Star Wars*. A large number of Dark Horse comics are limited series. Among the children's titles are *The Mighty Skullboy Army, The Dare Detective, Go! Girl,* and *Shadow Rock.* Dark Horse also has a line of manga, and among the other titles for children are collections of the old *Little Lulu, Casper,* and *Richie Rich* comic books.

Image

Another major independent, Image Comics was founded in 1992 by former Marvel Comics artists. Image's longest running titles are *Spawn* and *Savage Dragon,* both of which have been around since the early 1990s and have been made into animated series and/or movies. Comics and graphic novels for children include *Tommysaurus Rex, Death Jr., Leave It to Chance,* and *Lions, Tigers, and Bears.*

Tokyopop

Tokyopop is one of the major publishers of manga in America. Some of its juvenile titles include *Kingdom Hearts, Pixie Pops, Angelic Layer,* and *Kamichama Karin.* Tokyopop also published a number of OEL manga, including *Peach Fuzz, Mail Order Ninja,* and *Kat and Mouse,* as well as the cine-manga series of books. Incorporated in Japan, Tokyopop was founded as Mixx in 1997 and has branches in Los Angeles, Germany, and the United Kingdom.

Viz

Another major manga publisher, the San Francisco–based Viz, which is owned by one of Japan's largest publishers of manga, is the home of such popular books as *Ranma 1/2, Dragon Ball Z, Pokemon, Inu-Yasha, Yu-Gi-Oh, Prince of Tennis*, *Whistle!*, and a series of animanga based on anime films. Viz is also the publisher of *Shonen Jump* and *Shojo Beat*.

Disney Press and Gemstone

Disney Press puts out trades with comics taken from the *Disney Adventures Magazine*. The Disney imprint Hyperion also published graphic novels, including novels based on the *W.I.T.C.H.* series of books, the adaptation of *Artemis Fowl*, and the OGN *Biker Girl*.

The Baltimore-based Gemstone is another publisher of Disney characters, including Mickey Mouse, Donald Duck, and Uncle Scrooge. Gemstone's parent company is Diamond Distributors.

Top Shelf

Founded in 1997, the Georgia-based Top Shelf is the home of such notable graphic novels as the multiple award-winning *Blankets* and the children's books *Grampa and Julie Shark Hunters*, *Korgi*, *Monkey vs. Robot*, and the *Owly* series.

Antarctic Press

Besides comics such as *Neotopia* and manga-style adaptations of *The Wizard of Oz* and *Alice in Wonderland*, this Texas-based company also publishes books such as the *How to Draw Manga* series.

Archie Comics

For more than 60 years, Archie, Jughead, Betty, Veronica, and the rest of the gang have been appearing in kid-friendly stories in both comic book and digest form. Whereas many comics are generally found in comic shops and bookstores, Archie still appears on newsstands and even among the impulse items at the grocery store. This has helped Archie Comics be among the top comics publishers in America.

Bongo Comics

Co-owned by *Simpsons* creator Matt Groening, Bongo's major titles are comics based on *The Simpsons* and various spin-offs. However, the trades of their comics are published by HarperCollins.

Devil's Due Publishing

Devil's Due published comic versions of many licensed properties, such as *GI Joe* and *Army of Darkness*, and children's titles that include *Patrick the Wolf Boy*.

Fantagraphics Books

The publishers of *The Comics Journal*, Fantagraphics has put out myriad works for adults, including *Ghost World*, *King*; books in the "Love and Rockets" series; and titles for younger readers, including *Castle Waiting*. They are also the publishers of *The Complete Peanuts* and are reprinting the entire run of this classic comic strip.

IDW Publishing

IDW is known for its horror comics (*30 Days of Night, Dawn of the Dead*) and licensed properties (*CSI, Angel*), and for the children's graphic novels *Adventures in Oz, The Vanishers,* and *Grumpy Old Monsters*.

Oni

Founded in 1997, the Oregon-based Oni published comics and graphic novels for all ages. Titles for younger readers include *Banana Sunday, Mutant Texas, Polly and the Pirates,* and the *Allison Dare* and *Courtney Crumrin* books.

Slave Labor Graphics (SLG)

Slave Labor puts out such popular oddball titles as *Milk and Cheese* and *Gloomcookie*. Its Amaze Ink imprint is for titles that are more appropriate for younger readers, including Disney-owned properties such as *Gargoyles* and *Haunted Mansion* and the graphic novels *Gordon Yamamoto and the King of the Geeks, Jet Pack Pets,* and *Little Gloomy*.

ADV

ADV (AD Vision) distributes both anime and manga, including both versions of *Azumanga Daioh* and the manga *Yotsuba&!*

Digital Manga Publishing (DMP)

Digital Manga publishes manga for all ages, including the "edu-manga" series of biographies.

NBM/Papercutz

The New York–based Nantier Beall Minoustchine Publishing, Inc., has been publishing graphic novels since 1976, often translating works from France and Belgium. Publications for younger readers include *Mister O, Cryptozoo Crew,* and literary and fairy tale adaptations. Papercutz is an imprint of NBM, which publishes original *Hardy Boys* and *Nancy Drew* graphic novels and adaptations of the animated *Totally Spies*.

Intercompany Crossovers

Sometimes companies will cross over. DC's and Marvel's characters have been meeting each other since the 1970s. In 1996 the fans got to answer the question of who would win a fight between the DC and Marvel heroes with the "DC vs. Marvel" limited series.[2] There have been crossovers between superheroes and

Exhibit 6-1. Crossgen Comics

Debuting in 2000, Crossgeneration Comics, better known as Crossgen, put out comics in a variety of genres, created by many popular writers and artists. Many of their titles had a tenuous link to one another due to a mysterious sigil possessed by a character in each book. Titles included the science fiction title *Sigil*; the fantasy *Meridian, Ruse*, which featured a Sherlock Holmes–like detective; the horror title *Route 666*; and the Samurai story *The Path*. Their titles were collected in both regular and digest-sized trades, and two monthly trade anthologies, *Forge* and *Edge* (also called *Vector*), reprinted issues of various series.

Crossgen also worked with schools and libraries. The company created teacher's guides to its trade editions along with a program for the schools. Crossgen was one of the first comic companies on the GNLIB list and among the publishers at the 2002 YALSA Graphic Novel Preconference.

Unfortunately, Crossgen went out of business in 2004, and most of its books never finished their ongoing storylines. Disney later purchased many of Crossgen's assets and in June 2006 began to publish the fantasy series *Abadazad* for their Hyperion imprint, in which comic pages were mixed in with "regular" story. It saw only three comic book issues.

In 2007 Checker Publishing began to publish trades containing previously uncollected stories. The numbering of the volumes continued from those put out by Crossgen (for example *Sigil* is "restarting" at Volume 5). Whether those stories that have already been collected will be collected again and put back in print remains to be seen.

of Roaring Brook Press, includes among its titles the *Sardine in Outer Space* series and the highly acclaimed and award-winning *American Born Chinese*. Christian publisher Zondervan has begun putting out graphic novels through its Zonderkidz line. Stone Arch Books, which publishes for eight- to fourteen-year-olds, puts out "safe graphic novels," in five lines: Graphic Sparks, Graphix Trax, Graphic Quest, Graphic Revolve (adaptations of novels), and Ridge Riders. Other companies that have adapted classic books include Penguin (the Puffin Graphics series and its Philomel imprint, whose adaptations include Anthony Horowitz's *Stormbreaker* and Brian Jacques's *Redwall*), Abdo, and Gareth Stevens. School Specialty Publishing has a series called "The Critter Kids Adventure Series," based on characters created by Mercer Mayer and aimed at the elementary school level.

Del Rey, which is part of Random House, has its own manga imprint, as does the Hachette Book Group, which has created a new imprint, Yen Press. Instead of creating a separate imprint, Simon & Schuster's Children Publishing undertook a division-wide effort in 2007 to encourage the publication of graphic novels throughout its various imprints. The first book in this effort, *Chiggers*, by Hope Larson, about two 13-year-old girls, came out in 2008. Other books target both middle and high school and come out in a variety of genres and subjects. The rise in "graphic nonfiction" has led to publishers of juvenile nonfiction, such as Rosen, Capstone, Lerner, Gareth Stevens, School Specialty, and Osprey, to create new graphic lines dealing with history, biography, mythology, and other nonfiction topics (see Exhibit 6-2).

licensed characters (*Batman vs. Predator*, *Superman vs. the* ?
Trek/X-Men, etc.), and in a very unusual crossover, Marvel'.
vigilante the Punisher met "All-American" Teenager Archie.[3]

Publisher Changes

Sometimes a title will change publishers. In the case of licensed pi
simply because a new company has acquired the rights to that proper
as mentioned in Chapter 2, has switched publishers a number of ti
times this results in a new comic book, while in others the existing
retains its original numbering. *Walt Disney's Comics and Stories* publ.
been Dell Comics (for #1–#264, 1940–1962), Gold Key Comics (for #?
with #474–#510 under Gold Key's "Whitman" imprint 1962–198
stone Publishing (for #511–#547, 1962–1984), Disney Comics (for #5∢
1990–1993), Gladstone Publishing again (for #586–#633, 1993–19.
the current publisher Gemstone Publishing (since #634, 2003).

Another reason for switching publishers is because it is a creator-
property and the creator, for one reason or another, has brought it to
publisher. For similar reasons, sometimes a comic book will be put out I
publisher, but the collected trade will be put out by another, even thoug
original publisher is still around. Dark Horse Comics, for example
published trades for *Star Wars* collected from comics originally put ou
Marvel. A further reason is that the original publisher has gone out of busin
Many comic book publishers have done so over the years. Some of the m
recent examples include Crossgen (see Exhibit 6-1), Tekno Comics, Kitch
Sink, and Broadway. Defunct publishers may have the rights to their characte
and their comics purchased by another publisher. DC comics now owns char
acters once published by Fawcett (Shazam), Charlton (Blue Beetle, Captair
Atom), and Quality (Blackhawk). Checker Book Publishing Group has recently
put out collections of Gold Key's *Star Trek* title and several series from
Crossgen, and Dark Horse is collecting the children's titles from Harvey
Comics. Unfortunately, if their properties are not purchased elsewhere, any
graphic novels that they have put out will become unavailable and any comic
books that they have published will remain uncollected.

Graphic Novels from Noncomics Publishers

Some mainstream publishing companies have begun their own graphic novel
lines. Scholastic has a line of juvenile and young adult graphic novels called
Graphix. Besides color versions of Jeff Smith's *Bone* collections (originally
published by Cartoon Books) and adaptations of the chapter book series
Goosebumps and *The Baby-sitter's Club*, Graphix also publishes original fiction, including Chynna Clugston's *Queen Bee*. First Second Books, an imprint

While they may not have a specific line of graphic novels, many mainstream fiction publishers also put out the occasional graphic novel. Many of the more acclaimed graphic novels for adults have come from these companies, including *Fun Home* (Houghton Mifflin) and *Persepolis* (Pantheon). Mainstream publishers have also helped publishers such as Tokyopop and Viz distribute their books to bookstores. HarperCollins, which works with Tokyopop, has a copublishing deal that allows Tokyopop to develop manga based on HarperCollins's authors, starting in 2007 with *Warriors: The Lost Warrior* based on Erin Hunter's children book series *Warriors*.

Even though many foreign-language graphic novels are translated before publication in the United States, some are distributed in their original language, and American and international graphic novels are also translated into Spanish and other languages and sold in the United States. American distributors of foreign language graphic novels both foreign and American include Public Square Books, which publishes books in Spanish. These can be helpful in attracting immigrants to your library and may even be helpful in programs that help people learn English (see Chapter 8).

A large number of original graphic novels, trade editions, and volumes of manga series are released each year. DC and Marvel alone put out more than 400 titles in 2006, and more than 1,400 volumes of manga came out in 2007 ("Manga Releases Up," 2007). Also, with trade editions, it is not just collections of recent comic books that are being published; comics that came out prior to

---

Exhibit 6-2. Same Subject, Different Publishers

Just as with nongraphic nonfiction, more than one publisher will put out a book on a particular subject. Librarians must decide which ones to purchase, or even if they wish to purchase every book on a particular topic, especially if that topic is a popular one. Here are some of the repeated subjects that are found in Appendix A.

Subject	No. of books	Subject	No. of books
Christopher Columbus	4	The Battle of Gettysburg	4*
George Washington	4		
Jackie Robinson	3	Lewis and Clark	2
The Wright Brothers	4	Rosa Parks and the Bus Boycott	3
Abraham Lincoln	4		
Battle of the Alamo	3	Anne Frank	4
Harriet Tubman	3	The First Moon Landing	3
The Attack on Pearl Harbor	4*	Robin Hood	3
		Martin Luther King	2

* Since the interior of the Rosen and Osprey books on this topic is the same, they are only counted once.

Even literary adaptations are put out by multiple publishers. Appendix A lists five versions of *Frankenstein*, four of *Moby Dick*, and three versions of *Treasure Island* and *The Wizard of Oz*. These range from a more than 150-page adaptation (Puffin) to a 16-page version (Gareth Stevens Publishing's Bank Street 3-in-1 series).

Exhibit 6-3. Older DC and Marvel Books in 2006

Looking at 416 trade editions put out by DC Comics and Marvel Comics in 2006, the decade by decade breakdown is as follows:

Stories originally published between	No. of books	Stories originally published between	No. of books
1930–1939	1	1980–1989	29
1940–1949	11	1990–1999	25
1950–1959	4	2000–2006	260
1960–1969	24	Multiple decades	35
1970–1979	28		

Of the 35 trades with stories from multiple decades,[4] the breakdown is this:

Decade of original publication	No. of titles with stories from that decade	Decade of original publication	No. of titles with stories from that decade
1930–1939	0	1970–1979	14
1940–1949	4	1980–1989	21
1950–1959	5	1990–1999	10
1960–1969	12	2000–2006	11

2000 are being collected in greater numbers than they were at the beginning of the decade. For example, more than 35 percent of DC and Marvel's 2006 trade output contained pre-2000 material (see Exhibit 6-3). As you can see, this means that a ten-year-old boy can come into the library and read a recent Superman story. Then he could read a story that his father read as a ten-year-old, followed by one his grandfather read at that age, and possibly even a Superman story that his *great*-grandfather read when he was ten back during the "Golden Age." And all four stories could conceivably be in the same book!

It's not just recent releases that you can choose from. Many publishers have a backlist with years' worth of graphic novels to choose from. DC Comics for example has more than 1,500 titles to choose from. It is very beneficial to libraries that publishers keep older material in print. Not only does it help when the library needs to replace a lost or damaged book, but when starting a collection, a complete, or at least up-to-date, collection of a trade or manga series can be put together.

Review Sources

So with hundreds of new titles each year to choose from and thousands of older titles still available, how do you decide what to buy? The catalogs will give basic descriptions, but won't tell you more than that. If you are unfamiliar with the material, what can you do? It is rare for graphic novels to produce review copies prior to general publication, but fortunately there should be much less immediate demand for the newest book as there would be with, say, a new

Harry Potter book, or the latest by an adult author such as John Grisham. Luckily, once they come out, there are many review sources, some of which may already be in your library.

Library periodicals have been reviewing graphic novels for years, first on an occasional basis, but eventually with regular columns. One of the first was *VOYA*, which has featured Kat Kan's "Graphically Speaking" since 1994, and it appears in every issue, along with the occasional article. *Library Journal* has featured bimonthly reviews by Steve Raiteri and others since 2002, and *School Library Journal* began regular graphic novel reviews a few years later. *Booklist* has an annual graphic novel issue, and all of these publications also intermix graphic novel reviews with reviews for other books.

There are also a number of periodicals that deal with comic books and graphic novels and often have reviews including *The Comic Buyer's Guide*, *Wizard*, and *The Comics Journal*, though the latter often concentrates on material for older readers. Of course these publications only review a small percentage of the comics and graphic novels that come out each year. Besides the reviews, there is also news, which includes information on upcoming titles, interviews with people in the industry, and columns. Mainstream periodicals, including *Entertainment Weekly* occasionally review graphic novels, and *Publishers Weekly* has a regularly updated graphic novel related Web page.

A large number of online sources—Web pages, message boards, and mailing lists—will help you to find news and reviews on comic and graphic novels. One of the best resources is the listserv GNLIB-L, a list dedicated to the subject of graphic novels in libraries. Founded by Steve Miller in 1999, GNLIB-L counts among its participants many of the people who have written books and articles about graphic novels in libraries (including Kan and Raiteri, as well representatives from publishers, vendors, and even a few creators). From the beginning, participants on GNLIB-L have recommended titles (the list's second post on October 11, 1999, by librarian Georgia Wages requested, "We are just beginning to buy graphic novels for our library system. Any recommendations on what is popular would be appreciated"), given advice when books have been challenged, and discussed issues of cataloging, shelving, preservation, and programming. *Publisher's Weekly*, *Comic Buyer's Guide*, and ICv2 are among the sources that send news and reviews directly to your e-mail inbox.

Besides the various Web sites that list, discuss, and review graphic novels, some sites created by librarians, including the popular No Flying No Tights. This site (www.noflyingnotights.com), created by librarian Robin Brenner who, among other accomplishments, was named by ICv2 as the eleventh most powerful person in the manga industry, includes a section of graphic novels for children. Several of the sites that sell graphic novels also include reviews. Diamond's, for example, has reviews by Kat Kan, who has also prepared the titles for H.W. Wilson's new "Graphic Novels Core Collection: A Selection Guide" database. Features of this database (available by subscription either by itself or grouped with other Wilson products) include being able to search in various areas including genres, subjects, awards, and, most important, age-appropriateness. Discussion and some reviews can also be found on Usenet's various rec.arts.comics newsgroups and various comic (and related) message boards. Appendix C lists some of the online sources. Some resources may review only individual comic book issues, but this can be very helpful when those individual issues are collected into a trade and you are able to have a review source for the collected work prior to its publication.

Appendix A provides a list of recommended titles, which will also be helpful in picking books. Other books on graphic novels in schools and libraries also contain helpful booklists. These and other print resources can be found in Appendix B.

As you would purchase a book for your collection that has won a Newbery, Caldecott, or other juvenile literary award, the same can apply to age-appropriate winners of the graphic novel–related awards (see Exhibit 6-4) as well as the winners of "mainstream" awards such as *American Born Chinese*. The same goes for any appropriate items on various "best" lists, such as YALSA's "Great Graphic Novels for Teens" list. Besides *American Born Chinese*, other middle-school appropriate titles on the inaugural list in 2007 included *To Dance: A Ballerina's Graphic Novel*; *Plastic Man*, Volume 2: *Rubber Bandits*; *Baby-sitter's Club: Kristy's Great Idea*; and *Death Jr.*

If your school or the schools that are served by your library use the Accelerated Reader program, see whether any of the hundreds of graphic novels for which they provide tests are on the school's list of books. If you are in a school media center, you may even be able to convince those who choose the list's titles for your school to include graphic novels. A list of titles can be found by going to www.renlearn.com/store/quiz_advanced.asp and doing a topic search for "graphic novel/comics & cartoons." Not everything listed there, however, is a graphic novel.

If you have a good working relationship with a comic book store, employees may be able to recommend titles or let you look through the new books. Bookstores are also a good location for you to examine recent graphic novels. The larger chains such as Borders and Barnes & Noble have large collections and don't mind customers sitting at a table and looking at books. You may not have the time to read an entire graphic novel, but you can at least flip through to see if there are any problematic images. You can also see how the company has rated the book to determine if it is age-appropriate.

Graphic novel publishers have been regular vendors at the American Library Association Annual Conference for years, and since 2005 there has

Exhibit 6-4. Comic Book Awards

Comics have long had their own awards. Some have been voted on by fans, while other winners have been chosen by people in the industry. Early versions included the fan-based Alley Awards (1961–1969) and the Shazam! Award from the Academy of Comic Book Arts (1971–1975). Comics-themed publications have annual awards with winners chosen by their readers, and the rise of online comics fandom led to awards including the "Squiddy Awards" from Usenet's rec.arts.comics groups.

Two of today's major comic book awards come from the same original source. In 1985 the Jack Kirby Awards were begun, but a dispute over ownership two years later resulted in the creation of two new awards—the Eisner Awards and the Harvey Awards.

Named for the comics legend, the Will Eisner Comic Achievement Awards are presented yearly at Comic-Con International and are considered to be the "Oscars" of the comic book industry. Nominees are chosen by a five-person panel—which in recent years has included librarians such as Kat Kan and Robin Brenner—and voted on by people in the industry, including creative personnel, publishers, retailers, and distributors. Besides awards for creative personnel (writers, artists, colorists, letterers, etc.) and comic book stories, limited series, and ongoing titles, there are also awards for "Best Graphic Album–New" (original graphic novels) and "Best Graphic Album–Reprint" (trade edition). In addition, there is also an award for "Best Publication for a Younger Audience." Recent winners of this award include *Owly*, *Herobear and the Kid*, and *Walt Disney's Uncle Scrooge*. Until his death in 2005, Eisner took part in the ceremonies and also won five Eisner Awards of his own.

Named for Harvey Kurtzman, whose works included early issues of *Mad*, the Harvey Awards have been presented at a variety of conventions. Nominations are done by an open vote among comic professionals, with the top five vote-getters placed on a final ballot. Award categories are similar to those in the Eisners, and although the awards do not include a category specifically for youth-aimed comics, they do have one for humor. Other awards include the Ignatz Awards (for small-press or creator-owned works), the Eagle Awards (presented by fans in the United Kingdom), the Lulu Awards (for female creators or stories with female protagonists), the Reuben Awards (from the National Cartoonists Society), and the Glyph Comics Awards (for black creators and characters).

The following books/series listed in Appendix A have won or have been nominated for at least one award. Those with an asterisk (*) are recommended for middle school readers.

Amelia Rules	*The Life and Times of*	*Project X* *
American Born Chinese *	*Scrooge McDuck*	*Spiral-Bound*
Bone	*The Lone and Level Sands* *	*To Dance*
Castle Waiting *	*Mouse Guard*	*Usagi Yojimbo*
Courageous Princess	*Nancy Drew*	*Walt Disney's Uncle*
Herobear and the Kid	*Owly*	*Scrooge*
Leave It to Chance	*Plastic Man*	*Yotsuba&!*

even been a designated "Graphic Novel Alley," where catalogs, review copies, and even creative personnel can be found. As mentioned in the previous chapter, publishers and even creators have taken part in "graphic novels in the library" panels while at ALA. If there is a comic book convention in your area (see Exhibit 6-5), this might also provide the opportunity to talk to creators and publishers. Sometimes the two are even combined. Several conventions have held panels dealing with the issue of comics in libraries, and the New York

---

Exhibit 6-5. Comic Book Conventions

The first comic book convention was held in New York City on July 27, 1964, put together by fan Bernie Bubnis. On that Monday afternoon a few hundred attendees got to meet people from Marvel Comics. Today there are conventions all over the world that are attended by tens of thousands of attendees. Some of these conventions are primarily comics-themed, while others include guests from movies, television, and literature. Attendees get to meet comic book creators, get comic books signed, acquire original drawings by artists, learn about what's going on in comics, and get the chance to purchase old and new comics and other related items. Besides the New York Comic Con, other major conventions include Megacon in Orlando, Wizard World in Chicago, the Baltimore Comicon, the Mid-Ohio Con, Heroes Convention in Charlotte, Motor City Comic Com in Detroit, Wondercon in San Francisco, and, of course, the San Diego's Comic-Con International.

Also known as the San Diego Comic-Con, what later became Comic-Con International was first held between August 1–3, 1970, with 300 fans gathering at the U.S. Grant Hotel to see such guests as comics legend Jack Kirby and author Ray Bradbury. The convention has grown in size over the years, and the 2006 event filled the San Diego Convention Center to capacity with 125,000 attendees (a number that increased the following year). In addition, there were 12,000 people from the comic book and entertainment industries; 600 hours of panels, films, and programs—including the Eisner Awards—and 970 exhibitors filling 52 aisles, which, if put out end to end, would be three miles long. Comic-Con International has also become a place for science fiction, fantasy, comic-based, and other related films and television shows to be hyped, with major actors appearing, occasionally unannounced (Rowe, 2006). Along with other programming, the convention has also held several panels on graphic novels in libraries.

Comic Con has had graphic novel conferences affiliated with it, which brought together publishers, distributors, retailers, and librarians. Sponsored by ICv2, topics at these conferences have included Graphic Novel Growth and Diversification; Graphic Novels—The New Literature?; Anime and Manga—Looking Forward; Superheroes and Manga: Making Room for Both at Your Library; Formats and Genres: Understanding Comics, Superheroes, Sci-Fi, Fantasy, Manga, ComicsLit, Humor, and Web Comics; and Graphic Novel Classics Every (School and Public) Library Should Shelve and Circulate. Even contacting the publisher directly might be helpful if you are concerned about age suitability. Some of the vendors will allow you to preview a book prior to purchase, such as BWI's SNAP (selection, notification, and acquisition plan), and also allow you to send it back if it is unsuitable for your library.

If the book has been out for while, interlibrary loan is also an option. Not only can you examine the title, but you also get a chance to see how another library catalogs and processes their graphic novels. As one librarian put it, "It's cheaper to reject an ILL than a purchase." If you are a school media specialist, it might be a simple as going to your local public library branch and finding the book in question on the shelf. The public library might also have someone who can give you great suggestions.

If you are able to view the book, what are the best ways to decide if you want it for your collection? Besides checking for age-inappropriate materials, there are other things to check when evaluating a graphic novel. Gail de Vos (2005) in her article "ABCs of Graphic Novels" suggests checking for such things as:

- What is the story and how is it being communicated by the text and the illustrations?
- How do the comic book elements such as facial expressions, clothing, background details, lettering, and panel composition help to tell the story?
- Is the art appropriate to the story?
- Does it detract from the text or vice versa?
- Are the panels easy to follow?

Of course if you don't want to look for these items, the most basic way to quickly judge a book that you are able to view is to do what you probably do with the nongraphic titles: skim through it and listen to the advice of reviewers.

In-house reviews can also be helpful. You may not be familiar with comics and graphic novels, but there might be someone else on your staff or in your library system who is. You can go to this person for advice, or, if possible, even give him or her the responsibility of collection development. If multiple people are available, then a graphic novel committee can be set up to share the work. The library's users can be a source of ideas as well. Suggestions by patrons of all ages can at least give you an idea of what might be popular, and if your library has a teen advisory board, anime/manga club, etc., these can also be a wonderful source of help, even if you are looking for books for a younger age.

Besides graphic novels, many related books are available that you can purchase for your library. Dorling Kindersley (DK) has a number of books that talk about various comic book characters (Batman, Spider-Man, Superman, etc.), as well as nonfiction books that the characters are a part of, including *Superman's Guide to the Universe* and *Green Lantern's Book of Great Inventions*. Rosen Publishing has a line of "Action Heroes" books that discuss the creation of several Marvel Comics heroes. A number of books deal with drawing manga-style artwork. Other books deal with the history of the medium, though many of those tend to be cataloged in the adult section. There are also works of fiction that feature characters from comic books, sometimes as adaptations and other times in original stories, in both beginning reader and chapter book levels, and some books that follow comic-book-type themes. Also Tokyopop offers a series of "Manga Chapters," which are middle-elementary level chapter books with occasional manga-style drawings, and Stone Arch's "Graphic Flash" line has historical fiction mixed in with comic-style drawings. A list of titles can be found in Appendix A and Appendix B.

Several periodicals can be purchased for your children's area that tie in to the graphic novel collections, especially the American versions of *Shonen Jump* and *Shojo Beat* from Viz, which contain various chapters of popular manga titles, including *Yu-Gi-Oh, Dragon Ball Z,* and *Absolute Boyfriend.* Many of the books that collect these stories will have the *Shonen Jump/Shojo Beat* label on them. You may wish to examine a few issues before purchasing a subscription to ensure that the contents are suitable for your library. At best, they are for middle schools and above.

If your budget allows it, your library can subscribe to certain age-appropriate comic books. A cheaper alternative available at many comic book shops is a "bin" with cheap, older comics. If you purchase these, then the low cost helps to make them more "disposable" and less worrisome if they are stolen or fall apart due to excessive use.

Some audiovisual products also could be purchased to tie into your collection. The various age-appropriate films and collected television shows, both animated and live action, can be collected on DVD, as could the anime films and television shows that are connected with the manga in your collection. There are even comic books on CD-ROM. More than 40 years of *The Amazing Spider-Man, The Fantastic Four, The X-Men,* and other comics have been scanned and put onto the discs. If your library lends out video games, the ones with comics characters can also tie in to the new collection.

What Not to Buy

If you are creating a graphic novel collection for your library, you have thousands of volumes to choose from. However, if you are creating a collection intended primarily for children and tweens, your selection, while still very large, is also limited. Overly violent or sexual images, foul language, and mature themes—these are reasons for you not to buy a book for your collection. It is not because these books are bad—far from it; many of the best books out there are for older readers, but they are inappropriate for this particular age range. Even though the perception persists that comics are for kids, there has been much discussion in articles and message boards over the fact that there are less comics for children than there once were. Gail de Vos makes this observation: "The term comic for comic books is probably more inappropriate than at any time in history as there are very few titles intended for young readers" (de Vos, 2005), while author Michael Chabon has commented, "Children did not abandon comics; comics, in their drive to attain respect and artistic accomplishments abandoned children" (Chabon, 2004).

Ratings systems, such as the those on Marvel's and Tokyopop's books, can be helpful (see Exhibit 6-6). If you see a parental advisory or a teen plus label, it should give you pause. And a Marvel max or mature rating or a title from an

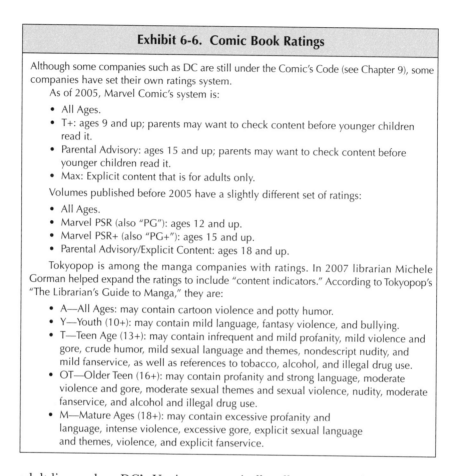

Exhibit 6-6. Comic Book Ratings

Although some companies such as DC are still under the Comic's Code (see Chapter 9), some companies have set their own ratings system.

As of 2005, Marvel Comic's system is:

- All Ages.
- T+: ages 9 and up; parents may want to check content before younger children read it.
- Parental Advisory: ages 15 and up; parents may want to check content before younger children read it.
- Max: Explicit content that is for adults only.

Volumes published before 2005 have a slightly different set of ratings:

- All Ages.
- Marvel PSR (also "PG"): ages 12 and up.
- Marvel PSR+ (also "PG+"): ages 15 and up.
- Parental Advisory/Explicit Content: ages 18 and up.

Tokyopop is among the manga companies with ratings. In 2007 librarian Michele Gorman helped expand the ratings to include "content indicators." According to Tokyopop's "The Librarian's Guide to Manga," they are:

- A—All Ages: may contain cartoon violence and potty humor.
- Y—Youth (10+): may contain mild language, fantasy violence, and bullying.
- T—Teen Age (13+): may contain infrequent and mild profanity, mild violence and gore, crude humor, mild sexual language and themes, nondescript nudity, and mild fanservice, as well as references to tobacco, alcohol, and illegal drug use.
- OT—Older Teen (16+): may contain profanity and strong language, moderate violence and gore, moderate sexual themes and sexual violence, nudity, moderate fanservice, and alcohol and illegal drug use.
- M—Mature Ages (18+): may contain excessive profanity and language, intense violence, excessive gore, explicit sexual language and themes, violence, and explicit fanservice.

adult line such as DC's Vertigo automatically tells you not to buy. But even ratings can't always help. Sometimes an ongoing series will "jump" ratings, and although the first five volumes may be at an appropriate level, the sixth may move up a rating, and the series then may become inappropriate for your collection. This is not exclusive to graphic novels. The early volumes of Phyllis Reynolds Naylor's *Alice* series are perfect for younger readers, but the later editions are considered to be much more appropriate for young adults, and the latter volumes in the *Harry Potter* series are certainly darker and more mature than the earlier books. Ratings can also be subjective, and what the person who applies the rating feels is suitable for children may be different from how you feel. As with other materials, what is acceptable in one community may not be acceptable in another. Of course, as with any ratings system, some might still find "appropriate" materials inappropriate.

Even superhero comics can be inappropriate due to their subject matter. A major plot point of *Identity Crisis*, which stars most of the DC Comics heroes, was that while investigating the murder of the Elongated Man's wife Sue, it is revealed that several years earlier she was raped by the supervillain Dr. Light. In the "Sins Past" story line in the Spider-Man titles it was revealed that Peter Parker's first girlfriend Gwen Stacy had a one-night stand with, and was impregnated by, Norman Osborn, a man not only old enough to be her father, but who was secretly the villainous Green Goblin who killed her soon after. Younger children might be attracted to these books after seeing Batman or Spider-Man on the covers, and their parents may not want them to read about these subjects yet. Even characterization can be different from book to book. The Batman of *The Batman Strikes!* and the Captain America of *Marvel Adventures: The Avengers* are much more child friendly than their counterparts in *All-Star Batman and Robin* and *The Ultimates*.

Another good example of "never judge a book by its cover," or at least its premise, are the *Barry Ween* books by Judd Winick. The basic description is the adventures of a ten-year-old supergenius and his friends. Sounds like *Dexter's Laboratory* or *Jimmy Neutron*, right? Well the amount of four-letter words that these children say make the books extremely unsuitable for a children's section.

Most libraries have collection development policies. Some have ones specifically for their graphic novel collection, others include them in their general policy as they would their audiovisual of foreign language items, and some do not mention them at all (see Exhibit 6-7). Even if your library is among the latter, following the same basic procedures that you would use for any other age-appropriate fiction or non-book fiction should be all right. Regardless of how you do it, you should have a policy. Not having one at all can be problematic in case of a challenge.

Making Your Final Decisions

You know how to order, find out what's available, evaluate a book, how to find reviews, and what definitely not to buy. Now the question is what to purchase for the children and tweens who use your library. Unfortunately, there is no one answer. Are you purchasing for an elementary or middle school media center? Are you purchasing for the children's section of a public library, or for multiple branches of a library system? If it is for a school you know that the only readers of the material will be children or tweens, while with the public library you also have to consider how it may fit in with the young adult and adult collections (see Chapter 7 for cataloging and shelving issues).

Of course your budget and shelf space will be a factor in how much you can buy for your library, but so is how often you are intending to purchase graphic novels. Is this a one-time thing, an occasional purchase, or will they be something that you plan to order every month? The frequency of your purchases can be a factor in deciding what to buy.

Exhibit 6-7. Excerpts from the Collection Development Policy for the Youth Services Department for the Duluth (MN) Public Library (see www.duluth.lib.mn.us/Policies/YouthServices.html)

Graphic Novels

Collection overview: The graphic novel is a format in which a narrative is conveyed with sequential art. The graphic novel format holds great appeal for reluctant and avid readers alike. While this format has been in existence for many decades, its acceptance in the United States as an important and popular format has only recently been recognized.

The graphic novel format includes a wide variety of genres and subjects. Graphic novels can be nonfiction, adaptations of classic novels, science fiction, realistic fiction, fantasy, horror, romance or superheroes. Graphic novels can be found in the Juvenile Fiction, Juvenile Science Fiction, Juvenile Nonfiction, Young Adult Fiction and Young Adult Nonfiction collections.

The graphic novel has worldwide popularity, with many foreign books being translated into English, particularly from France, Japan, and Korea. Readers should be aware that there may be cultural differences reflected in both the art and writing of the graphic novel.

Youth Services staff members are trained to assist children and adults with choosing developmentally appropriate materials for young people, but it is the responsibility of the parents or other caregiving adults to determine which materials are appropriate for their child.

Selection plan: When considering titles for purchase, standard selection review journals are consulted as well as other magazine and newspaper reviews and online resources. Patron suggestions for purchase are also considered. Individual titles and series that are popular may be purchased in multiples.

Retention and weeding: Graphic novels are retained as long as they are in good condition and continue to circulate. Worn copies of classic or popular titles may be repaired or replaced depending on availability. If a publisher produces books with bindings that do not stand up to typical library use, these books are not purchased or replaced.

The graphic novels section of their collection development policy is similar to other sections in the policy.

Take for example the "chronological" type of trade edition in which a volume reprints issues A and B, and the next volume begins with the issue after "B." These titles tend to come out two to three times a year. However, in most cases, any story arc will be contained in one volume, and while some subplot story lines will be carried over, skipping a volume will not cause the reader to not get the whole story. After all, someone reading his or her first *X-Men* comic in 2006 does not necessarily have know the team's 40-plus year history (though with the Internet it's much easier to get background information). It is the same with many book series. For example, with the *Harry Potter* or the *Lemony Snicket* titles, the books, especially those later in the series, depend on the reader being familiar with the previous volumes, while in others series, such as *Junie B. Jones* or *The Hardy Boys*, reading the previous books helps but is not as vital.

Manga can be more problematic. Not only do the books in manga series come out more frequently, sometimes on a bimonthly basis, but many of them have a continuing story line, which makes it very helpful, if not absolutely necessary, for the reader to have read the previous volumes if they want to understand and enjoy the story. The need to get future editions of a title can be a factor in getting that title in the first place. For that matter, in purchasing an existing series in which the main plotline continues in future volumes, it may become necessary to purchase the preceding editions as well (see Exhibit 6-8).

It's not only ongoing trade and manga series for which one volume affects another. Within the comic book universes a crossover story line, especially one tied in to an event-limited series, can be featured in many different volumes. The stories connected to Marvel's big 2006–2007 event *Civil War* filled 21 books. Of those, 15 contain reprints from ongoing series, with the others collecting the main *Civil War* limited series and additional limited series and specials. Is it necessary to get all 21 books? In this case, no, but if you would normally get any of the ongoing series collections, your readers may at least want the main *Civil War* collection to better understand what is going on.

Exhibit 6-8. Author's Picks

I have reviewed a large number of graphic novels—original works, trade editions, and both Asian and OEL manga—and most of them are listed in Appendix A. My 25 favorites are below. Those best for middle-school-aged readers are marked with an asterisk.

Adventures in Oz by Eric Shanower
While there have been many adaptations of *The Wizard of Oz*, Shanower takes elements from the later Oz books and creates five new stories with both familiar and new characters.

Amelia Rules by Jimmy Gownley
This wonderful series about a nine-year-old girl and her friends and family has been collected in four volumes with more to come.

American Born Chinese by Gene Luen Yang*
This multi-award-winning original graphic novel deals with issues of race, identity, stereotypes, and self-acceptance.

Bone series by Jeff Smith
An award-winning fantasy, told over nine volumes, with reluctant heroes, hidden princesses, dragons, monsters, evil magicians, and everything that makes fantasy fun.

Bone Sharps, Cowboys, and Thunder Lizards by Jim Ottaviani
A "docudrama" about the early discoveries of dinosaur bones.

Castle Waiting series by Linda Medley*
In the castle once lived in by Sleeping Beauty dwells talking animals, bearded nuns, and all sorts of people and creatures.

Clan Apis by Jay Hosler
Read about the life of a bee and end up learning something.

Courageous Princess by Rod Espinosa
Kidnapped by a dragon, Princess Mabelrose escapes and must find her way back to her kingdom.

(Cont'd.)

Exhibit 6-8. Author's Picks *(Continued)*

Courtney Crumrin series by Ted Naifeh*
A young girl goes to live with her uncle and finds herself in a world of magic.

Days Like This by J. Torres
Set in the early 1960s, three girls find their dreams of being a singing group come true.

Dreamland Chronicles by Scott Christian Sava
When Alexander was young he dreamed about a fantasy land. Now he's older and has found that his "Dreamland" companions have aged along with him.

Edu-manga series by various artists
These biographies, told in a story format, give a great deal of information about the subjects and in an entertaining manner.

Essential and Showcase series by various artists
These black-and-white, 500+ page books from DC and Marvel contain decades' worth of stories—some of them classics—for a low price. Characters ranging from the famous to semiobscure appear.

Grease Monkey by Tim Eldred*
Set in the future on a space-battlecrusier, Robin Plotnik is an assistant mechanic working under a mentally accelerated gorilla.

Imaginaries by Mike S. Miller and Ben Avery with art by various artists
What happens to imaginary friends when they are no longer imagined? Superhero G finds himself in the Imagined Nation and must fight against the dictatorial Ice Queen.

Lions, Tigers, and Bears by Mike Bullock and illustrated by Jack Lawrence
An award-winning title, young Joey finds that his stuffed animals come to life to protect him from the "monsters in the closet."

Mail Order Ninja by Joshua Elder
In this OEL manga, Timmy is an outcast until he orders a ninja out of a catalog. But his newfound popularity infuriates "queen of the school," Felicity.

Puffin Graphics series by various artists
The most "complete" of the book adaptations, each book also includes information on its creation.

PS238 by Aaron Williams
In this secret elementary school, the super folks of the future are being taught and getting into all sorts of misadventures.

Sardine series by Emmanuel Guibert and illustrated by Joann Sfar
A humorous outer space adventure from France. Young Sardine travels through space with her pirate uncle Captain Yellow Shoulder fighting the menace of Supermuscleman.

Simpsons by various artists
New adventures of everyone's favorite animated family

Spider-Girl by Tom DeFalco and various artists*
In the near future, Spider-Man's daughter follows in her father's wall-crawling footsteps.

To Dance: A Ballerina's Graphic Novel by Siena Cherson Siegel and drawn by Mark Siegel
An autobiographical tale of how a young girl became a ballerina.

Tommysaurus Rex by Doug TenNapel
After young Ely's dog is killed he goes to visit his grandfather's farm. Will the dinosaur he finds there replace his lost pet?

Vögelein: Clockwork Fairies by Jane Irwin
After the man who takes care of her dies, a living clockwork fairy must find a new caretaker.

So now you know the why, the how, and the what. You've chosen your books and placed the order. There are still some choices that must be made, and the next chapter will cover some of those.

Notes

1. Some sources call the first issue *Fun: The Big Comic Magazine*. The title changed to *More Fun Comics* in 1936 and ran until #127 (1947).

2. Also known as *Marvel vs. DC*, this led to a series of one-shots called *Amalgam* in which the characters were merged together to create new characters, such as Super Soldier (Superman and Captain America) and Dark Claw (Batman and Wolverine).

3. This 1994 comic book was published by Archie as *Archie Meets the Punisher* and by Marvel as *The Punisher Meets Archie*.

4. One of the best examples of a multidecade collection from 2006 is *Superman vs. Lex Luthor*, which reprinted *Action Comics* #23 (1940); *Superman*, Volume 1 #90 (1954); *Adventure Comics* #271 (1960); *Superboy* #86 (1961); *Superman*, Volume 1 #164 (1963); *Superboy* #139 (1967); *Superman*, Volume 1 #292 (1975); *Action Comics* #544 (1983); *Superman*, Volume 1 #416 (1986); *Man of Steel* #4 (1986); *Superman*, Volume 2 #9 (1987) and #131 (1998); and *Superman: Lex 2000!* (2000).

References

Chabon, Michael. "Keynote Speech 2004 Eisner Awards." Comic-Con International. Available: www.comic-con.org/cci/cci_eisners04keynote.shtml.

de Vos, Gail. 2005. "ABCs of Graphic Novels." *Resource Links* 10, no. 3 (February). Available: www.resourcelinks.ca/features/feb05.htm.

"Manga Releases Up 16% in 2007 According to ICv2 Guide." ICv2.com (February 7, 2007). Available: www.icv2.com/articles/news/10034.html.

Rowe, Peter. 2006. "Invasion of the Comic Fanatics." *Union-Tribune*, July 16. Available: www.signonsandiego.com/news/features/20060716-9999-1n16comicon.html. Accessed: July 17, 2006.

PART III

Managing, Promoting, and Maintaining a Graphic Novel Collection

Chapter 7

Collection Management

In between the time that you order your books and the time that you put them on the shelves there are some additional decisions that will have to be made as to how the books will be cataloged, bound, and processed. Depending on your library, this work may be done by a vendor, a central processing department, your own circulation department, or even yourself. Regardless of who does it, hopefully you will, at the very least, be able to provide input into these areas.

Cataloging Options: 741, Fiction, and Other Ways

Among the proponents of graphic novels in libraries, one of the biggest debates is the best way to catalog them. This is an issue that will also affect how they are shelved. Some choose to treat them as nonfiction while others feel that they should be considered, and cataloged as, fiction. Under nonfiction, the vast majority of graphic novels are placed in the 741.5 or 741.59 areas alongside collected comic strips, books on comics and comic-related topics, and books on drawing. Most are cataloged even more specifically under 741.59XX, with "XX" being 73 for American books, 52 for manga, 51 for manhua and manhwa (which can be further cataloged as 741.595195), 41 for British books, 71 for Canadian, and 44 for translated French titles, with French-language titles from Belgium such as *Tintin* also being cataloged as 741.59493. With the recent explosion of graphic novels in libraries, OCLC has been discussing making additional changes to the rules, including classifying comic strip collections as 741.569XX to separate them from graphic novels. Universities and other libraries that use Library of Congress cataloging generally put graphic novels in the PN6700s.

Even before Capstone, Rosen, and the others began their lines of graphic nonfiction, libraries were putting certain graphic novels in other nonfiction areas. And now with more and more publishers creating nonfiction series, graphic novels are popping up all throughout the areas of the Dewey Decimal System. Besides a large number of books for the biography section, graphic nonfiction can be found in the 000s (graphic mysteries), 200s and 300s (graphic myths and legends), 500s (graphic science, natural disasters), 600s (inventions), 800s (literary adaptations), and 900s (history).

The biggest advantage to keeping the bulk of the graphic novels in the 741s is that it makes it easier for someone who is specifically looking for graphic novels to find them when they are all placed together in one area. The argument against placing them there is that these graphic novels are works of fiction and should be treated as such. Although there are some fictional works such as fairy tales and plays that are placed in the nonfiction area (398s and 800s), some feel that graphic novels are being regulated to the 741s due not to their content, but instead to their format. If a "regular" novel by Neil Gaiman, Holly Black, or Peter David is placed in the fiction section, then a "graphic" novel by these same authors should be placed in fiction as well.

The "graphic novels are fiction too" argument is the main reason for cataloging them in this manner. The main argument against this is that if someone is specifically looking for graphic novels and they do not have a particular book in mind, they may have a harder time finding them if they are mixed in with all of the other fiction titles. There is, however, a counter argument, which points out that someone who is browsing the fiction section might come upon a graphic novel and decide to check it out, which is something that they might not have done had the graphic novels been "segregated" in the 741s.

Some libraries have a "compromised" cataloging technique for graphic novels, cataloging them as "graphic" or "graphic novel," and some have bypassed the issue by shelving all graphic novels, regardless of how they are cataloged, in one particular area of the library (more on that later in this chapter). Obviously age prefixes (J, YA, teen, etc.) are used when needed in all three cases, and unless you are in a media center or an age-specific library, you should always make sure that the proper age prefix is included to avoid potential problems.

Cutter Choices

Regardless of the method used, another important cataloging issue is the cutter numbers or the name or word used after "fiction," "graphic," etc. Often the usual rules of cataloging are followed, where if a title has a solo or primary author, that author's last name is used (*Amelia Rules: The Whole World's Crazy* by Jimmy Gownley would be under 741.5973 GO, Fic Gownley, etc.), and if it's an anthology then the title provides the word (*The Greatest Batman Stories Ever Told* under 741.5973 GR or Fic Greatest). This is fine for original graphic novels, trades that are not part of a series, or for a multivolume series that only had one author, but for some long-running series there could be problems.

A good example is Marvel's *Ultimate X-Men* series, a YA title, in which Volumes 7, 8, and 9 are written by Mark Millar, Brian Michael Bendis, and Brian K. Vaughn, respectively. So, if your library used Dewey then these three consecutive volumes would be cataloged under 741.5973 MI, 741.5973 BE, and 741.5973 VA, and, depending on the size of your graphic novel collection and the presence of other 741 titles, could be placed on different shelves of the bookcase or, with a large collection, one or more bookcases over. If cataloged FIC MILLAR, FIC BENDIS, and FIC VAUGHAN, they might be several rows of bookcases apart from one another, with hundreds if not thousands of other books separating the three volumes. In some cases this might not be a problem. For example, novels based on *Star Wars* are spread out among the fiction area. But when the events of Volume 6 have a direct effect on the story in Volume 10, it can be very helpful to have these books found in the same location.

One solution to this would be to use the series title as the cutter, so that all of the title's trades would be under 741.5973 ULT or Fiction Ultimate. This would keep the books in close proximity to one another, allowing patrons to easily find all of the volumes. Those shelving the books can also take care not to intermix the *Ultimate X-Men* volumes with *Ultimate Spider-Man*, *Ultimate Fantastic Four*, or any other graphic novel series that started with "Ultimate." If the series title is used as the cutter, then the biggest problem would be what to do in the event that the title changed its name, such as when *Marvel Knights Spider-Man*, which has four collections, changed its name to *Sensational Spider-Man*. A second solution, especially for the superhero titles, would be to use the name of the title character (or team) as the cutter. For example, 741.5973 SPI or Fiction SPIDER would put all of the Spider-Man titles together in the same area, whether they are from a multivolume series, a collected limited series, a collected story line from the various Spider-Man books, or a theme book of old Spider-Man stories.[1]

Regardless of which way the graphic novels are cataloged, the most important thing is to make sure that your library's patrons can find them. If your catalog is computerized and allows for keyword searches, make sure that "graphic novels" is listed as one of the searchable terms (this would be line 650 in MARC Records). Other possible terms could be "manga," or the names of the primary characters or teams (Batman, X-Men, etc.). If done properly, the patron will not only know the way in which your library catalogs its graphic novels, but also the extent of its collection.

Title Choices

Another cataloging issue that might come up is what title to use for certain books. Although it's easy to know how to proceed with a solo original graphic novel, or a one-shot trade such as *Megamorphs*, or even with a series that does not use subtitles in its editions, for example, *Dragon Ball Z*, Volume 24. With subtitled series you do have a few options. The seventh *Ultimate X-Men* book could be listed as *Ultimate X-Men*, Volume 7: *Blockbuster*, *Ultimate X-Men*, Volume 7, or even simply as *Blockbuster*. (Just *Ultimate X-Men* is also a possibility but would be confusing if you own multiple volumes.) If you were to just use the subtitle *Blockbuster*, having *Ultimate X-Men* as a searchable term would also be a good idea.

If at all possible, try to keep each volume cataloged in the same manner. It can be very confusing to both staff and patrons if, for example, the six volumes of *Essential Fantastic Four* were listed in the catalog as follows:

- *Essential Fantastic Four*, Volume 1
- *Stan Lee Presents Essential Fantastic Four*, Volume 2
- *Essential Fantastic Four*, Volume 3: *Collecting Fantastic Four 41–63 and Annuals 3–4*
- *Essential Fantastic Four*
- *Fantastic Four*, Volume 5
- *Essential Fantastic Four*, Volume 6

This is another instance where it will have to be decided in advance which cutter to use—"Essential" (ES), "Fantastic" (FAN), or the author name? Stan Lee wrote most of what is in the first six volumes, but he was followed by Roy Thomas, Gerry Conway, and other writers. If the first six are cataloged 741.5973 LE or Fiction LEE, will patrons have to search around for the location of future volumes? For that matter, it could be very confusing if the full name and subtitle of a book are not provided. If a library's catalog lists *X-Factor*, Volume 2, to which book is it referring? *Essential X-Factor*, Volume 2, which collects issues #17–#35 of the 1980s *X-Men* spin-off? *X-Factor Visionaries*, Volume 2, which collects later issues of that series that were written by Peter David? Or is it *X-Factor*, Volume 2: *Life and Death Matters*, the second volume of the new X-Factor series?

One last issue is whether to catalog a volume of an ongoing series as a part of a serial or as a monograph. Some feel, especially in the case of manga, that the volumes are serial products and not individual books and therefore should be cataloged on one serial bibliographic record, with each volume distinguished by its number. In this way, all volumes are in one entry, and problems such as differences in the cataloged name or cutter number can be avoided (Brenner, 2007: 20). On the other hand, some feel that each volume of an ongoing series is a separate book with its own ISBN number and that it should be treated as such and given its own entry in the catalog. In addition, with certain online catalogs, it can be difficult for a patron or librarian to place a "hold" on one particular volume if they are all in the same catalog entry.

Processing

After deciding how to catalog, the next issue deals with the book itself, and how it will be prepared and processed before going onto your library's shelves. One minor item to keep an eye on is where the "due date card" pocket is to be placed. If it is your library's custom to put that card on the last page of the book, be aware that there are times when the last page of a graphic novel contains the end of the story or additional artwork or text that the card would block. In these cases, the pocket should be placed elsewhere, such as the inside of the back cover, to avoid problems. In the case of an unflopped manga, the question becomes what should be considered the back of the book. The issue of which is the front cover and which is the back can also be an issue in deciding where to place a barcode, a sticker with the library's name, or anything else that your library puts on the front or back covers of the books in its collection.

The main area of processing a graphic novel concentrates on how to make the book last longer. Graphic novels are not the sturdiest of books. The majority are soft-covered books that were designed to be read every now and then, but generally spending the bulk of their existence on a shelf. They were not designed to be read dozens of times a year and to fall into book drops, sometimes opening in the process, with other, heavier books piling on top of them. Broken spines and loose pages are a result of this. Graphic novel publishers are aware of this, and have made attempts at improvement, but there are other solutions that a library can use.

If you are purchasing your graphic novels from a comic shop or bookstore, then there are certain devices, such as Kapco's Easy Cover Self Adhesive Book Covers, that can help keep your books together. If you use a vendor, various forms of library binding are available. In vinabinding, the original paperback cover is removed, protected by polyvinyl lamination, and then bound to binders board. Additional improvements are made to the binding and the spine. The completed book has the general appearance of the original and is expected to last much longer.

There are also a number of ways of turning the paperback book into a hardback. Some, such as textbound and textmount, transform the book, and sometimes retain the cover art, but leave the spine looking unappealing, which may cause a potential reader to skip it (though a book jacket that reprints the covers could be created to help with this). Others, such as BWI's FolletBound books, will retain the front, back, and spine artwork, making the books both appealing and durable. There are a few negatives to binding, including that at times rebinding causes the gutters (the space between panel borders) closest to the spine to shrink, which then may obscure some art and/or text. All bindings will of course cost extra, which will affect your budget, but in most cases it will cost significantly less than it would to replace the book every few months. Some books, for various reasons, cannot be bound.

Weeding and Replacing the Collection

Speaking of replacing, we now move into the area of collection management that happens after the books have gone on the shelf and circulated—weeding and replacing your graphic novel collection. Despite whatever methods you've used to reinforce them, whether it's from constant use or the little kid with the magic marker, some of your books will be damaged. Sometimes a loose page can be tipped back in or a cover glued back on, but the rest of the time a replacement is needed. Many of the companies that provide binding have some kind of warranty, including a lifetime warranty for BWI Books, but they will not be applicable if the books are lost, stolen, or not returned (see Chapter 9). These titles will also have to be replaced.

In choosing what to weed and/or replace, you should treat the graphic novels with the same criteria you use for any other book in your library. Can you afford to replace the book? Has the book circulated enough to warrant replacing? Is it part of series? If so, would a missing volume affect the overall story (this is not always the case)? And, most important, is the book still in print? Many graphic novel publishers keep a backlist of older volumes, but titles do go out of print for one reason or another. Manga titles and licensed works can stop if the publisher loses the rights, and, as seen in Chapter 6, there are publishers who go out of business. In these cases the books that you need can be replaced only if you can find a place, such as a comic shop or an online site, that might still have them in stock, or if a new publisher has picked up the series and reprinted the older volumes. In addition, the original publisher may simply release a new, and possibly even improved, edition.

The Future of the Collection

The final aspect of collection management is the future of the collection. If you plan to continue to purchase graphic novels for your library, there are some decisions that you will have to make. Some of these will be based on what is in your collection. If the title is a series, do you plan on continuing it? With many manga series and some Western titles, the latter volumes are needed to complete the story. In this case you are committing yourself to purchasing up to six volumes of the manga (until the story ends) and two to three volumes of the Western titles each year, and this will affect both your budget and shelving. Do you want to begin a new series? If a particular series has low circulation, should you continue purchasing new volumes for the sake of those still checking it out?

Additional decisions may have to be made regarding your vendor. Are you happy with how they have handled things? If you want to change vendors are you able to? Do you need to change the way the books are processed? Do you want to expand your collection? Do you want to cut down on the number of titles? Some of these decisions will be affected by factors such as increases or cuts in your budget or even the policies of your library. Others will be based on how well the collection has been circulating. Hopefully both high circulation and a healthy budget will allow your library to have a great graphic novel collection for years to come.

Note

1. For 2006, that included 23 volumes, including ten ongoing series, five "Essentials," and two limited series.

Reference

Brenner, Robin. 2007. *Understanding Manga and Anime*. Westport CT: Libraries Unlimited.

Chapter 8

Displaying, Promoting, and Working with the Collection

Shelving Options

The graphic novels have been ordered, processed, and are ready to go on your library's shelves. So now what? How you display the books can help your patrons find them easier and therefore help your circulation. Basically, there are two main ways to shelve your graphic novel collection: by how they were cataloged or in a special area.

If you are following the two most common cataloging styles—as fiction or as 741.5—shelving is relatively easy, with your major decision being, if you work in a library that makes this distinction, whether or not to catalog a particular title "J" or "YA" (or "Juv" and "Teen" or whatever particular terms your library uses). Most of the titles included in this book also appeal to teens (and many to adults as well), and this should be a factor in your shelving decision.

If you are shelving your graphic novels in the nonfiction section, then most of them will probably be going in the 741 area of your collection. So you can assume, especially if you are planning to order a large number of titles and then continue to order more, that that section will be growing. Even if many of the titles will be off the shelf due to high circulation, eventually, given time, they will find their way back to the shelf. In this case, you may want to do some preemptive "shifting" of the other books in the area in order to prepare for the influx of new titles.

Another consideration involves the graphic novels that are truly nonfiction—histories, biographies, and so forth. Even if they had been cataloged with other numbers, do you want to have them changed to a 741 in order to keep more of your graphic novels in the same area and therefore make them easier to find? What about graphic novel adaptations of books? Should a graphic novel version of *Black Beauty* be cataloged under Anna Sewell or under the name of the person who wrote the adaptation? If it's the former, could there be a problem if someone requests the book from another library branch and they get the graphic and abridged version? If it's the latter, should you put it in the juvenile fiction section, the 741s, or even in the 823 area with other books on or about British literature?

A third item to consider depends on how your library is set up. Are the J and/or YA nonfiction books separate from the adult nonfiction collection, or is the collection interfiled? If it's the latter, then what else is nearby? Not only might there be graphic novels for adults located right next to the ones for children, but some of the nearby drawing and photography books might also not be "child friendly," with books on drawing nudes as close as the 743s. This will be covered further in Chapter 9. There are fewer concerns when it comes to shelving with fiction, other than that the graphic novels are more spread out. Fiction is already age segregated, so the only problem will be deciding what goes in juvenile and what goes into young adult.

As mentioned earlier, some libraries have created special catalog designations for graphic novels, and placed them in a special area in the same way that some libraries have created special areas for fiction genres such as romance, Western, or science fiction (if your library does have this sort of genre separation, then you may also have to decide whether romance, Western, or science fiction graphic novels should be placed in them—remember, graphic novels are a format, not a genre). However, even if your graphic novels are cataloged in the traditional way, there is no reason that you still cannot put them on their own shelf in a special area of the library. Besides making the graphic novels easy to find, this setup has other advantages. If your graphic novels are cataloged in the 741s and you regularly order a large number of titles, having them in a different area avoids the need to continually shift the books in the 740s.

Once you have moved the books to their new location, you can shelve them however you wish. If you want to keep them in the proper Dewey/author order, then you can. If you want to place them in the order of the cutter, then you can. If you want to separate manga from nonmanga books, then you can. If you want to separate ongoing titles from collected limited series, original graphic novels, and one-shot trades, then you can. If you want to divide the books up by character and have the Superman books in one place and the Fantastic Four books in another, then you can. If you put the graphic novels in a special area, be sure that your library's staff—both reference services and circulation—is aware of both the location of the collection and of your shelving preferences for it.

Where you put the graphic novels section is also something to consider. If there is more than one section—where the "mature audience" titles are kept in one place and the "kid friendly" in another—then remember that there will be older teens and adults who are interested in the books found in the "kid friendly" area. Although there is adult interest in some juvenile fiction (the *Harry Potter* books being the best example), there will be much more when it comes to the graphic novels, with the probable exception of most of the non-fiction and titles aimed at very young ages, such as Tokyopop's "cine-manga" books or series such as *Fashion Kitty* or *Babymouse*. One suggestion is, if possible, to put the graphic novels section on the outer border of the children's section. This way, adults won't feel weird going into the children's section, and you do not have to worry about adults hanging around inside the children's area.

Promoting the Collection

As with cataloging, the most important aspect of shelving is making sure that your patrons can easily locate the books. If the majority of your graphic novels are together, either in the 741s or in a special section, then you can put up a sign indicating that the graphic novels can be found there. You can hang one of ALA's comics-related posters (see Figure 8-1), DEMCO's poster (see Figure 8-2), or place DEMCO's graphic novels standee (see Figure 8-3) on top of a bookcase or on a table by the collection. A very simple way to advertise the collection is to have some of them facing out, either on the shelf, on top of the bookcase, or on an "end cap." The colorful covers can be very eye-catching and even attract a patron who is just passing by. Some companies, including DEMCO and Brodart also sell special shelving for graphic novels (see Figure 8-4). If the graphic novels are intermixed in the fiction area, then putting the posters on the wall or on a bookcase in that section can also help to let patrons know about them.

Stickers can also be very helpful. DEMCO and Brodart are among those companies that provide them (see Figure 8-5). Putting stickers on your graphic novels can be helpful no matter which method of shelving you use. If they are intermixed among the fiction books, then the stickers will help them stand out. This can also be the case if they are in the 741s, where at a glance they can be distinguished from the drawing, cartoon, and other related books, and just as with placing graphic novels in the fiction section, placing the stickers on the non-741 nonfiction graphic novels will help them to stand out as well.

If you have special shelving with all of your graphic novels together, then the stickers will help the staff members who shelve the books know which books go in the special area and which do not. If you choose to include related, non–graphic novel titles, such as books on drawing manga and anime characters or DK's series of superhero-related books, in with your graphic novels in the special area, then the stickers will also help the shelvers know which of these books to put in the special area and which to place on the regular nonfiction shelves.

Besides knowing where the graphic novels are located and what gets shelved where, you may also wish to make sure that the rest of the staff knows a

Figure 8-1. Examples of ALA Superhero Posters

Also available from ALA are posters with Neil Gaiman's DC/Vertigo character, the Sandman, characters from Megatokyo (available at www.megatokyo.com with collections published by DC's CMX Manga line), Marvel's X-Men, and the main character from the manga *Cantarella* (published in the United States by Go! Comi). Go to www.alastore.ala.org for more information.

34" x 22" poster of the DC Universe of the late 1990s; also available as a 13 1/4" x 8 1/2" mini-poster. *Source:* ™ and © DC Comics. All rights reserved. Used with Permission.

22" x 28" poster of former librarian Barbara Gordon aka Batgirl and Oracle; art by Gene Ha. *Source:* ™ and © DC Comics. All rights reserved. Used with Permission.

(Cont'd.)

Figure 8-1. Examples of ALA Superhero Posters *(Continued)*

Two 17" x 38" posters; art by Alex Ross. *Source:* ™ and © DC Comics.
All rights reserved. Used with Permission.

22" x 28" poster of the Teen Titans from the
popular *Teen Titans* cartoon series; also
available in a pack of 4" x 6" postcards.
Source: ™ and © DC Comics. All rights
reserved. Used with Permission.

Figure 8-2. DEMCO Graphic Novel Poster

Source: Dist. DEMCO, Inc. demco.com. 800-356-1200.

Figure 8-3. DEMCO Graphic Novel Standee

Source: Dist. DEMCO, Inc. demco.com. 800-356-1200.

Figure 8-4. Special Graphic Novels Shelving Sold by Companies Such as DEMCO and Brodart

Source: Dist. DEMCO, Inc. demco.com. 800-356-1200.

little more about graphic novels, so they are not like the librarian who, when asked about them for a *Time* magazine article replied, "You mean like pornographic?" (Arnold, 2003). At the very least the staff members who deal with the public should know what graphic novels are, that certain titles may not be appropriate for certain ages, and that patrons may ask for them not only as graphic novels but as "comics" and "manga" as well.

Figure 8-5. DEMCO Graphic Novel Stickers

Source: Dist. DEMCO, Inc. demco.com. 800-356-1200.

There are a number of ways to advertise the graphic novel collection, especially if you have just established one. ALA and DEMCO have bookmarks, usually with the same pictures as the posters (see Figure 8-6), which could be given out at the reference, children's, and checkout desks. Book displays are also a good thing, and not just a display of graphic novels. If doing a display on a certain subject, include any graphic novels in the collection that fit that subject. If you have any lists of "If you liked 'A' try 'B,'" include graphic novels on the "B" list. If the new collection has a large number of books, a press release that your library is now carrying graphic novels can help to publicize the collection, as will press releases about other comics-related events and programs.

Programming

There are many events and programs at your library that will allow you to both promote and work with your graphic novel collection. For example, you can have an event for Free Comic Book Day (FCBD). Sponsored by Diamond, the first Free Comic Book Day was on May 4, 2002, the day after the first *Spider-Man* movie premiered. The next few were also around the same time as a new comic-book based movie, but more recently it has been held on the first Saturday in May. Many comic companies put out a special comic for FCBD, some reprinting one of their regular comics, and others creating a special comic book. Not all FCBD titles are appropriate for all ages, though many are perfect for younger readers. Libraries can get free comics directly through Diamond (see www.freecomicbookday.com for more information), or they can arrange to get some from a local comic shop. Even though the comics are free to their customers, the stores do pay for the FCBD books, so if you go through them it might be nice to, for example, buy a graphic novel to be raffled off at your event, and be sure to promote them both at your event and in any signs or press releases. They can also promote your event and collection.

Figure 8-6. Bookmarks

The additional ALA posters are also available as bookmarks.

Source: Dist. DEMCO, Inc. demco.com. 800-356-1200. *(Cont'd.)*

Figure 8-6. Bookmarks *(Continued)*

Source: ™ and © DC Comics. All rights reserved. Used with Permission.

Many libraries have had events and promotions that tied into Free Comic Book Day. In San Diego on Free Comic Book Day in 2006 comic shop Comickaze gave everyone four comics, but if someone showed a library card he or she got two more. Four branches of the Hawaii State Public Library System teamed with store Collector Maniacs to give free comics to library card holders as well ("Library Cards," 2006).

Some libraries have been fortunate enough to get comic book professionals to appear at their libraries, and even have their own comic book conventions. The library in McHenry, Illinois, has made the "McHenry Comicon" a regular event. If there is enough interest, a graphic novel and/or manga or anime/manga club could be formed. Titles could be discussed and reviewed, and the children could even have a "comics swap" in which they exchange issues and books. Contests, such as "create your own comic book character," can also make kids interested in the collection. It could even be a regular program (see Exhibit 8-1), similar to the month-long creating comics workshop held by the Tampa-Hillsborough library system in 2003. Some professionals even have their own comic workshops including graphic novel writer/artist Paul Sizer (*Little White Mouse*).[1] Many comics professionals are online and could be contacted through e-mail. Other ways to contact them are through their publishers or even by asking for contact information on the GNLIB-L listserv.

Besides press releases, other external means of promoting your collection are available. When you do book talks at schools, camps, afterschool programs, and so forth, bring graphic novels along with the other books and talk about them as well. Suggest them to patrons and students who you think might be interested. A child who is reading a book in a particular genre can be shown a graphic novel in the same genre. And of course the opposite is also true, as a child reading a graphic novel of a particular genre can then also be shown a "text" book of that same genre. A child whose clothing, backpacks, etc., feature characters from American comics or manga is also someone who would very probably be interested in graphic novels.

There are also several outside places that can help to promote your library and its graphic novel collection. Comic book stores are one of these places. Besides being a source for comics, books, etc., they can help to promote your programs (and not just for Free Comic Book Day) and encourage people to visit your library. Besides the shops mentioned previously, another successful store/library partnership is the store in Phoenix, Arizona, which teamed up with both the library and the local newspaper to publish serialized excerpts

---

Exhibit 8-1. Teen Read Week Miniconvention

In 2002 the Broward County (Florida) Library System celebrated Teen Read Week (the theme of which was Get Graphic @ Your Library), with both a contest to create a superhero character and a miniconvention. The free convention, whose lineup included comics legend Will Eisner and author Adam-Troy Castro, both of whom lived in the area, was also an opportunity for the library system to show off its new expanded graphic novel collection. Local comic book store Tate's Comics was set up as a vendor, with some proceeds going back to the library, and also provided free comic books to the attendees.

from kid-friendly comic books. This tied into the library's summer reading program, where comics were given out as prizes (Banks, 2006).

One of the more interesting library–comic store partnerships is Night Flight Comics in Salt Lake City, Utah, which is actually located *inside* the main library. Besides hosting appearances by comics professionals, the store was featured in an issue of *Archie* (*Archie* #570, October 2006) in which Archie and the gang visited the library to get ideas on how to improve their own library. Both store and library personnel were featured, and writer George Gladir, who has worked on *Archie* since 1959 and created *Sabrina, the Teenage Witch*, spoke at the library's Literary Luminaries event.

Even the comic book companies can be a source of partnership. As part of its 2006 Summer Reading Program, the Los Angeles Public Library joined with Tokyopop to create the Manga Madness Summer Reading Club to encourage teens ages 11 to 18 to read. Participants who signed up at the libraries received a free folder, book bag, reading log, and bookmarks.

If the graphic novels are in your school media center or even in a classroom in your school, then there are many ways that you can use them in an educational setting.

Graphic Novels in the Classroom

Teachers across the country have found ways to incorporate comics and graphic novels in the classroom, both as part of the class and as special programs. Some came from their own ideas, while others are from other sources, and some are part of a city or even statewide program. Some examples from the past few years:

- Beginning with a pilot program in Hartford County, and later spreading across the state, schools in Maryland have been using comics and graphic novels in the classroom. It began as a three week reading and writing unit that was intended to "motivate struggling readers and stir the imagination of more advanced readers by using a mutisensory approach in the reading/writing process." One of the program's creators, fifth-grade teacher Erin Rebhorn, found that the program was good for struggling readers because "the colorful panels of a comic with simple blurbs of text motivates their interest in the reading process," and for better readers, the comics "allow them to use their higher level thinking and reading skills." Among other aspects of the program, students in fifth grade are reading Jim Ottivanni's *Dignifying Science*, which discusses famous woman scientists and which, among other things, helped to fit the program into the voluntary state curriculum by showing that graphic novels can support other subject areas (Mui, 2004: B1). Other members of the creative team were award-wining teachers, reading specialists, educational administrators, comic book writers and publishers, and distributors, including Disney and Diamond ("Maryland's Comic Book Project," 2005).

- In Ithaca, New York, teacher Sharon Nelson used a grant to create a program called "Go Graphic! Hook Those Reluctant Readers and Writers" in which fourth-graders are introduced to an "innovative approach to reaching and writing using graphic novels" ("Ithaca Public Education Initiative," 2007: 3B). She is among a number of teachers who have gotten grants for similar programs.

- In Coral Springs, Florida, a $4,000 grant allowed 40 fourth- and fifth-grade students to form an after-school "Superhero Club" where they learned about writing scripts, drawing characters, coloring pages, and other skills to create a comic book. Both boys and girls participated in the program, and as part of their activities the students had to work together to create the book. The only rules for the comic were that the story be appropriate for elementary schools and contain no guns, blood, or death. The grant helped to offset some printing costs, and the comic book was sold to cover the rest (Abraham, 2007: 4). Many other schools have also had a class or after-school program similar to the one in Coral Springs.

- The Comic Book Project (www.comicbookproject.org) originally began as a pilot project in New York City through Columbia University's Teacher College and focused on "reinforcing urban youth's literary skills" through the development of original comic books. In 2002, 733 elementary and middle school students from 33 locations were selected, many of whom had low academic performance, and more than half were English language learners. The children went through the process of creating a comic using characters from Dark Horse Comics. When the students were later surveyed, it was found that as a result of the program 82 percent knew more words, 78 percent needed less help reading, 76 percent got better at reading, and 69 percent understood most of what they read. The children also reported a heightened interest in reading. Writing was also improved, with a high interest in continuing creative writing, and 76 percent felt that their writing had improved and 70 percent felt they needed less help. In addition, 87 percent learned to use pictures to give clues to the stories (Bitz, 2003). Since then the project has received several grants and has expanded to schools around the country. Themes for the comics have included conflict resolution, leadership, and community. Some of the comics can be seen at www.comicbookproject. org/pubsnf.htm.

- An elementary school teacher in Carson, California, Rachael Sawyer Perkins uses comics to teach punctuation for dialogue. She has found that comics provide "an extremely visual way of getting across the concept of using quotation marks around narrative text spoken by individuals." The students were able to figure out that when they saw a dialogue balloon it meant that it was spoken dialogue that in a book would have quotation marks around it ("Using Comics," 2005).

Ideas for Lessons

Many programs, books, and online sources are available with ideas on how to use comics in the classroom. Some currently inactive programs include Crossgen's (see Chapter 6) and C.O.M.I.C.S. C.O.M.I.C.S, which stood for Challenging Objective Minds: An Instructional Comicbook Series, was a popular program started by Brooklyn teacher Daniel Tandarich for the now defunct New York City Comic Book Museum and had been used by more than 50 schools across the United States. It was an eight-lesson program, with the first half dealing with what a comic book was, including genres, "what makes a comic book unique," and the vocabulary associated with comic books, and the second half having the students create a comic book, including writing, storyboarding, page layouts, working on characters, and editing (Tandarich 2007).[2]

The following are other sources for getting lesson plans and ideas:

- Comicsintheclassroom.net, a site created by Scott Tingley, an early years teacher in New Brunswick, Canada. The site includes lesson plans in language arts, social studies, and science.
- The U.S. Department of Education (DOE) created *Spider-Man in Amazing Adventures*, which has high interest supplemental language activities to engage more young children and families in reading activities. The master copy was developed jointly by the DOE and the National Dairy Council in the 1990s as part of President Clinton's America Reads Challenge: Read*Write*Now! initiative. It provides activities for educators, parents, and learning partners for grades K–6, and the activities encourage fun with words and help to sharpen reading and oral and written communication skills. The activities, found at www.ed.gov/inits/america reads/spidey/index.html, are not copyrighted.
- Diamond has lesson plans for elementary and middle school classes using Donald Duck, Superman, and Ultimate Spider-Man comics. These cover vocabulary, reading, and story comprehension, and other ideas. These are available through Diamond's library guides, or online in the schools section of Diamond Bookshelf (http://bookshelf.diamondcomics.com/public/). Diamond also has a monthly newsletter for librarians and teachers.
- Scholastic has produced *Using Graphic Novels with Children and Teens: A Guide for Teachers and Librarians* (available at http://teacher.scholastic. com/products/tradebooks/boneville_using_graphic_novels.pdf), which includes ideas on how to use the series *Bone*, which is in their Graphix

line, in the classroom. Their Web page for *Goosebumps* (www.scholastic. com/goosebumpsgraphix) has an online game in which users can "create" comics by clicking on characters, settings, objects, and word balloons, and adding their own dialogue.

- The Secret Origins of Good Readers (www.night-flight.com/secretorigin/ SOGR2004.pdf), which was originally presented at the 2004 Comic-Con International, has a number of helpful comic book–related classroom activities.

Additional books that discuss comics and graphic novels in the classroom and provide lesson plans can be found in Appendix B.

Other ways comics can be used in the classroom include the following:

- Using a comic book story, have students find various kinds of words, whether they be parts of speech or examples of onomatopoeia.
- Have a story with the words in the balloons missing. Using the pictures, have the children create their own dialogue.
- Take a story written in another decade and use it in a discussion of that time, pointing out fashions, slang, gender roles, the type or amount of violence, portrayal of minorities, or the background behind the story (Cary, 2004: 120-121). For example, the *Best of the Seventies* volume of the *Archie Americana* series has stories that deal with such issues as student protests, 1970s fashion, the oil crisis, women's liberation, the bicentennial celebration, CBs, and early video games.
- Cut out the panels of a comic book. Have the children put them in the proper order using both dialogue and visual clues.
- Begin but do not finish the story, or use a "to be continued" story. Have the children give ideas as to what happens next.
- Take a comic book story and have the students convert it into a text story, or, for more advanced students, have them convert it into a comic book script.
- If your school uses the Accelerated Reader List, include the graphic novels that are on that list.
- Allow comic books and graphic novels during "sustained silent reading" or any similar program, such as D.E.A.R. (Drop Everything and Read), that your school might use. This has been used elsewhere, including as part of the project in Maryland (Maryland's Comic Book Project, 2005).
- Allow graphic novels to be used in book reports. If you wish, you can allow them with conditions such as word or page count, genre, or subject.
- Use the words in the stories for spelling and/or vocabulary lessons.
- Use a comic or graphic novel in a foreign language to help teach words in that language, especially if you can find both an English-language title and its foreign language counterpart.

The graphic novels have been ordered, processed, and shelved. They are being checked out and being used in programs or in the classroom and perhaps you've already ordered more. Is that all? Possibly. Unfortunately, you have some problems that will be caused by the presence of graphic novels in your library or media center, and that is the topic of Chapter 9.

Notes

1. www.paulsizer.com/matrix/workshops.htm.

2. For more information on the program, contact Daniel Tandarich at yellowjacket 74@hotmail.com.

References

Abraham, Randy. 2007. "Superhero Club Members Work to Create Comic Book." *South Florida Sun-Sentinel*, February 4. People Section, p. 4.

Arnold, Andrew D. "The Graphic Novel Silver Anniversary." Time.com (November 14, 2003). Available: www.time.com/time/columnist/arnold/article/0,9565,542579,00. html.

Banks, Mike. "Mike Banks of Samurai Comics on Partnering With Libraries." ICv2.com (May 30, 2006). Available: www.icv2.com/articles/indepth/8752.html. Accessed: July 5, 2006.

Bitz, Michael. 2003. *A Profile of the Evaluation of the Comic Book Project—New York City Pilot*. Cambridge, MA: Harvard Family Research Project. Available: www.gse.harvard.edu/~hfrp/projects/afterschool/mott/cbp.pdf.

Cary, Stephen. 2004. *Going Graphic: Comics at Work in the Multilingual Classroom*. Portsmouth, NH: Heinemann.

"Ithaca Public Education Initiative 2007 Teacher Grants." 2007. *The Ithaca Journal*, January 24, p. 3B.

"Library Cards Get Bonus on Free Comic Book Day." 2006. *Library Journal*, May 11. Available: www.libraryjournal.com/article/CA6333717.html.

Maryland's Comic Book Project Receives Innovation Award." News Release (October 23, 2005). Maryland State Department of Education. Available: www.maryland public-schools.org/NR/exeres/95DB79BE-780C-49BE-BB6B-78A5321D8DD8.

Mui, Ylan Q. 2004. "Schools Turn to Comics as Trial Balloon." *Washington Post*, December 13, p. B1.

"Using Comics and Graphic Novels in the Classroom." *The Council Chronicle* (September 2005). Available: www.ncte.org/pubs/chron/highlights/122031.htm. Accessed: October 16, 2006.

Chapter 9

Dealing with Potential Problems

Yes, graphic novels are wonderful. They will help your collection, they will increase circulation, and they are educational. However, there are still some problems that you might—and probably will—encounter with having a graphic novel collection in your library.

Theft and Vandalism

The first issues to consider are theft and vandalism of the materials. It has been said that graphic novels in libraries do not "walk"—they "run." It is almost a certainty that some of the graphic novels in your collection will disappear. They are popular items, and popular items do have a habit of being stolen. Will they be stolen at a higher rate than other popular items? It's hard to say, though discussions on GNLIB-L and elsewhere seem to indicate that they disappear about as often, and sometimes less often than other "hot" items, such as DVDs, CDs, and books on popular or controversial topics. With graphic novels, it may simply be more apparent to you that they are missing. Obviously, it is easier to notice if volume four of an eight-volume manga series is no longer available as opposed to some other book in the nonfiction area, whose absence you may notice only when a patron is asks for it.

So what can be done? Normal antitheft devices, such as the targets put in books that cause the security gates to "beep," can help, but on the other hand they can be foiled if, for example, the thief tears out the page with the target. Even having the books in a very visible location can't prevent all theft, since all that the thief has to do is take the book to a more hidden part of the library before tearing out the page. Some librarians have taken more creative methods to prevent theft, including placing a sign warning that not only wouldn't stolen titles be replaced, but future volumes would not be purchased. Although this has not entirely prevented theft, it has, in some cases, cut down on it, and some missing volumes have even found their way back to the library.

Sometimes patrons, who for one reason or another cannot check out the graphic novel, will actually hide a book that they are reading elsewhere in the library so that only they will have a chance to read it. With luck, the book will be found before you have to go through the general "lost book" procedure. Converting a graphic novel for library use—reinforcing the cover, stamping the library's name, adding stickers and call numbers, and so forth—can at least prevent the thief from selling the book to a local comic book or used book stories. Sadly, it will not stop them if they want it for their own private collection or if they want to put it on eBay.

Vandalism of comics can also be a problem, though the motives may be slightly purer than the simple destruction of library property. A person may tear or cut out a page in order to get themselves a free poster or pictures of characters they like. A small child may even treat a black-and-white graphic novel as if it were a coloring book. If a book is stolen, damaged beyond repair, or lost in another way, such as a patron who checks out a book and doesn't return it, you will have to decide whether or not to replace it. While you will make this decision on the same criteria that you would a book that has fallen apart (whether by normal wear and tear or by someone accidentally or deliberately removing pages), the fact that the book was stolen once already will be on your mind. If the replacement copy also disappears, it can be difficult to decide whether it is worthwhile to purchase a third copy.

Complaints and Challenges

There is a bigger potential problem in regard to complaints about the material. Parents may object to the material in the graphic novels that their children are reading, or in some cases, what other people's children might have access to. In some instances however, their criticisms can be valid. For example, in the case of collection in which the adult, YA, and juvenile are intermixed, there is a chance that are child will, accidentally or deliberately, pick up a book with R-rated material, including gore, foul language, and nudity, and even some PG-13 material might cause problems. Children may see the comic book style and be attracted to it, and besides the format, it might have other similarities to age-appropriate titles. For instance, Marvel's *Supreme Power* features superheroes, but also nudity and foul language. And as mentioned in Chapter 6, Oni's *Barry Ween* series may look like it's about a ten-year old super genius and his friends, but the dialogue would make the kids from *South Park* blush.

Even items in the graphic novels intended for children, tweens, and teens can lead to complaints. There are many possible causes for complaint, and with graphic novels it is not just content of the story that could cause problems, it can also be the artwork. Long cited in complaints has been the visual depiction of women, often portrayed as "full figured" and wearing tight or revealing outfits.

The fact that violent acts or sexual imagery can be seen rather than described can also be cause for complaint. This has been referred to as the "naked buns" effect. There is no problem if it is mentioned in a book that someone is naked below the waist, but if it shown, even from the back, then problems can arise (Cary, 2004: 45). And of course the same complaints that are made about other juvenile titles—the content in the story, that it features "antisocial" activities, etc.—can also be made in regard to graphic novels.

Another relevant fact is that since the average comic reader is in his or her twenties, comic book writers will take this into account while creating their scripts. Many of the "recommended for teens titles," including the vast majority of the current superhero titles, may have elements that some parents would not want younger children exposed to. In Chapter 3, the cultural differences in dealing with foreign titles was discussed, including how nudity, especially non-sexual nudity such as a character bathing or changing clothes, is not as big a deal in places such as Japan as it is in the United States. Again, the reactions of American audiences to these scenes may be different than those of readers from the book's original country.

Even if adult-level titles are located in a separate area of the library, there is a chance that an adult will complain even if children do not find them. They may be under the mistaken impression that all comics and graphic novels are for children, and if the library has this book in the collection then obviously they intended it for children despite it being both cataloged and shelved as an adult title. "Comics are for kids" has been used not only by complaining patrons, but even by prosecuting attorneys in cases in which comic book shops have been charged with selling adult materials to adults.

If there is complaint toward a graphic novel, then it should be handled in the same manner as a complaint toward any other item in the collection. If graphic novels are included in your collection development policy, this can be helpful when responding to the complaint. At the very least you should have collection development policy to show to complaining patrons. Not having any policy can cause you to additional problems during a challenge. Sometimes all that is asked for is that the title be moved from the children's to the adult section, and depending on the book and on your community, this may not be an unreasonable request, especially if access to the materials is not an issue. If the complaint asks for the total removal of the title from the collection, then the normal reconsideration procedures for your library should be followed.

Luckily it has become easier to defend a graphic novel from a patron complaint. As more mainstream sources are covering graphic novels, there are many more positive reviews to be found, and a positive review in a publication such as *Time* may hold more weight with the decision makers than if the review were from a magazine about comics. The librarians at GNLIB-L can also provide not only information on reviews, some of which were written by list members, but also information on how the title has been received by the patrons of their own libraries.

Complaints may not even be from adults. A student at Deering High School in Portland, Maine, wrote an article in 2005 for her school paper asking why tax dollars were being spent on certain graphic novels found in the school's library. The student complained about "written garbage" such as the mangas *Tokyo Mew Mew* (a rated Y title) and *Peach Girl* (rated T) that featured female characters who wore "sexy outfits" and acted in "sexist" ways. The school librarian defended the books, pointing out that, among other things, *Peach Girl* was recommended by ALA (Bell, 2005).

While reported challenges have been relatively low—in a 2005 survey only 35 of 178 librarians reported challenges (National Coalition Against Censorship, the American Library Association, and the Comic Book Legal Defense Fund. 2006)—when they do happen, additional problems can be caused if the local media gets wind of it and blows it out of proportion (usually with headlines in the nature of "Pow! Bam! Guess What Your Kids Are Reading!"). The 2006 complaint toward two adult-themed graphic novels in a Missouri library (*Blankets* and *Fun Home*, which were shelved in the YA and adults sections, respectively) was reported in newspapers all across America. In this case, it was generally the same Associated Press story with minor modifications, including discussions about graphic novels in libraries, along with other examples of challenges.

To help librarians who might not be sure how to handle graphic novel challenges, the American Library Association, the National Coalition Against Censorship, and the Comic Book Legal Defense Fund (see Exhibit 9-1) have created *Graphic Novels: Suggestions for Librarians*, which can be found at various Web sites, including www.ala.org/ala/oif/ifissues/graphicnovels_1.pdf. This nine-page document not only covers what graphic novels are and answers shelving questions, but also provides recommendations on dealing with challenges. This includes how to field complaints, talking with the media, and sample answers for questions including "why do libraries have to buy graphic novels?" Many of their suggestions are adapted from other ALA "dealing-with-challenges" documents, which again shows that graphic novels should be treated the same way as only other library material.

As is the case when people complain about other items in the library, when you receive complaints about graphic novels you sometimes can see their point, while on other occasions the reason for the complaint can surprise you. In 2005 an anti-immigrant group in Denver complained about the library's collection of fotonovelas—photo-illustrated comics for adults, similar to animanga—just because they were in Spanish ("Anti-Immigrant Criticism in Denver," 2005). As with any other item in the library, one never knows what someone will complain

---

Exhibit 9-1. The Comic Book Legal Defense Fund

The Comic Book Legal Defense Fund (CBLDF) is a nonprofit organization dedicated to protecting the First Amendment rights of comic book creators, publishers, and retailers. This is often done by helping to cover legal expenses, but has also included writing "friend of the court" briefs or other letters of support (such as the one they wrote for the Missouri library).

The CBLDF began in 1986 as a way to help Michael Correa, manager of the Lansing, Illinois, comic book store Friendly Franks, who had been arrested and convicted on obscenity charges after selling adult comic books to adults. The sentence was overturned on appeal only after two years and thousands of dollars in legal fees. The fees were offset after comics publisher Dennis Kitchen (of the now defunct Kitchen Sink Publishing) helped organize support from creators, retailers, and fans. Following the resolution of the Friendly Frank's Case, as it has come to be known, CBLDF was officially incorporated and has acted as a watchdog organization ever since.

The CBLDF has come to the aid of many companies and individuals since then, sometimes meeting with success, and other times with failure. Notable cases included those of Mike Diana and Jesus Castillo. Diana was a Florida cartoonist who was convicted of obscenity for his comic book *Boiled Angel*. His sentence included psychosocial testing at his own expense, no contact with children under 18 years of age, and his residence being "subject to inspection, without warning or warrant, to determine if he is in possession of, or is creating obscene material." Castillo worked in a comic shop in Dallas, Texas, and was convicted of selling an adult comic book to an adult undercover police officer. In her closing argument, the prosecuting attorney used the reasoning that, despite what the expert testimony had claimed, comic books were for kids.

Although the CBLDF has not defended librarians in court, it has joined with ALA, the ACLU, and other groups in cases to overturn Internet filtering laws (including the Children's Internet Protection Act), material access laws, and other related issues. Board members include publishers, creators, and others in the industry, and besides membership fees and donations, additional money is raised through the sale of materials created or donated by some of the best-known people in the industry. In addition, the CBLDF puts out a quarterly publication called *Busted!* that discusses not only attacks on comic books but on all free speech issues. The summer 2003 edition, created in time for Banned Books Week, had library issues as its cover story. More information can be found at www.cbldf.org.

---

about and what their reasoning will be. Even books about comics have come under fire. Paul Gravett's adult-level book *Manga: Sixty Years of Japanese Comics* was challenged, and then removed, from a California library after a 16-year-old boy looked through it and found images from pornographic manga reprinted on a few pages. The headline in one newspaper? "Good Grief, Charlie Brown! Family Stunned by Porn Comics at Library" (Gonzalez, 2006).

Internal Problems

One final potential problem is difficulties from library personnel. It could be that the administrator, despite the positive reasons given in Chapter 4, still does not think that graphic novels belong in the library or media center. Or it might be someone else on the staff who feels that the money in the book-buying budget or the limited amount of shelf space available should be allotted to something other than graphic novels. Perhaps the biggest problem is an administrator or other staff member who feels that a certain title is inappropriate, and either raises a fuss or, worse, takes it upon himself or herself to remove it from the shelf. Librarians who purchase graphic novels have told of certain times in which a person who is processing the book or is in the circulation department will find a particular graphic novel objectionable and prevent it from going back out. This tends to be done without any of the reconsideration process that the library would normally go through had a patron complained about the book. It is up to you as to how such a situation is to be handled within the proper procedures of your library. If there is a "higher authority" to complain to, you may do so, unless you feel that this would cause additional problems for you, or, in the worse-case scenario, the person at the top may be the one with the objection.

Of course complaints about comic books are nothing new. Similar to movies, rock and roll, video games, Dungeons and Dragons, Myspace, and whatever this year's controversial item is, comic books have been something that adults have had to "protect" children from.

Comic Book Censorship: A Brief History

The modern comic book had been around for only a few years when complaints began in newspapers, magazines, and journals, including library publications, and some who were involved in attacking or defending comics also had, or would have, literary success of their own.

In May 1940, Sterling North, a literary critic who later wrote the 1963 Newbery Honor book *Rascal*, wrote an article in the *Chicago Daily News* titled "A National Disgrace." In it, he stated:

> Virtually every child in America is reading color "comic" magazines—a poisonous mushroom growth of the last few years. Ten million copies of these sex horror serials are sold every month. One million dollars are taken from the pockets of America's children in exchange for graphic insanity. The bulk of these lurid publications depend for their appeal upon mayhem, murder, torture, and abduction—often with a child as the victim. Superman heroics, voluptuous females in scanty attire, blazing machine guns, hooded "justice," and cheap political propaganda are to be found on almost every page. The old dime novels in which an occasional red skin bit the dust were classic literature compared to the sadistic drivel pouring from the presses today.
>
> Badly drawn, badly written, and badly printed, a strain on young eyes and young nervous systems—the affect of these pulp-paper nightmares is that of a violent stimulant. Their crude blacks and reds spoil the child's natural sense of color; their hypodermic injection of sex and murder make the child impatient with better, though quieter, stories. Unless we want a coming generation ever more ferocious than the present one, parents and teachers throughout America must band together to break the "comic" magazine. (Maxwell, 1943: 60)

North went on to advise parents to use bookstores and libraries as an "antidote" to comics, saying, "the parent who does not acquire that antidote for his child is guilty of criminal negligence." More than 40 newspapers and magazines reprinted this, and the *Chicago Daily News* reportedly received 25 million requests to reprint it for distribution in churches and schools (Nyberg, 1998: 4). There was also much discussion of it in other publications.

One of those publications was *The Wilson Library Bulletin*, in which future Pulitzer Prize winner and U.S. Poet Laureate Stanley Kunitz had a column titled "The Roving Eye." In April 1941, under the heading "Librarians To Arms," Kunitz talked about North's editorial, and he dismissed the effect of the "good" comics such as *True Comics* as well as the findings of a study by a Columbia University professor that comics might help reading and learning. Kunitz said that "a child conditioned by the jerky, jiggling, inflamed world of the comics in a damaged child, incapacitated for enjoyment of the more serene pleasures of the imagination. The chances are that a child who likes *True Comics* will be even more delighted with the 'false' comics." Kunitz also doubted that the reverse was true, and claimed that comics were nothing more than a "training-school for young impressionable minds" and could spawn only "a generation of Storm Troopers, Gauleiter [the party leader of the regional branch of the Nazi party], and coarse, audacious Supermen." He closed by asking librarians what they planned to do about it. Ironically, in the same edition of "The Roving Eye," he praised the fact that a California library had lifted its ban on *The Grapes of Wrath* (Kunitz, 1941b).

Kunitz followed this up two months later, in "The Comic Menace" (1941a), in which he told the tale of a librarian who was ordered by the library board to stock the children's room with "as fine and fancy a collection of these gaudy comics as you ever saw," and every attempt she made to remove the comics she objected to had been "frustrated," and that she was told to "knuckle under and stop being so hifalutin—or else." He then quoted her letter:

> I was informed in no uncertain terms that I was to put the comics out in the juvenile room every week, that there was no harm in them, they helped the backward children learn to read and other equally inane and maudlin sentiments. "You are expected to cooperate with Board in all matter of library policy."
>
> Now the comics grace the children's room reading table once more, and the librarian listens to the objectionable language taken directly from them tossed back and forth among the readers or even directed at herself. Her hands are completely tied until another library position is available in the state or elsewhere. (Kunitz, 1941a)

He also told of another librarian who was waging an "unspectacular and simple, but successful campaign against the highly colored enemy" by having books on the shelf labeled "Funny Books" and "Heroes and Superman." When children asked about Superman books, she told them they didn't have them, but that they instead could read about Robin Hood and other legendary heroes (Kunitz, 1941a). Today, of course, librarians know that they can recommend both.

Comics did have their defenders. In 1942, an article appeared in *Library Journal* titled "They Like It Rough," written by a children's librarian from a public library, Gweneira Williams, who would go on to write *Timid Timothy: The Cat Who Learned to Be Brave*, and Jane Wilson, a librarian from a junior high school. They felt that at least some of the concern over comics was something that occurs every generation: children have a love for things that their parents think are bad for them.

In response to the question of what should be done about comics, Williams and Wilson replied, "Why should anything be done?" adding that many children's librarians felt that nothing could be done, and given their popularity among children, it was very difficult to "entice Johnny away from *Batman* with a copy of *Kidnapped*." They surveyed 125 junior high students about what they liked about the comics, and many responses had to do with the normal love of excitement, adventure, and hero worship. Their reasons for liking Superman and Batman included because they stopped bad guys and helped to defend America. In the authors' opinion, valid objections included sensational plots and action; cheap paper, format, and art; the amount of crime; "the fantastic" and the occasional "sloppy sentimental" story shown; and grammar that was "not the best." They found "little difference emotionally between watching a knight of Arthurian romance being violently unhorsed and a gangster being hailed to Justice by Superman," and found that, compared to some heroes in fairy tales, Superman's morals were "impeccably pure" (Williams and Wilson, 1942).

Objections at the time ranged from the quality of the print (which admittedly could be quite poor) to the content of the stories, especially in the crime and horror comics. Articles such as *The Hartford Courant*'s "Depravity for Children—10 Cents a Copy" warned parents that any child could buy a "short course in murder, mayhem, robbery, rape, cannibalism, carnage, sex, sadism, and worse" (Nyberg, 1998: 29). All of these articles helped to spawn community and parents groups that would monitor and if necessary attempt to ban "objectionable" comics. The targets of these groups were not only the publishers, but also the newsstand vendors and owners of drugstores or supermarkets who sold comics (Nyberg, 1998: 23).

Some of these committees would create lists of acceptable and unacceptable titles. Reviewers of the material included librarians, and *Parents' Magazine* and similar publications would then print the lists. At first the lists would cover those comics with sex and violence, but later they also looked at cultural and moral values. Different groups had different criteria as to what was objectionable. For example, in one list was an objection to a Superman comic because it showed a criminal act, despite that fact that the criminal was caught, and there were times when a title was rated acceptable on one group's list but unacceptable on another's (Nyberg, 1998: 30–31).

Library publications continued to discuss comics, such as the 1948 *Library Journal* article "Youth's Librarian's Can Defeat Comics" written by former children's librarian Jean Gray Harker. The article reflected many of the criticisms of the time. She complained about the quality of the stories and art, which had "poor grammar, poor word choice, garish pictures, and objectionable subject matter" that "retard the development of reading skill," "strain children's eyes," "arrest their mental development," and "debase their morals." She also criticized the "cheesecake art" and complained that the "wonder comics" such as Superman did not present a "realistic attitude towards crime." In addition, she echoed a complaint of the time that crime comics led to juvenile delinquency, showing young readers not that, as one popular comic book's title proclaimed, *Crime Does Not Pay*, but instead gave them ideas about how to pull off a crime successfully. Harker also argued that children's librarians should better train themselves to help improve the ways they deal with children so to better influence them, countering the effects of the comics. "How long must the public wait before our children's librarians are as well trained as our teachers?" she asked. "It's no wonder that our children are reading the comics!" (Harker, 1948).

The comic book publishers did try to alleviate fears, and as early as 1941 would set up editorial boards that included psychiatrists (including Wonder Woman's creator William Moulton Marston), educators, and even celebrities such as Shirley Temple. It was hoped that these boards, whose membership were listed in the comics, would convince concerned adults that the titles were wholesome. In 1948, they took a step toward self-regulation with the creation of the Association of Comics Magazine Publishers (ACMP). The ACMP created a publisher's code, and if a title met with code approval, then a "seal of approval" could be placed on its cover, informing potential readers (and their parents) that this was a "safe" comic. Among the code's rules were "no drawing should show a female indecently or unduly exposed," "crime should not be presented in such a way as to throw sympathy against the law and justice or to inspire others with the desire for imitation," and "slang should be kept to a minimum and used only when essential to the story" (Nyberg, 1998: 165). However, many publishers did not join the ACMP, others such as EC dropped out, and some of the remaining publishers would use the seal without going through the approval process. Although this attempt at self-regulation failed, more would come soon.

Despite their attempt, strong anticomic feeling persisted in 1948, with a comic book burning reported at the end of the year. A debate on the effect of comic books had been broadcast earlier that year, and more anticomics articles were appearing in magazines, including one in the *Saturday Review of Literature* that called them "the marijuana of the nursery; the bane of the bassinet; the horror of the house; the curse of the kids; and a threat to the future" (Brown, 1948).

Also in 1948 a man whose name is forever linked with the anticomics feeling of the time came on the scene, Dr. Fredric Wertham. A psychiatrist, Wertham had worked with troubled youth, and he began to examine a link between juvenile delinquency and comic books, finding that many troubled children read comics. In 1948, he moderated a panel in Manhattan for the Association for the Advancement of Psychotherapy called "The Psycho-Pathology of Comic Books." Wertham, quoting a two-year study of comics that he headed, concluded that comics were "sexually aggressive in an abnormal way" and that they glorified violence and undermined morals, and added that "comic book reading was a distinct influencing factor in the case of every single delinquent or disturbed child" (Goulart, 2004: 298). His views gained him publicity, and he wrote about them in such diverse publications as *Collier's Weekly* ("Horror in the Nursery") and *The American Journal of Psychotherapy* ("The Psychopathology of Comic Books"), but his most memorable attack on comics came in 1954 with his book *Seduction of the Innocent*.[1]

Seduction attacked crime and horror comics and blamed juvenile delinquency on them, forgetting that although it may be true that bad kids read comics, it was also true that good kids were reading them as well. While there were some elements in those books that were cause for concern and in some cases may have been intended for older audiences, some of his best-known attacks were also the some of the more absurd. He claimed, for example, that he saw erotic images "hidden" in artwork, and that there was a homosexual connotation in the relationship between Batman and Robin.

Wertham also covered the issue of comics and reading skills, going against many published studies by claiming that "severe reading difficulties and maximum comic book reading go hand in hand, that far from being a help to reading, comic books are a casual and reinforcing factor in children's reading disorders" (Krashen, 2004: 97).

Seduction of the Innocent was very popular, and was cited and discussed in the media, including *Library Journal*. Another result of the additional anticomic feeling that *Seduction* caused were hearings on comic books and juvenile delinquency held by the U.S. Senate. State and local governments had previously investigated the issue on their own, with some discussion of regulation and censorship, and there were even ordinances passed in some communities prohibiting the sale of some titles to juveniles. The Senate Judiciary Committee created a special Subcommittee on Juvenile Delinquency headed by Senator Estes Kefauver of Tennessee, which in 1954 held hearings on the topic of how comic books affected juvenile delinquency. Among those who testified were Wertham and EC publisher William Gaines.

The subcommittee's interim report the following year was balanced, discounting some of Wertham's claims and rejecting the idea of legislated censorship (Lavin, 2002). It did criticize some aspects, especially the crime and horror titles (see Exhibit 9-2). Superhero titles were also criticized because in them "law and order are maintained by supernatural and superhuman heroes, and officers of the law, ineffective in apprehending criminals, must depend on aide from fantastic characters. The law-enforcement officials who do solve cases often succeed through 'accidental events.'" The committee felt that this portrayed real police in a poor light.

While it "flatly rejected" the idea of government censorship, the subcommittee did laud the efforts of the community groups that worked at the local level to boycott and protest against certain comics, and recommended that the industry self-regulate itself. Perhaps anticipating this, the previous year publishers had formed the Comics Magazine Association of America (CMAA), the second attempt at self-regulation. Many more companies joined the CMAA, which then set up the Comics Code Authority (CCA). Members would submit their comics to the CCA, which would make sure that the art and text adhered to the code. If there was a problem they would recommend changes, and once the changes were complete, or if there was nothing that needed to be changed, the comic would get the seal for the cover saying "Approved by the Comics Code Authority." Of course a publisher did not have to get the CCA seal, but it made financial sense to join, since newsstand owners who didn't carry only code-approved titles would face the wrath of "Concerned Mothers Against Comics" or whatever such group was in his or her city. The only publishers who could afford not to join were those who were already known to be "clean."

The new code had similarities to the 1947 code. The first part covered the portrayal of crime, the second part covered horror, and the third dealt

---

Exhibit 9-2. Comics and Communism?

Under the heading "The Exportation of Crime and Horror Comic Books," the subcommittee claimed that "there is evidence that comic books are being utilized by the U.S.S.R. to undermine the morale of youth in many countries by pointing to crime and horror as portrayed in American comics as one of the end results of the most successful capitalist nation in the world."

with dialogue, portrayals of religion, "costume," marriage and sex, and advertising material. Some notable rules included, "Crimes shall never be presented in such a way as to create sympathy for the criminal, to promote distrust of the forces of law and justice, or to inspire others with a desire to imitate criminals," "policemen, judges, government officials, and respected institutions shall never be presented in such a way as to create disrespect for established authority," "in every instance good shall triumph over evil and the criminal punished for his misdeeds," and "no comic magazine shall use the word 'horror' or 'terror' in its title," as well a prohibition against vampires, werewolves, zombies, and many other aspects of horror (Nyberg, 1998: 166–169).

Some companies adapted to the code, while others had problems, the most notable being EC. Due to the new rules, it could no longer continue publishing comics with titles such as *The Vault of Horror* and *The Crypt of Terror*, and the remaining titles ended up having their material censored by CCA. EC ended up canceling many titles, and started new ones, including *Incredible Science Fiction, Extra!* (which was about newspapermen), and the humor comic *Mad*.

Although EC attempted to stay within code guidelines, problems still arose. For example, the code forced EC to add a "happy ending" to an alien invasion story, and the extra page cost them a page worth of ads. The final straw occurred when EC submitted *Incredible Science Fiction* #33 (January–February 1956), in which a story from 1953 titled "Judgment Day" was reprinted. In this highly regarded story, an earthman visited a planet of robots to see if they were ready to join the Galactic Republic. The orange robots thought that the blue ones were inferior and discriminated against them, which caused the earthman to decide that they were not yet ready for membership. He then left the planet, and in the final panel he took off the helmet he had worn throughout the story, revealing to the audience that he was black. The CCA insisted that EC change the art to make the astronaut white. Gaines told them they were bigots, said he would print it as is, and if they objected he would publicize the reason. Interestingly, the reprint was being reviewed because another story had been rejected by the CCA (Thompson and Lupoff, 1998: 310). Following this, EC cancelled all of its titles except for *Mad*, which it turned into the magazine that is still around today.

As children's comics entered the Silver Age, they mainly did so under the watchful eye of the CCA. But times changed, and circumstances led the code to change as well. In 1971, the U.S. Department of Health, Education, and Welfare asked Marvel to create a story detailing the dangers of drug abuse. A three-part Spider-Man story was written that included a storyline in which a friend of Spider-Man's has a bad reaction to LSD. Despite showing drugs as being a bad thing the CCA rejected the story. Marvel editor in chief Stan Lee, who wrote the story, consulted his publisher, and got permission to print the story anyway without the CCA's seal of approval in *Amazing Spider-Man* #96 to #98.[2]

This helped lead to modifications in the code in 1971. Among the significant changes were that "narcotics or drug addiction shall not be presented *except as a vicious habit*" and that "vampires, ghouls and werewolves shall be permitted to be used when handled in the classic tradition such as Frankenstein, Dracula, and other high calibre literary works . . . read in schools around the world" (Nyberg, 1998: 170–174).

Marvel was among those who took advantage of the second rule, creating code-approved comics featuring Dracula, Frankenstein's Monster, and the "Werewolf by Night." Since zombies still couldn't be used, the walking dead, or at least those who seemed to be walking dead but were actually mind controlled, were referred to in Marvel Comics as "zuvembies."

By the 1980s, the Comic Code Authority's power had weakened with the creation of the direct market and the rise in the independent publishers, many of whom did not submit their titles. Even members such as DC started up lines for mature audiences that were not submitted for code approval. The code was again revised in 1989, and among the changes, were that depictions of homosexuality were now approved as long it was not displayed in a graphic or stereotypical way. The 1989 revision also stated that:

> The members of the Comics Magazine Association of America include publishers who elect to publish comics that are not intended to bear the Code Seal, and that therefore need not go through the approval process described above. Among the comics in this category may be titles intended for adult readers. Member publishers hereby affirm that we will distribute these publications only through distribution channels in which it is possible to notify retailers and distributors of their content, and thus help the publications reach their intended audiences. The member publishers agree to refrain from distributing these publications through those distribution channels that, like the traditional newsstand, are serviced by individuals who are unaware of the content of specific publications before placing them on display." (Nyberg, 1998: 178)

In 2001, Marvel Comics withdrew from the CCA and began its own ratings system, and as of 2007 the only major companies that are still members are Archie (which is generally known to be "safe"), DC (which submits it only for some superhero comics and all of the Johnny DC titles), and Dark Horse (which submits comics that will appear only on newsstands as well as in comic shops). In addition to Marvel, other companies such as Tokyopop and Viz have their own in-house ratings systems that can serve as a guide.

The period between 1940 and 1955 was the heyday of anticomics feelings, with the "save our children" crusaders moving on to other issues. There were still complaints here and there, but on a small, local level, not in the nationwide organized manner that occurred during that period. In many cases, especially in recent years, complaints have been about adult materials being sold to adults in comic book stores, since, in the minds of some, comics are only for kids. However, there have been some children-related issues. As of this writing, Rome, Georgia, comic shop owner Gordon Lee is being prosecuted for misdemeanor charge of exhibition of harmful materials to a minor for a 2004 incident in which he allegedly gave a minor a free copy of *Alternative Comics* #2. This comic featured several panels in which Pablo Picasso is shown naked from the front, though there was no sexual content.[3] On two occasions charges were dropped, but new charges followed. The CBLDF is aiding in paying Lee's legal expenses (Comic Book Legal Defense Fund Web site). Another controversy appeared in 2007 when a teacher in Connecticut gave a high school freshman an issue of the comic book *Eightball* by Daniel Clowes, which featured, among other things, foul language and brief nudity. This case drew some media attention, with both pro and con articles, including the typical "comics aren't just for kids anymore" stories.

In addition to having their own ratings systems, some publishers will occasionally indulge in special editing to make their works more suitable for younger ages. For example, during the 1970s, besides its code-approved *Dracula* comic, Marvel also has a black-and-white non-code-approved magazine titled called *Tomb of Dracula* that was aimed at an adult audience. When these stories were collected for an essential edition both code- and non-code-approved stories were mixed together, so the art was changed for some stories, covering up images of nudity that had appeared in the magazine ("Marvel Edits 'Tomb of Dracula' for *Essential Dracula* Reprint," 2006). The same has happened to some manga, in which some scenes were "toned down" for the American editions (MacDonald, 2006).

Graphic novels can be a source of problems in your library or media center. Luckily, the advantages of having graphic novels in your collection far outweigh any of the disadvantages. Do not be discouraged by any stories of past or current problems, though. If you did not have something in your library that *somebody* would find it objectionable, then you would have a very small collection indeed, and theft—while annoying and even costly—can also be an indication of the popularity of graphic novels in your library.

Notes

1. Originally published by Holt, Reinhart, and Winston.
2. The story has been reprinted and collected in the trade editions *The Death of Gwen Stacy* and *The Essential Amazing Spider-Man*, Volume 5.
3. This story has been collected into the graphic novel *The Salon* by Nick Bertozzi (St. Martin's Griffin, 2007).

References

"Anti-Immigrant Criticism in Denver Extends to Library Fotonovelas." *Library Journal* (August 18, 2005). Available: www.libraryjournal.com/article/CA635920.html.

Bell, Tom. 2005. "Racy Fluff or Reading Aid?" *Portland Press Herald*, March 14, p. B1.

Brown, John Mason. 1948. "The Case Against Comics." *Saturday Review of Literature*, March 20, pp. 32–33.

Cary, Stephen. 2004. *Going Graphic: Comics at Work in the Multilingual Classroom.* Portsmouth, NH: Heinemann.

Comic Book Legal Defense Fund. Available: www.cbldf.org.

Gonzalez, Miguel. 2006. "Good Grief, Charlie Brown! Family Stunned by Porn Comics at Library." *Daily Press* [Victorville, CA], April 12. Available: http://archive.vvdaily press.com/2006/11448553316.html.

Goulart, Ron. 2004. *Comic Book Encyclopedia: The Ultimate Guide to Characters, Graphic Novels, Writers, and Artists in the Comic Book Universe.* New York: HarperCollins.

Harker, Jean Gray. 1948. "Youth's Librarians Can Defeat Comics." *Library Journal* (December 1): 705–1707, 1720.

Krashen, Stephen D. 2004. *The Power of Reading*, 2nd ed. Westport, CT: Libraries Unlimited.

Kunitz, Stanley J. [As SJK]. 1941a. "The Comic Menace." *Wilson Library Bulletin* 15: 846–847.

Kunitz, Stanley J. [As SJK]. 1941b. "Libraries to Arms!" *Wilson Library Bulletin* 15: 670–671.

Lavin, Michael R. "The Comics Code Authority" (April 11, 2002). Available: http://ublib.buffalo.edu/libraries/projects/comics/cca.html.

MacDonald, Heidi. 2006. "Manga Alternations/Censorship." *The Beat*, June 26. Available: www.comicon.com/thebeat/2006/06/manga_alterationscensorship.html.

"Marvel Edits 'Tomb of Dracula' for *Essential Dracula* Reprint." ICV2.com (September 22, 2006). Available www.icv2.com/articles/news/9357.html.

Maxwell, Arthur S. 1943. *Great Prophecies for Our Time.* Mountain View, CA: Pacific Publishing Association.

National Coalition Against Censorship, the American Library Association, and the Comic Book Legal Defense Fund. 2006. *Graphic Novels: Suggestions for Librarians.* Available: www.ala.org/ala/oif/ifissues/graphicnovels_1.pdf.

Nyberg, Amy Kiste. 1998. *Seal of Approval: The History of the Comics Code.* Jackson, MS: University Press of Mississippi.

Thompson, Don and Dick Lupoff. 1998. *The Comic-Book Book*, revised ed. Iola, WI: Krause Publications.

Williams, Gweneira and Jane Wilson. 1942. "They Like It Rough: In Defense of Comics." *Library Journal* (March 1): 204–206.

Chapter 10

A Final Word

So this is where graphic novels have been and where they are. But where are they going? Things are looking good for this once-maligned format. More and more publishers are putting out graphic novels, either individually or as part of a line, and at least some of them are for younger readers. Graphic novels are winning awards and have gained respectability. Librarians who just a few years ago didn't even know what a graphic novel was are now recommending them and using them in programs.

But what does the future bring? David Saylor, editorial director of Scholastic's Graphix line is optimistic. "I believe we're in the midst of another golden age of comics," he said in a 2007 interview.

> The talent, energy, and passion of comics-creators is dovetailing with a burgeoning new audience. In the next ten years I think we're going to see a tremendous growth in graphic novels for adults and children. They'll be read, discussed, and have the same popularity as other forms of literature. And partly it's because Scholastic and other publishers are creating an audience of kids that will grow up to love the graphic novel form and will continue reading them life-long. It's like a trickle-up effect. Kids today are changing the future of publishing. (Hunt, 2007)

Hopefully all publishers will see this and continue to create graphic novels that are suitable for children and tweens, and hopefully libraries will not only provide them to the readers but pick out the best books for their libraries. Some material to consider starts in Appendix A. The final words go to graphic novel writer/artist Jeff Smith, who said of libraries and graphic novels:

> It's something I've wanted to have happen all along. I've always felt that graphic novels as an art form could get a better audience. I feel librarians a lot of times represent the front line of our culture. They stand up for art. They stand up for literature. And I think if librarians are saying there's something to these comics, to graphic novels, I think it has some weight. I think that means something. (Beardsley, 2002)

References

Beardsley, Nancy. "Graphic Novels Gain Popularity with American Teenagers." Washington: American Library Association (October 19, 2002). Available: www1.voanews.com/article.cfm?objectID=98EDEF8B-C27B-4F9E-B8C1F0D516752029.

Hunt, Jonathan. 2007. "The Trickle-up Effect: An Interview with David Saylor." *Children and Libraries: The Journal of the Association for Library Service to Children* 5, no. 1: 8–11.

Annotated Suggested Graphic Novel Booklist

Introduction

In choosing the books for this list, I have either read the book, read a representational sample of the series (for both fiction and nonfictions series), or been familiar enough with the material to include it in the list. These titles are in my personal collection (including in comic book form), were provided by the publishers or creators, or were checked out from the Broward County Library System or from other systems via interlibrary loan.

The following list is therefore not a list of all graphic novels appropriate for children or tweens, nor is it necessarily a "best of" list. It is, however, a look at the vast spectrum of genres and titles available to librarians and media specialists. Not all of the titles listed will be available through all vendors, and some may go in and out of print, acquire new publishers, be collected in new ways, etc. Additional books and Web sites that contain booklists are found in Appendix B and Appendix C. Recommended books are indicated.

The titles in this list are listed alphabetically, but in three different ways:

- **Title:** For a stand-alone book. This is for both an original graphic novel and a for a one-volume trade edition.
- **Series**: These are alphabetical by the series name, which includes going by the publisher's name (e.g., Capstone's Graphic Nonfiction). Individual titles and/or subtitles will be included in the body of the entry.
- **Character(s):** All books and series in which a certain character or characters are the "star" will be grouped together, such as books with Batman, Spider-Man, Archie, and the Simpsons. Series titles, individual titles, and/or subtitles will be included in the body of the entry. Specific titles can also be located in the title index, where their page numbers are listed in bold.

For this list I have stretched the definition of tween to include early teens, since many 12-year-olds are in the same school as 13- and 14-year-olds and share libraries. Therefore, a few titles that are suitable for readers in their early teens are also included and will have a **[T]** after their description. Titles with a **[C]** are for younger elementary age readers, and their content or reading level might not appeal to older readers. Those marked with a **[B]** are generally appropriate for both older elementary and middle/intermediate/junior high students, though they still may also be acceptable for younger readers as well. Books/titles that are appropriate for all ages but would appeal more to elementary-age readers than those in middle/intermediate/junior high are marked with an **[E]**. Additional notes on age suitability and interest will also be found in the series/book description. However, please remember that this is a general and broad list. Only you can properly judge what books are appropriate for your community, library, and readers.

All titles on this list were out or had their publication announced by July 2008. The price listed is the original price. Publishers and vendors may sell them at a discount.

Graphic Novels and Publishers

Abdo Publishing

At first the only graphic novels published by Abdo were hardcover, enlarged (7" × 10½") versions of various kid-friendly Marvel and Archie comic books put out by their Spotlight imprint. Although many of these stories are also found in the digest-sized trades put out by Marvel, the books are found by their Abdo title on some Accelerated Reader lists. **[B]**

Beginning in 2007, Abdo began a Graphic Planet line as part of their Magic Wagon imprint. These books cover nonfiction topics (biography and history) and literary adaptations (both general classics and famous horror stories). Each 32-page book includes a glossary, a timeline (in the nonfiction books), and author biography (in the adaptations). Several comic book creators have worked on these books, including Rod Espinosa and Ben Dunn. Additional titles are expected. **[E]**

Magic Wagon Graphic Planet

$18.95 each.

Bio-Graphics Series

> *Abraham Lincoln.* Written by Joe Dunn. Illustrated by Rod Espinosa.
> *Anne Frank.* Written by Joe Dunn. Illustrated by Ben Dunn.
> *Benjamin Franklin.* By Rod Espinosa.
> *George Washington.* By Rod Espinosa.
> *Jackie Robinson.* Written by Joe Dunn. Illustrated by Rod Espinosa.
> *Lewis and Clark.* By Rod Espinosa.
> *Patrick Henry.* By Rod Espinosa.
> *The Wright Brothers.* Written by Joe Dunn. Illustrated by Ben Dunn.

Graphic History Series

> *The Battle of the Alamo.* By Rod Espinosa.
> *The Bombing of Pearl Harbor.* Written by Joe Dunn. Illustrated by Joseph Wight and Rod Espinosa.
> *The Boston Tea Party.* By Rod Espinosa.
> *The California Gold Rush.* Written by Joe Dunn. Illustrated by Ben Dunn.
> *Miracle on Ice.* Written by Joe Dunn. Illustrated by Ben Dunn.
> *Moon Landing.* Written by Joe Dunn. Illustrated by Joseph Wight and Rod Espinosa.

The Titanic. Written by Joe Dunn. Illustrated by Ben Dunn.
Underground Planet. By Rod Espinosa.

Graphic Classics Series

Around the World in 80 Days. Adapted by Rod Espinosa.
Moby Dick. Adapted by Rod Espinosa.
Peter Pan. Adapted by Rod Espinosa.
Robin Hood. Adapted by Joe Dunn. Illustrated by Ben Dunn.
The Time Machine. Adapted by Joe Dunn. Illustrated by Ben Dunn.
White Fang. Adapted by Joe Dunn. Illustrated by Ben Dunn.

Graphic Horror Series

The Creature from the Depths. Adapted by Mark Kidwell.
Frankenstein. Adapted by Elizabeth Genco. Illustrated by Jason Ho.
Dr. Jekyll and Mr. Hyde. Adapted by Jason Ho.
The Legend of Sleepy Hollow. Adapted by Jeff Zornow.
Mummy. Adapted by Bart A. Thompson. Illustrated by Brian Miroglio.
Werewolf. By Jeff Zornow.

Abdo Spotlight Books

$21.95 (Marvel titles) and $24.21 (*Archie*).

These books feature (from their Marvel Age titles) Spider-Man, Spider-Girl, Power Pack, the Hulk, the X-Men, Mary Jane (Spider-Man's friend), the Fantastic Four, and characters from Archie Comics (see the entries for these characters elsewhere in this list).

The Abomination! (Hulk)
Am I Blue (X-Men)
The Apple Doesn't Fall Far! (Fantastic Four)
Bedeviled (Spider-Girl)
Big Green Men (Hulk)
Big Trouble at the Big Top! (X-Men/Power Pack)
Bugs (Hulk)
Captain America: Stars, Stripes, and Spiders! (Spider-Man)
Choices (Spider-Girl)
Color Blind (Archie)
The Coming of the Scorpion (Spider-Man)
Costumes On! (X-Men/Power Pack)
Cowboys and Robots (Hulk)
A Day to Remember (Archie)
The Diabolical Dr. Santos (Fantastic Four)
Duel to the Death with the Vulture (Spider-Man)
Duel with Daredevil! (Spider-Man)
End of the Rainbow (Power Pack)
The Enforcers! (Spider-Man)

Face-to-Face with the Lizard! (Spider-Man)

Family Photos (Archie)

Fantastic Four: The Chameleon Strikes! (Spider-Man)

Fantastic Four: The Menace of Monster Isle! (Spider-Man)

Fool Proof (Archie)

Fore! (Archie)

Fun 'N' Games with the Fantastic Five! (Spider-Girl)

The Grotesque Adventure of the Green Goblin! (Spider-Man)

Hearing Things (X-Men)

Help Wanted (Archie)

His Latest Flame (Fantastic Four)

I Know What We Did That Summer (Power Pack)

It's Slobberin' Time! (Fantastic Four)

Jet-Ski Scandal (Archie)

Kitty Pryde: Down with the Monsters! (Spider-Man)

Kraven the Hunter (Spider-Man)

The Last Word (Archie)

Leader of the Pack (X-Men/Power Pack)

Legacy . . . In Black and White (Spider-Girl)

Lines in the Sand (X-Men)

The Loyalty Thing (Mary Jane)

Lucky Day (Archie)

Mammoth Madness (Archie)

The Man Called Electro! (Spider-Man)

Marked for Destruction by Dr. Doom (Spider-Man)

The Menace of Mysterio (Spider-Man)

Mind Over Matter (X-Men/Power Pack)

Misadventures in Babysitting (Power Pack)

The Money Thing (Mary Jane)

Nothing Can Stop the Sandman! (Spider-Man)

A Plague of One (Fantastic Four)

Power Play (Archie)

Pup-ularity Contest (Archie)

Quiet Please (Archie)

The Real Thing (Mary Jane)

The Rival (Archie)

Seeing Clearly (X-Men)

Shortcut (Fantastic Four)

Snack Swap (Archie)

Snooze Button (Archie)

Spider-Girl Battles the Deadly Dragon King (Spider-Girl)

Spider-Man and the Terrible Threat of the Living Brain! (Spider-Man)

Spider-Man versus Doctor Octopus (Spider-Man)

Spidey Strikes Back! (Spider-Man)

Stampede (Archie)
Storm: Change the Weather (Spider-Man)
Strange Change (Archie)
A Test Case (Archie)
The Things Below (Fantastic Four)
Thor: Out of Time! (Spider-Man)
Top This (Archie)
Touch of Venom (Spider-Girl)
Trendsetter (Archie)
The Trust Thing (Mary Jane)
The Ugly Truth (Archie)
The Unexpected (Archie)
Unmasked by Doctor Octopus! (Spider-Man)
Vacation of Doom! (Power Pack)
Where Flies the Beetle . . . ! (Spider-Man)
Wish Fulfillment (Archie)
Women Are from Venus, Men Are from Atlantis (Fantastic Four)

Adventures in Oz

Eric Shanower. IDW (2006). $39.99. **[B]**. Recommended.

Unlike the other adaptations of *The Wizard of Oz*, this color graphic novel creates new stories based not only the first book, but on the entire Oz series. *Adventures in Oz* collects five graphic novels put out between 1986 and 1992. All of the familiar characters appear, including Dorothy, who was a made a princess of Oz, and the Wizard who also returned to Oz after learning real magic.

Akiko

Mark Crilley. Sirius Entertainment. **[B]**

Akiko is a young Japanese-American girl who goes on adventures in outer space in this enjoyable, Eisner-nominated black-and-white series. Accompanying Akiko on her adventures are the wise Mr. Beeba; the adventurer (and braggart) Spuckler; Gax the Robot; Poog, a round flying creature; and, on occasion, the young Prince Froptoppit, who has a crush on her. Several of the graphic novels have also been adapted into a text series from Random House, which has continued with original stories. The earlier collections have been "reformatted" as "pocket size" volumes. Volume 1 is on Diamond's list of recommended titles for elementary schools.

Pocket Size

All $9.95.

The Menace of Alia Rellapor, Volumes 1–3
The Story Tree, Volume 4
Bornstone's Elixir, Volume 5

Volumes 6 and 7 are larger and cost $14.95.

Alia's Mission: Saving the Books of Iraq

Mark Alan Stamaty. Alfred A. Knopf (2004). $12.95.**[B]**

A short, black-and-white book about a librarian in Baghdad who helped save more than 30,000 books in the Baghdad library in the weeks before it was destroyed by fighting.

Alice (*aka* Lela Dowling's Alice)

Adapted by Chris Weiman. Art by Lela Dowling. About Comics (2004). $8.95. **[B]**

One of the *Alice and Wonderland* adaptations on this list. There are no "typical" panels, but most pages have four images placed in a diagonal left-right-left order.

A.L.I.E.E.E.N.

Lewis Trondheim. First Second (2006). $12.95. **[B]**

Originally published in France, this graphic novel is wordless except for alien languages. The title is actually an acronym for "Archives of Lost Issues and Earthly Editions of Extraterrestrial Novelties," and the basic premise of this odd book is that it is the contents of a comic book left behind by visiting aliens. There is a small amount of violence and scatological humor, and although the book is wordless, older readers may be better at understanding what is happening.

Amelia Earhart Free in the Skies *and* Into the Air: The Story of the Wright Brothers' First Flight

Robert Burleigh. Illustrated by Bill Wylie. Silver Whistle, an imprint of Harcourt. $16.00 (hardcover), $5.95 (softcover). **[E]**

Short biographies of these pioneers of flight. Each page has generally one to three panels, and has both narration boxes and word and thought balloons. The Wright Brothers book covers much of their lives, while Earhart's covers through to her famous flight, with a brief summary of the rest of her life, including her disappearance, on the final page.

Amelia Rules

Jimmy Gownley. Renaissance Press (2003–). $24.95 (hardcover) and $14.95 (softcover). **[B]**. Highly recommended.

In this wonderful comic, nine-year-old Amelia Louise McBride moves with her divorced mother to live with her (cool) Aunt Tanner. In her new town she makes some new (and strange) friends including Reggie, who dreams of being superhero, and the ever-silent "Pajamaman." The first volume is on Diamond's list of recommended titles for elementary schools, and the series has been nominated for and won several awards.

Current books in the series are:

> Volume 1: *Amelia Rules: The Whole World's Crazy*
> Volume 2: *Amelia Rules: What Makes You Happy*
> Volume 3: *Amelia Rules: Super Heroes*
> Volume 4: *When the Past Is a Present*

American Born Chinese

Gene Luen Yang. First Second Books (2006). $16.95. **[T]**. Recommended.

A recent hit, *American Born Chinese* has aided in the perception of graphic novels as literature. It was the first graphic novel to be nominated for the National Book Award, and the first to win the Michael L. Printz award for young adult literature. It has also been on a number of "best graphic novel" lists and has won a number of other awards. It was also on both Diamond's list of recommended titles for middle schools and in the top ten of YALSA's Great Graphic Novels for Teens List. The book has three story lines that start separately but eventually intersect. The first is about Jin Wang, one of the few Asian children in his school. The second is based on the old Chinese legend of the Monkey King. The third, told in the style of a sitcom, complete with laugh track, is about Danny, a Caucasian teen who is forced to change schools each year following the yearly visit of his cousin Chin-Kee, who incorporates every negative Chinese stereotype and is a great embarrassment to Danny. It is a wonderful book that deals with issues of race, identity, stereotypes, and self-acceptance. Some elements in the book make them more appealing to the older age range.

Angelic Layer

Clamp. Tokyopop (2002–2003). $9.99. **[B]**

A five-volume series that inspired anime series *Angelic Layer*, it is about 12-year-old Misaki Suzuhara who moves to Tokyo to live with her aunt. At the time the most popular pastime is the hit arcade game Angelic Layer, in which players mentally control robots that compete against one another. She soon builds her own "angel," Hikaru, and although it is smaller and weaker than others, it does well due to Misaki's will and determination. The series is rated **A** for all ages.

Archie

Archie Comics Publications. **[B]**

For more than 60 years, teenager Archie Andrews and his friends Jughead, Reggie, Betty, and Veronica have entertained readers with their adventures in the town of Riverdale. They, and their spin-offs, including Josie and the Pussycats and Sabrina, the Teenage Witch, have appeared in a number of comic books and digests, as well as on television, in the movies, and elsewhere. Despite their long history, currently only a handful of trade editions are available, which collect the stories from over the decades.

Archie Americana Series

Each book has Archie stories from a particular decade.

Best of the Forties, $11.95   *Best of the Sixties*, $9.95
Best of the Forties Book Two, $10.95   *Best of the Seventies*, $9.95
Best of the Fifties, $10.95   *Best of the Eighties*, $10.95
Best of the Fifties Book Two, $10.95

Other Collections

Archie's Camp Tales, Volume 1, $7.49

Sabrina the Teenage Witch: The Magic Revisited, $7.49

Archie's Classic Christmas Stories, Volume 1, $10.95

Archie Day by Day (a collection of the comic strip), $10.95

The Adventures of Little Archie (Archie and the gang as children), $10.95

Best of Josie and the Pussycats, $10.95

Betty and Veronica Summer Fun, $10.95

See also the entry for **Abdo Publishing**, **Abdo Spotlight Books**.

Artemis Fowl: The Graphic Novel

Adapted by Eoin Colfer and Andrew Donkin. Illustrated by Giovanni Rigano. Hyperion Books for Children (2007). $18.99 (hardcover), $9.99 (softcover). **[B]**

An adaptation of the first book in the popular *Artemis Fowl* series, which deals with 12-year-old genius and criminal mastermind Artemis Fowl and his plans, which often tend to involve an underground fairy race. More adaptations may be done.

Asterix

René Goscinny and Albert Uderzo. Orion Publishing Group (English translation) (1961–). $9.95–$12.95. **[B]**

This funny, internationally popular series from France is about Asterix and his friends, who live in Gaul in the first century BC and are doing their best to keep the Romans out. Asterix, who is short with a large mustache, and his friends, including the large Obelix and the druid Getafix, travel all over the ancient world in their adventures. The translations usually carry over the author's humor, even in the case of French puns, and even though it takes place more than 2,000 years ago, there are contemporary references thrown in as well. Asterix is distributed in the United States by Sterling Publishing.

In chronological order, the books in the series are:

Asterix the Gaul	*The Mansions of the Gods*
Asterix and the Golden Sickle	*Asterix and the Laurel Wreath*
Asterix and the Goths	*Asterix and the Soothsayer*
Asterix and the Gladiator	*Asterix in Corsica*
Asterix and the Banquet	*Asterix and the Caesar's Gift*
Asterix and the Cleopatra	*Asterix and the Great Crossing*
Asterix and the Big Fight	*Obelix and Co.*
Asterix in Britain	*Asterix in Belgium*
Asterix and the Normans	*Asterix and the Great Divide*
Asterix the Legionary	*Asterix and the Black Gold*
Asterix and the Chieftain's Shield	*Asterix and Son*
Asterix and the Olympic Games	*Asterix and the Magic Carpet*
Asterix and the Cauldron	*Asterix and the Secret Weapon*
Asterix in Spain	*Asterix and Obelix All at Sea*
	Asterix and the Actress

Asterix and the Roman Agent
Asterix in Switzerland
Asterix and the Falling Sky

Aseterix and the Class Act
Asterix and the Falling Sky

Babymouse Series

Jennifer L. Holm and Matthew Holm. Random House Books for Young Readers (2005–). $12.99 (hardcover), $5.95–$5.99 (softcover). **[C]**

Written by Newbery Honor book winner Jennifer Holm and illustrated by her brother, the Babymouse series are small, 96-plus-page books in black and white and pink. In a world of anthropomorphic animals, Babymouse is a young girl in elementary school who has all sorts of fun and funny adventures.

Current books in the series are:

Babymouse: Beach Babe
Babymouse: Heartbreaker
Babymouse: Monster Mash
Babymouse: Our Hero
Babymouse: Puppy Love

Babymouse: Queen of the World
Babymouse: Rock Star
Babymouse: Skater Girl
Camp Babymouse

More volumes are expected.

The Baby-sitter's Club

Adapted by Raina Telgemeier. Scholastic/Graphix (2006–) $16.99 (hardcover), $8.99 (softcover). **[B]**

Based on the popular paperback series by Ann M. Martin about four girls who set up a baby-sitting service while also handling the problems of their own lives. The first volume is on YALSA's Great Graphic Novels for Teens List.

Volume 1: *Kristy's Great Idea*
Volume 2: *The Truth About Stacy*

Volume 3: *Mary Anne Saves the Day*
Volume 4: *Claudia and Mean Janine*

Additional volumes are planned.

Banana Sunday

Root Nibot. Illustrated by Colleen Coover. Oni Press (2006). $11.95. **[B]**

Teenager Kirby Steinberg is starting at a new high school, but what makes her different than the average new student is that she is coming to school with monkeys—monkeys who can talk. The monkeys are highly intelligent Chuck, the romantic Knobby, and Go-Go, a strong, but simple, gorilla. Amazing as they are, the truth behind them is even more fantastic than everyone thinks. This book is on YALSA's Great Graphic Novels for Teens List.

Barron's Graphic Classics

These books from Barron's Publishing provide short (32–34 pages) adaptations of works of classic literature. Each page has a number of comic panels, but instead of word balloons, the text is below the panels, making this book closer to a hybrid graphic novel. In addition to the adaptation, an additional fourteen to sixteen pages include information on the author, on the setting of the story (for example, *The Hunchback of Notre Dame* includes information on medieval Paris and the history of the cathedral), and of the history of the book itself. The series is available in hard ($15.99) and soft-cover ($8.99). All titles in the series are illustrated by Penko Gelev. **[B]**

> *The Hunchback of Notre Dame.* Adapted by Michael Ford.
> *Journey to the Center of the Earth.* Adapted by Fiona Macdonald.
> *Kidnapped.* Adapted by Fiona Macdonald.
> *Moby Dick.* Adapted by Sophie Furse.
> *Oliver Twist.* Adapted by John Malam.
> *Treasure Island.* Adapted by Fiona Macdonald.

Additional art on *Moby Dick*, *Hunchback*, and *Kidnapped* by Sotir Gelev.

Batman

DC Comics. **[B]**

A well-known character since 1939, Batman has appeared in many different comic books and many different collections including:

Batman Chronicles, Volumes 1–5, $14.99 each. Collections of Batman stories from the later 1930s and early 1940s. The art may be different than what some children are used to. Additional volumes may come out.

> Best of the decade collections, $19.95 each.

> | | |
> |---|---|
> | *Batman in the Forties* | *Batman in the Seventies* |
> | *Batman in the Fifties* | *Batman in the Eighties* |
> | *Batman in the Sixties* | |

Batman: The Greatest Stories Ever Told, Volumes 1–2, $19.99

The various animated *Batman* programs of the past 20 years have been turned into comic books which have since been collected.

> Collections include:
>
> *Batman: The Dark Knight Adventures.* Written by Kelley Puckett. Art by Mike Parobeck and Rick Burchett. $7.95.
> *Batman: Harley and Ivy.* Written by Judd Winick, Paul Dini. Illustrated by various artists. $14.99.
> *Batman Adventures*, Volume 1: Rogue's Gallery by various writers and artists. $6.95.
> *Batman Adventures*, Volume 2: Shadows & Masks by various writers and artists. $6.95.
> *The Batman Jam-Packed Action!* By various writers and artists. $7.99.
> *The Batman Strikes!* Written by Bill Matheny. Illustrated by Christopher Jones and Terry Beatty.
>> Volume 1: *Crime Time*. $6.99. This volume is on Diamond's list of recommended titles for elementary schools.
>> Volume 2: *In Darkest Knight*. $6.99.
> *Duty Calls.* Written by J. Torres. $12.99.

See also the Batman titles under **DC Archive Editions**.

Beet the Vandel Buster

Riku Sanjo. Art by Koji Inada. Viz (2004–). **[B]**

A manga series that has inspired both an anime television series and a video game, *Beet* takes place in the future in a time known as "The Age of Darkness," when alien monsters called Vandels rule the world. They are opposed by humans called Vandel Busters. Beet has once tried to join the group the Zenon Warriors, but after their defeat he began his own group, the Beet Warriors. The series is rated **A** for all ages, and as of 2007, 12 volumes have come out.

Beyblade

Takao Aoki. Viz (2004–). $7.99. **[B]**

This 14-volume, all-ages series has led to an anime series, video games, and toys. The beyblades are spinning tops enchanted with the spirits of mystical creatures that people compete with against each other. Tyler wants to be the best, and with the mysterious beyblade he has acquired he just might be. But the team known as the Blade Sharks is in the way and willing to do whatever it takes to win.

The Big Book of Horror

Steve Niles. Illustrated by various artists. IDW (2006). $19.99. **[T]**

A collection of the three *Little Books of Horror* adaptations of *Dracula, Frankenstein,* and *War of the Worlds*. A hybrid, each page is illustrated, sometimes with one picture spread over two pages, with the text also on the page.

Big Fat Little Lit

Edited by Art Spiegelman and Francoise Mouly. Puffin Books (2006). **[B]**

This softcover book collects stories from the three previously published "Little Lit" books: *Little Lit: Folklore and Fairy Tale Funnies* (2000), *Little Lit: Strange Stories for Strange Kids* (2001), and *Little Lit: It Was a Dark and Silly Night* (2003). These books featured both new material and reprints of older work. Other well-known writers and artists whose work appears in the compilation include Crockett Johnson, Ian Falconer, Neil Gaiman, Walt Kelly, Jules Feiffer, Gahan Wilson, David Macauly, Lemony Snicket, David Sedaris, Lewis Trondheim, and Art Spiegelman.

Biker Girl

Written and illustrated by "Misako Rocks!" (Misaka Takashima). Hyperion (2006). $7.99. **[T]**

An OEL shōjo manga (though the creator is originally from Japan) about Aki, a shy, glasses-wearing teenage girl who transforms with the help of a magical motorcycle into a superhero, the latest in the family line of "bike heroes." She must face off against a gang of evil bikers, one of whom has a link to her past.

A Bit Haywire

Scott Zirkel. Art by Courtney Huddleston and Jeff Dabu. Viper Comics (2006). $11.95 **[B]**

Ten-year-old Owen Bryce is a normal kid who learns he has superpowers: speed (if he holds his breath), flight (if he shuts his eyes), laser vision (when he's cold), and others. In addition, he finds out his parents are superheroes, who for the time being want him to stay undercover. But even the costume they give him is no help if his clothes disappear whenever someone takes his picture.

The Black Belt Club

Dawn Barnes. Art by Bernard Chang. Scholastic/Blue Sky Press (2005–). $16.95 (hardcover), $4.99 (softcover). **[E]**

This series of children's books is hybrid, with the text intermixed with comic panels and even entire pages of comic art. In the books, Max and his friends in the secret Black Belt Club go on missions to fight evil.

> *Beware the Haunted Eye*
> *Night on the Mountain of Fear*
> *Seven Wheels of Power*

Bone

Jeff Smith. **[B]**. Highly recommended.

Jeff Smith's multi-award-winning fantasy series was one the first ongoing titles to be collected. The main protagonist of the series is Fone Bone, who along with his scheming cousin Phoney Bone and his simplistic cousin Smiley were forced to escape from their home of Boneville after one of Phoney's schemes went wrong. They end up in a strange valley, and in an adventure that includes lost princesses, evil sorcerers, dragons, talking animals, and the "rat creatures." The black-and-white series was originally collected into nine volumes published by Smith's company Cartoon Books. They were very popular, especially in libraries. This led Scholastic to reprint color editions of the trades as the first book in their Graphix line. Scholastic will be reprinting the final volume in 2009, but the black-and-white editions may still be found in comic book stores and elsewhere. In addition, Cartoon Books has produced and kept in print *Bone: The One Volume Edition*. More than 1,300 pages long, this book collects the entire original black-and-white series. It is also on Diamond's list of recommended titles for elementary schools, and on *Time* magazine's list of the "10 Greatest Graphic Novels of All Time."

The color Scholastic Graphix Editions are available in both hard ($18.99) and softcover ($9.99), and have the same names as their black-and-white counterparts:

> Volume 1: *Out from Boneville*
> Volume 2: *The Great Cow Race*
> Volume 3: *Eyes of the Storm*
> Volume 4: *The Dragonslayer*
> Volume 5: *Rock Jaw: Master of the Eastern Border*
>
> Volume 6: *Old Man's Cave*
> Volume 7: *Ghost Circles* (2008)
> Volume 8: *Treasure Hunters* (2008)
> Volume 9: *Crown of Horns* (2009)

Besides the *Bone: The One-Volume Edition* ($39.95), Cartoon Books also published two prequels: *Rose* ($19.95), an original color graphic novel by Smith and artist Charles Vess, and *Stupid, Stupid Rat Tails: The Adventures of Big Johnson Bone, Frontier Hero* ($9.99), an original black-and-white graphic novel, with two stories written by Tom Sniegoski and art by Smith and Stan Sakai.

Bone Sharps, Cowboys, and Thunder Lizards.

Jim Ottaviani and "Big Time Attic." GT Labs (2005). $22.95. [**B**]. Recommended.

A "fictional nonfiction title," *Bone Sharps* tells the story of paleontologists Edward Drinker Cope and Othniel Charles Marsh, who were in the "bone war," the attempt to find the most dinosaur bones. Other characters in the book include P.T. Barnum, Ulysses Grant, Buffalo Bill Cody, Alexander Graham Bell, and artist Charles R. Knight, who was known for his painting of dinosaurs. Ottaviani also includes a "fact or fiction" section at the end of the book, explaining which elements of the story were real.

Buzzboy

Written and penciled by John Gallagher. Various inkers. Sky Dog Press (2002–). [**B**]

A humorous superhero series. In the first collected volume, which is on Diamond's list of recommended titles for elementary schools, Buzzboy returns after many years after his mentor Ultra becomes a dictator. Additional volumes contain shorts stories and adventures.

Current collections are:

Buzzboy: Trouble in Paradise ($11.95)
Buzzboy: Monsters, Dreams, & Milkshakes ($11.95)
Buzzboy: Sidekicks Rule ($12.95)

Capstone Graphic Library

Capstone's Graphic Library series covers history, biography, and science. Each 32-page book is in the same general format: a 24-page story followed by extra facts about the subject, a glossary, a link to Internet sites via facthound.com, additional related titles, a bibliography, and an index. The stories are told in a combination of caption boxes and dialogue balloons, and direct quotations from primary sources are indicated when they appear in the text. Each book lists a consultant or consultants in the field that the book is about. Although these books may not be the best choice for the chief source for report, they are helpful for the child who needs additional titles, cannot find any additional titles in the library, or just wants a quick and fun way to learn about a person or subject. Each volume comes in paperback ($7.95) and hardcover ($25.28). Several titles are on Accelerated Reader lists and are available in Spanish, and there are CD-ROM versions of some of the books that include audio along with a slightly animated version of the story. Librarians have the option of putting these in the 741s, or in the appropriate nonfiction Dewey area (500s, 900s, biographies, etc.). Some of the creators have experience in the comic book industry. Additional titles are expected. [**E**]

Graphic Biographies Series

Amelia Earhart: Legendary Aviator. Written by Jameson Anderson. Illustrated by Rod Whigham and Charles Barnett III. (2007)

Benedict Arnold: American Hero and Traitor. Written by Michael Burgan. Illustrated by Terry Beatty. (2007)

Benjamin Franklin: An American Genius. Written by Kay M. Olson.

Bessie Coleman: Daring Stunt Pilot. Written by Trina Robbins. Illustrated by Ken Steacy. (2007)

Booker T. Washington: Great American Educator. Written by Eric Braun. Illustrated by Cynthia Martin. (2006)

Cesar Chavez: Fighting for Farmworkers. Written by Eric Braun. Illustrated by Harry Roland and Al Milgrom. (2006)

Christopher Columbus: Famous Explorer. Written by Mary Dodson Wade. Illustrated by Charles Barnett III. (2007)

Clara Barton: Angel of the Battlefield. Written by Allison Lassieur. Illustrated by Brian Bascle. (2006)

Eleanor Roosevelt: First Lady of the World. Written by Ryan Jacobson. Illustrated by Barbara Schulz and Gordon Purcell. (2006)

Elizabeth Blackwell: America's First Woman Doctor. Written by Trina Robbins. Illustrated by Cynthia Martin. (2007)

Elizabeth Cady Stanton: Woman's Rights Pioneer. Written by Connie Colwell Miller. Illustrated by Cynthia Martin and Keith Tucker. (2006)

Florence Nightingale: Lady with the Lamp. Written by Trina Robbins. Illustrated by Anne Timmons. (2007)

George Washington: Leading a New Nation. Written by Matt Doeden. Illustrated by Cynthia Martin. (2006)

George Washington Carver: Ingenious Inventor. Written by Nathan Olson. Illustrated by Keith Tucker. (2006)

Helen Keller: Courageous Advocate. Written by Scott Welvaert. Illustrated by Cynthia Martin and Keith Tucker. (2006)

Jackie Robinson Baseball's Great Pioneer. Written by Jason Glaser. Illustrated by Bob Lentz. (2006)

Jane Goodall: Animal Scientist. Written by Katherine E. Krohn. Illustrated by Cynthia Martin and Anne Timmons. (2006)

John F. Kennedy: American Visionary. Written by Nathan Olson. Illustrated by Brain Bascle. (2007)

Martin Luther King Jr.: Great Civil Rights Leader. Written by Jennifer Fandel. Illustrated by Brian Bascle. (2007)

Matthew Henson Arctic Adventurer. Written by B.A. Hoena. Illustrated by Phil Miller and Charles Barnett III.

Molly Pitcher: Young American Patriot. Written by Jason Glaser. Illustrated by Todd Aaron Smith and Bill Anderson. (2006)

Mother Jones: Labor Leader. Written by Connie Colwell Miller. Illustrated by Steve Erwin and Charles Barnett III. (2007)

Nathan Hale: Revolutionary Spy. Written by Nathan Olson. Illustrated by
Cynthia Martin and Brent Schoonover. (2006)

Patrick Henry: Liberty or Death. Written by Jason Glaser. Illustrated by Peter
McDonnell. (2006)

Sacagawea: Journey to the West. Written by Jessica Gunderson. Illustrated by
Cynthia Martin. (2007)

Samuel Adams: Patriot and Statesman. Written by Matt Doeden. Illustrated by
Tod Smith and Charles Barnett III. (2007)

Theodore Roosevelt: Bear of a President. Written by Nathan Olson. Illustrated by
Mark Heike. (2007)

Thomas Jefferson: Great American. Written by Matt Doeden. Illustrated by
Gordon Purcell and Terry Beatty. (2006)

William Penn: Founder of Pennsylvania. Written by Ryan Jacobson. Illustrated by
Tim Stiles. (2007)

Wilma Rudolph: Olympic Track Star. Written by Lee Engfer. Illustrated by
Cynthia Martin and Anne Timmons. (2006)

Disasters in History

All published in 2006.

The Apollo 13 Mission. Written by Donald B. Lemke. Illustrated by Keith Tucker.

The Attack on Pearl Harbor. Written by Jane Sutcliffe. Illustrated by Bob Lentz.

The Challenger Explosion. By Heather Adamson. Art by Brian Bascle.

The Donner Party. Written by Scott Welvaert. Illustrated by Ron Frenz and
Charles Barnett III.

The Great Chicago Fire of 1871. Written by Kay M. Olson. Illustrated by Phil
Miller and Charles Barnett III.

The Hindenburg Disaster. Written by Matt Doeden. Illustrated by Steve Erwin,
Keith Williams, and Charles Barnett III.

Shackleton and the Lost Antarctic Expedition. Written by B.A. Hoena. Illustrated
by Ron Frenz and Charles Barnett III.

The Triangle Shirtwaist Factory Fire. Written by Jessica S. Gunderson.
Illustrated by Phil Miller and Charles Barnett III.

Graphic Science

The graphic science line is "hosted" by super-powered scientist Max Axiom, and have
the subtitle "With Max Axiom, Superscientist." All books published in 2007.

Adventures in Sound. Written by Emily Sohn. Illustrated by Cynthia Martin and
Anne Timmons.

The Attractive Story of Magnetism. By Andrea Gianopoulos.

A Crash Course in Forces and Motion. Written by Emily Sohn. Illustrated by
Shannon E. Denton.

Exploring Ecosystems. Written by Agnieszka Biskup. Illustrated by Tod Smith.

The Explosive World of Volcanoes. Written by Christopher L. Harbo. Illustrated
by Tod Smith.

The Illuminating World of Light. By Emily Sohn.

A Journey into Adaptation. Written by Agniesezka Biskup. Illustrated by Barbara Schulz.

Lessons in Science Safety. Written by Donald B. Lemke and Thomas K. Adamson. Illustrated by Bill Anderson.

The Shocking World of Electricity. Written by Liam O'Donnell. Illustrated by Richard Dominguez and Charles Barnett III.

Understanding Global Warming. By Andrea Gianopoulos.

Understanding Photosynthesis. Written by Liam O'Donnell. Illustrated by Richard Dominquez and Charles Barnett III.

The World of Food Chains. Written by Liam O'Donnell. Illustrated by Bill Anderson.

Inventions and Discovery

All published in 2007.

Alexander Graham Bell and the Telephone. Written by Jennifer Fandel. Illustrated by Keith Tucker.

Eli Whitney and the Cotton Gin. Written by Jessica Gunderson. Illustrated by Gerry Acerno.

George Eastman and the Kodak Camera. Written by Jennifer Fandel. Illustrated by Al Milgrom.

Hedy Lamarr and a Secret and a Secret Communication System. Written by Trina Robbins. Illustrated by Cynthia Martin.

Henry Ford and the Model T. Written by Michael O'Hearn. Illustrated by Phil Miller and Charles Barnett III.

Isaac Newton and the Laws of Motion. Written by Andrea Gianopoulos. Illustrated by Phil Miller and Charles Barnett III.

Jake Burton Carpenter and the Snowboard. Written by Michael O'Hearn. Illustrated by Ron Frenz and Charles Barnett III.

Johann Gutenberg and the Printing Press. Written by Kay M. Olson. Illustrated by Tod Smith.

Jonas Salk and the Polio Vaccine. Written by Katherine Krohn. Illustrated by Al Milgrom.

Levi Strauss and Blue Jeans. Written by Nathan Olson. Illustrated by Dave Hoover and Charles Barnett III.

Louis Pasteur and Pasteurization. Written by Jennifer Fandel. Illustrated by Keith Wilson.

Madame C.J. Walker and New Cosmetics. Written by Katherine Krohn. Illustrated by Richard Dominquez and Charles Barnett III.

Marie Curie and Radioactivity. Written by Connie Colwell Miller. Illustrated by Scott J. Larson.

Philo Farnsworth and the Television. Written by Ellen Sturm Niz. Illustrated by Keith Tucker.

Samuel Morse and the Telegraph. Written by David Seidman. Illustrated by Charles Barnett III.

Steve Jobs, Steve Wozniak, and the Personal Computer. Written by Donald B. Lemke. Illustrated by Tod Smith and Al Milgrom.

Thomas Edison and the Lightbulb. Written by Scott R. Welvaert. Illustrated by Phil Miller and Charles Barnett III.

The Wright Brothers and the Airplane. Written by Xavier Niz. Illustrated by Steve Erwin, Keith Williams, and Charles Barnett III.

Graphic History

The Adventures of Marco Polo. Written by Roger Smalley. Illustrated by Brian Bascle. (2005)

The Assassination of Abraham Lincoln. Written by Kay M. Olson. Illustrated by Otha Z.E. Lohse. (2005)

The Battle of the Alamo. Written by Matt Doeden. Illustrated by Charles Barnett III and Phil Miller. (2005)

The Battle of Gettysburg. Written by Michael Burgan. Illustrated by Steve Erwin, Keith Williams, and Charles Barnett III. (2006)

Betsy Ross and the American Flag. Written by Kay M. Olson. Illustrated by Anna Maria Cool, Sam Delarosa, and Charles Barnett III. (2006)

The Boston Massacre. Written by Michael Burgan. Illustrated by Charles Barnett III and Bob Wiacek. (2005)

The Boston Tea Party. Written by Matt Doeden. Illustrated by Charles Barnett III and Dave Hoover. (2005)

The Brave Escape of Ellen and William Craft. Written by Donnie Lemke. Illustrated by Charles Barnett III and Phil Miller. (2006)

The Buffalo Soldiers and the American West. Written by Jason Glaser. Illustrated by Tod Smith and Charles Barnett III. (2005)

The Building of the Transcontinental Railroad. Written by Nathan Olson. Illustrated by Richard Dominquez and Charles Barnett III. (2007)

The Creation of the U.S. Constitution. Written by Michael Burgan. Illustrated by Gordon Purcell and Terry Beatty. (2007)

The Curse of King Tut's Tomb. Written by Michael Burgan. Illustrated by Barbara Schulz. (2005)

Dolly Madison Saves History. Written by Roger Smalley. Illustrated by Anna Maria Cool, Scott Rosema, and Charles Barnett III. (2006)

The First Moon Landing. Written by Thomas K. Adamson. Illustrated by Gordon Purcell and Terry Beatty. (2007)

Harriet Tubman and the Underground Railroad. Written by Michael Martin. Illustrated by Dave Hoover and Bill Anderson. (2005)

John Brown's Raid on Harpers Ferry. Written by Jason Glaser. Illustrated by Charles Barnett III and Bill Anderson. (2006)

John Sutter and the California Gold Rush. Written by Matt Doeden. Illustrated by Charles Barnett III and Ron Frenz. (2006)

The Lewis and Clark Expedition. Written by Jessica Gunderson. Illustrated by Steve Erwin and Charles Barnett III. (2007)

Lords of the Sea The Vikings Explore the North Atlantic. Written by Allison Lassieur. Illustrated by Charles Barnett III and Ron Frenz. (2006)

The Mystery of the Roanoke Colony. Written by Xavier Niz. Illustrated by Shannon Eric Denton. (2007)

Nat Turner's Slave Rebellion. Written by Michael Burgan. Illustrated by Richard Dominquez, Bob Wiacek, and Charles Barnett III. (2006)

Paul Revere's Ride. Written by Xavier Niz. Illustrated by Brian Bascle. (2006)

The Pilgrims and the First Thanksgiving. Written by Mary Englar. Illustrated by Peter McDonnell. (2007)

Rosa Parks and the Montgomery Bus Boycott. Written by Connie Colwell Miller. Illustrated by Daniel Kalal. (2007)

The Salem Witch Trials. Written by Michael Martin. Illustrated by Brian Bascle. (2005)

The Sinking of the Titanic. Written by Matt Doeden. Illustrated by Charles Barnett III and Phil Miller. (2005)

The Story of Jamestown. Written by Eric Braun. Illustrated by Steve Erwin and Keith Williams. (2006)

The Story of the Star-Spangled Banner. Written by Ryan Jacobson. Illustrated by Cynthia Martin and Terry Beatty. (2006)

The Story of the Statue of Liberty. Written by Xavier Niz. Illustrated by Cynthia Martin and Brent Schoonover. (2006)

The Voyage of the Mayflower. Written by Allison Lassieur. Illustrated by Peter McDonnell. (2006)

Winter at Valley Forge. Written by Matt Doeden. Illustrated by Charles Barnett III and Ron Frenz. (2005)

Young Riders of the Pony Express. Written by Jessica Sarah Gunderson. Illustrated by Brian Bascle. (2006)

Castle Waiting

Linda Medley. Fantagraphics Books (2006). $29.95. **[T]**. Recommended.

What happened after Sleeping Beauty and her prince left the castle? Well, it became home to talking animals, people from fairy tales, refugee mothers, and a bearded nun, all with their own stories. The first version of *Castle Waiting* was published with a grant from the Xeric Foundation, and three volumes were published from Olio Press. These have been collected in this hardcover volume, with a new collection of stories published in 2008. An award winner, *Castle Waiting* has appeared on several "best" lists, including being in the top ten of YALSA's Great Graphic Novels for Teens List.

Chickenhare: The House of Klaus

Chris Grine. Dark Horse (2006). $9.95. **[B]**

Chickenhare (part chicken and part rabbit) and his friend Abe (a turtle with a beard) have been captured and brought to mad taxidermist Klaus. Can he and the other captured creatures escape? And what do the strange creatures called the Stromph have to do with it? Or the ghost of a goat for that matter? This strange and funny book got an Eisner nomination for best publication for a younger audience, and a sequel came out in 2008.

Cine-Manga

Tokyopop. $7.99. [C], [E], and [B] (depending on title)

As mentioned in Chapter 3, most of the cine-manga is pictures taken from animated or live-action television shows and movies, with captions and word balloons added. Although technically not graphic novels, they are very kid-safe. The junior cine-manga line is for an even younger age, with only two pictures on each page, and larger print. In the "Greatest Stars of the NBA" cine-manga, two cartoon characters tell about the player while pictures of the player in action are shown on the page.

Unless indicated, all titles are rated **A** for all-ages, and are 96 pages.

Aladdin (based on the feature film) (2004)
All Grown Up (based on Nickelodeon television series) (2005)
    Volume 1: *Suzie Sings the Blues*
    Volume 2: *Coup Deville*
The Amanda Show (2005)
Avatar, the Last Airbender (2006–2007)
Bambi (2005)
Barbie Fairytopia (2005)
Bratz! (48 pages, $5.99)
Cars (2006)
Chicken Little (film) (2005)
Cinderella (2005)
Cinderella III! (48 pages, $5.99) (2006)
Drake & Josh (2005)
Duel Masters (2004–2005)
    Volumes 1–5
The Fairly Odd Parents! (2004–2005)
    Volume 1: *Heroes and Monsters*
    Volume 2: *Beware the Babysitter*
    Volume 3: *Father Knows Less*
    Volume 4: *Let the Games Begin*
    Volume 5: *School Rules!*
Finding Nemo
Greatest Stars of the NBA (2004–2007)
    Volume 1: *Shaquille O'Neal* (2004)
    Volume 2: *Tim Duncan* (2004)
    Volume 3: *Jason Kidd* (2005)
    Volume 4: *Kevin Garnett* (2005)
    Volume 5: *Allen Iverson* (2005)
    Volume 6: *Future Greatest Stars of the NBA Dwayne Wade, Lebron James, Carmelo Anthony* (2005)

Volume 7: *Dynamic Duos Yao Ming, Tacy McGrady* (2006)
Volume 8: *All-Time Dunks* (2006)
Volume 9: *International Stars* (2007)
Volume 10: *Kobe Bryant* (2007)
Volume 11: *Greatest Guards* (2007)
Volume 12: *Greatest Forwards* (2007)
Hannah Montana (cataloged **Y**, 10+) (2007–)
    Volumes 1–2. Additional volumes announced.
Happy Feet (48 pages, $5.99) (2006)
Happy Feet Jr. Cine-Manga (30 pages, $3.99)
High School Musical (2007)
The Incredibles (2005) (not to be confused with the adaptation from Dark Horse
    Comics)
Kim Possible (rated **Y**) (2003–2004)
    Volumes 1–7
Lady and the Tramp Jr. Cine-Manga ($3.99)
Lilo & Stitch: The Series (2004–2005)
    Volumes 1–3
Lizzie McGuire (rated **Y**) (2003–2006)
    Volumes 1–14. Additional volumes may be produced.
The Lizzie McGuire Movie (2004)
Madagascar (2005)
Meet the Robinsons (48 pages, $5.99) (2007)
My Little Pony Jr. Cine-Manga (32 pages, $3.99)
    Volume 1: *Friends Are Never Far Away* (2005)
    Volume 2: *A Very Minty Christmas* (2005)
    Volume 3: *Dancing in the Clouds* (2006)
    Volume 4: *The Runaway Rainbow* (2006)
    Additional volumes are planned.
Pirates of the Caribbean Dead Man's Chest (rated **Y**, 48 pages, $5.99) (2007)
Pooh's Hefalump Movie (2005)
Princess Diaries 2 (2005)
Romeo (2005)
Sesame Street Jr Cine-Manga (32 pages, $3.99) (2005–2007)
    Volumes 1–5. Additional volumes may come out.
Shrek 2 (rated **Y**)
SpongeBob SquarePants (2003–2007)
    Another Day Another Sand Dollar
    Crime and Funishment
    Friends Forever
    Gone Jellyfishin'
    Gone Nutty
    Krusty Krab Adventures
    Meow—Like a Snail?

Mistaken Identity
Spongebob Saves the Day
SpongeBob SquarePants
Tales from Bikini Bottom
Who's Hungry—Patty Hype
The Spongebob SquarePants Movie (2005)
Spy Kids 3-D Game Over (2003)
Teenage Ninja Mutant Turtles
That's So Raven (2004–2005)
    Volume 1: *School Daze*
    Volume 2: *The Trouble with Boys*
    Volume 3: *Smother Dearest*
    Volume 4: *It's a Family Affair*
    Volume 5: *It Takes Two*
    Volume 6: *It's News to Me*
Totally Spies (**see also** the **Totally Spies** entry) (2004–2005)
    Volume 1: *Spies in Disguise*
    Volume 2: *Spies vs. Spy*
    Volume 3: *Trouble in the Tropics*
    Volume 4: *Time Spies When You're Having Fun*

City of Light, City of Dark: A Comic Book Novel

Avi. Art by Brian Floca. Scholastic (Orchard Books). **[B]**

Long ago when people settled on Manhattan they had to make a deal with beings called Kurbs. Each year on June 21 the Kurbs hid their power in the city in another form, and one of the people must find it and return it by December 21 or the city will freeze and the Kurbs will take it back. In recent times it has been in the form of a subway token. The current searcher is a woman who inherited it from her mother, and whose daughter was stolen years ago by her husband who works for a man who wants the power. A *Publisher's Weekly* best book of the year.

Clan Apis

Jay Hosler. Active Synapse (2000). $15.00. **[B]**. Recommended.

The life of a bee named Nyuki, the Swahili word for bee (in fact most of the bee names mean "bee"). By reading this wonderful "fictional nonfiction" graphic novel readers will learn all about bees without even realizing it. There is some additional text information at the end of the book.

The Collected Allison Dare: Little Miss Adventures

J. Torres. Illustrated by J. Bone. Oni Press (2002–). $11.95. **[B]**

These two paperback volumes collect the two *Allison Dare* limited series. Alison Dare is a 12-year-old girl attending St. Joan of Arc Academy for Girls. But when your mother is a famous archeologist and adventurer, your uncle is a super-spy, and your father is the superhero the Blue Scarab (who is a librarian in his secret identity), then you are not going to be an ordinary 12-year-old. She and her friend get into all sorts of adventures, sometimes along with her family, including dealing with genies, spies, and supervillians.

The Courageous Princess

Rob Espinosa. Dark Horse Comics (2007). $14.95. **[B]**. Recommended.

Princess Mabelrose is the daughter of the king and queen of New Tinsley, a smaller part of the land of the Hundred Kingdoms, a region that also includes the Charming Kingdom, the Slipper Kingdom, Beanstalk Land, and Swan Lake. Although not the fairest in the land, she is happy until she is kidnapped by a dragon who is holding her for ransom. Not really expecting her prince to come, she must escape and face other dangers on the way back home. This award-nominated book is on Diamond's list of recommended titles for elementary schools. This edition reprints *The Courageous Princess Masterpiece Edition* originally published by Antarctic Press.

Courtney Crumrin Series

Ted Naifeh. Oni (2000–) $11.95. **[T]**. Recommended.

Courtney has just moved with her parents into the creepy house of her uncle, Professor Aloysius Crumrin, and she's not happy about the house or her new school. Creepy occurrences are afoot, and Courtney encounters werewolves, trolls, fairies, goblins, and more. The digest-sized collections list them as being for ages 7+, but they are better for middle school readers. The first volume is on Diamond's list of recommended titles for middle schools.

> Volume 1: *Courtney Crumrin and the Night Things*
> Volume 2: *Courtney Crumrin and the Coven of Mystics*
> Volume 3: *Courtney Crumrin in the Twilight Kingdom*
> Volume 4: *Courtney Crumrin and the Fire-Thief's Tale*
> *Courtney Crumrin Tales: A Portrait of the Warlock as a Young Man*

Cryptozoo Crew

Allan Gross. Illustrated by Jerry Carr. NBM (2006). $12.95–$13.95, two volumes. **[B]**

Tork and Tara Darwyn are cryptozoologists who travel around the world studying hidden, mysterious, and undiscovered animals in their fun and often humorous adventures.

The Dare Detectives

Ben Caldwell. Dark Horse (2004–). $5.95–$6.95. **[B]**

Maria Dare is a reformed criminal now working as a detective. Along with Toby, the "muscle" of the group, and Jojo, a talking rabbit, they take on bizarre cases including the monkey Furious George, gangster pandas, and the evil Madame Bleu. A funny, digest-sized title.

> Volume 1: *The Snow Pea Plot*
> Volume 2: *The Royale Treatment*

Days Like This

J. Torres. Illustrated by Scott Chantler. Oni Press (2003). $8.95. **[B]**. Recommended.

A black-and-white original graphic novel about a trio of African-American teenage girls who are getting their start as music group called "Tina and the Tiaras." Elements of the story include a songwriter, a woman starting up her own record label, and Tina's attempt to get her father to accept her possible new career. Recommend this to tweens and other patrons who might check out the DVD of *Dreamgirls*.

DC Archive Editions *and* Showcase Presents Titles

DC Comics has two regular groups of books that collect older material. The *Archive Editions* are hardcover books in color that collect 200 to 300 pages worth of stories. The *Showcase* books, named after the comics book that introduced several major "Silver Age" characters, are more than 500 pages long, softcover, and the material is reprinted in black and white. The lack of color allows the high page count for a low price and generally does not affect the story. The collections are customarily the "chronological" type of trade collection, with each volume either collecting issues A and B of a particular series, or collecting the appearances of a character or team as they appeared in different comic books.

In many cases, stories that appear in *Archive* also appear in *Showcase*. For example, the first *Teen Titans Archive* contains their first three adventures and the first five issue of their own title, and the first *Showcase* edition has this plus an additional 13 issues of *Teen Titans*. In these cases, librarians may have to choose between color and hardcover sturdiness versus twice the pages at one-third the price. Since some of these books feature stories from the Golden Age, it should be noted that some may feature 1940s-era stereotypes. **See also** the **Marvel Masterworks and Essential Marvel** titles for Marvel Comics' versions of these books.

Most of the age-appropriate titles are listed below, grouped by character, and with stories from the 1940s through the 1980s. Most of the *Archive* books cost about $50.00, and the *Showcase* books are mainly $16.99. **[B]**. Recommended.

Adam Strange Archives, Volumes 1–3
Showcase Presents Adam Strange, Volume 1
> Archeologist Adam Strange is transported to the planet Rann and helps the people there in this science-fiction series.

Aquaman, Volume 1
Showcase Presents Aquaman, Volumes 1–2
> DC's underwater adventurer, keeping the oceans free from evil.

Atom Archives, Volumes 1–2
Showcase Presents the Atom, Volumes 1–2
> Scientist Ray Palmer invents a device that allows him to shrink down to a tiny size while retaining his full-sized mass and becomes The Atom.

Batman Archives, Volumes 1–7
Batman in World's Finest Archive, Volumes 1–2

Batman: The Dark Knight Archives, Volumes 1–5
Batman: The Dynamic Duo Archives, Volumes 1–2
Showcase Presents Batman, Volumes 1–3
Robin Archive, Volume 1
Showcase Presents Robin, the Boy Wonder, Volume 1
Showcase Presents Batgirl, Volume 1
Showcase Presents the Brave and the Bold: The Batman Team-Ups, Volume 1
> Except for *The Dynamic Duo Archives*, all of the other archives collect Batman and Robin stories from various 1940s comic books. The remaining *Archive* and *Showcase* books collect Batman and Robin stories from the 1960s along with the early adventures of Batgirl and Batman's team-ups and other heroes. **See also** the **Batman** entry.

The Brave and the Bold Team-Up Archives, Volume 1
> Before *The Brave and the Bold* became the adventures of "Batman & _____," other heroes teamed up with one another.

Showcase Presents Captain Carrot, Volume 1
> The complete run of the 1980s series. Captain Carrot and his Amazing Zoo Crew—Pig Iron, Yankee Poodle, Alley-Kat Abra, Rubberduck, and the super-speedy turtle Fastback—fight evil on taking place on Earth-C, where animals are like people.

Showcase Presents the Elongated Man, Volume 1
> Drinking an elixir called gingold gave Ralph Dibney the power to stretch, which he uses to solve both regular and super-mysteries.

The Flash Archives, Volumes 1–4
Showcase Presents the Flash, Volumes 1–2
> The exploits of the fastest man alive.

Showcase Presents Green Arrow, Volume 1
> A modern day Robin Hood, Green Arrow fights crime with trick arrows and his sidekick, Speedy.

Green Lantern Archives, Volumes 1–6
Showcase Presents Green Lantern, Volumes 1–3
> Armed with a power ring, whose emerald energy can form anything, Green Lantern fights evil both on earth and in space. This is one of the few times that the lack of color could be a problem, such as not being able to show that something is yellow, the one color his ring cannot affect.

Hawkman Archives, Volumes 1–2
Showcase Presents Hawkman, Volumes 1–2
> Police officers from the planet Thanagar, Hawkman and Hawkgirl come to earth on a case and decide to stay to fight evil here.

Showcase Presents the House of Mystery, Volumes 1–2
> DC's classic horror anthology series. **[T]**

Justice League of America Archives, Volumes 1–9

Showcase Presents Justice League of America, Volumes 1–3

> Superman, Batman, Wonder Woman, the Flash, Green Lantern, the Martian Manhunter, and other heroes team-up. **See also** the entry for **Justice League**.

Legion of Super-Heroes Archives, Volumes 1–12

Showcase Presents Legion of Super-Heroes, Volumes 1–2

> When Superman was a teenager he traveled 1,000 years into the future and joined the intergalactic team the Legion of Superheroes.

Showcase Presents Martian Manhunter, Volume 1

> J'onn J'onzz, a detective on Mars, is accidentally transported to earth. Trapped here, he uses his array of powers to carry on his work.

Plastic Man Archives, Volumes 1–8

> From the 1940s. Crook "Eel O'Brien" is splashed with a chemical that turns his body rubbery and allows it to stretch and change shape. He turns over a new leaf and uses his abilities to fight crime in often humorous adventures. **See also** the entry for **Plastic Man**.

Shazam! Archives, Volumes 1–4

The Shazam! Family Archives, Volume 1

Showcase Presents Shazam! Volume 1

> Young orphan Billy Batson is given powers by the Wizard Shazam. Whenever Billy says the wizard's name he is transformed to the adult Captain Marvel, the "World's Mightiest Mortal." Similar powers are soon given to his sister Mary (aka Mary Marvel) and to crippled newsboy Freddy Freeman (aka Captain Marvel Jr.). The *Archive* books collect the Marvel Family's 1940s stories in which they fight not only criminals such as evil scientist Dr. Sivana but also the Axis Powers, including Captain Nazi. The *Showcase* edition collects the 1970s that brought the Marvel Family back into comics after a nearly 20-year absence.

Superman in Action Comics Archives, Volumes 1–5

Superman Archives, Volumes 1–7

Superman: Man of Tomorrow Archives, Volumes 1–2

Supergirl Archives, Volumes 1–2

Showcase Presents Superman, Volumes 1–4

Showcase Presents Superman Family, Volumes 1–2

Showcase Presents Supergirl, Volume 1

> Since his debut in 1938, Superman has been one of the best known comic book heroes. The *Superman* and *Action Comics* archives reprint stories from the Golden Age, while *Man of Tomorrow* and the *Showcase* have stories from the 1960s. The *Supergirl* books collect the Silver Age adventures of Superman's cousin, while *Superman Family* chronicles the adventures (and misadventures) of "Superman's pal" Jimmy Olsen and "Superman's girlfriend" Lois Lane, with stories from their own Silver Age comic books. **See also** the entry for **Superman**.

The Silver Age Teen Titans Archive, Volume 1

Showcase Presents Teen Titans, Volumes 1–2

> Robin, Kid Flash, Wonder Girl, Speedy, Aqualad, and other teenaged heroes team up in these stories from the swinging sixties. **See also** the entry for **Teen Titans Go!**

Wonder Woman Archives, Volumes 1–4

Showcase Presents Wonder Woman, Volume 1

> Perhaps the best-known female superhero, the *Archive* books collect her Golden Age adventures, while *Showcase* reprints her early Silver Age exploits.

World's Finest Archives, Volumes 1–3

Showcase Presents World's Finest, Volume 1

> Superman and Batman team up in these stories from the 1950s.

Additional *Archive* and *Showcase* volumes are planned, both as continuations of the previously listed titles and introductions of new ones.

Death Jr.

Gary Whitta. Illustrated by Ted Naifeh. Image (2005–). $14.99, two volumes. **[B]**, **[T]**

It's hard enough to be the son of Death. Besides knowing that he'll eventually have to go into the family business, having a skull for a face, and all of his pets dying on him, DJ must also deal with elementary school. There he's grouped with other "odd" children, including supergenius conjoined twins Smith and Weston, Stigmartha, and Pandora, who has an obsession about opening boxes. When a trip to the Museum of Supernatural History unleashes an ancient evil, it is up to DJ and his friends to save the day. In Volume 2, DJ runs into trouble while working for his father. Horror, adventure, and humor mix together in these enjoyable books, which started off as a video game and have both been on YALSA's Great Graphic Novels for Teens List.

Dignifying Science: Stories About Woman Scientists

Jim Ottaviani. Illustrated by various artists. GT Labs (2003). $16.95. **[B]**

A host of well-known female artists help Ottaviani tell the lives of several female scientists, including Marie Curie, Rosalind Franklin, Barbara McClintock, and Hedy Lamarr (yes, the actress), in this Eisner-nominated work. Ottaviani also includes notes and references.

Disney/Gemstone

Both new and old Disney characters appear in comics and graphic novels published by both Disney Press and Gemstone Publications. **[B]**

Disney Press

Comic Zone (2006). $4.99.

> These four digest-sized books collect comic stories from Disney Adventures Magazine.
>> Volume 1: *Lilo and Stitch* by various.
>>> Based on the animated film and the subsequent television show.

Volume 2: *Gorilla Gorilla* by Art Baltazar.
Gorilla Gorilla is an ordinary gorilla who can become a giant.
Volume 3: *Disney's Tall Tails* by Glenn McCoy.
Mickey and Goofy in adaptations of stories from folklore.
Volume 4: *Kid Gravity* by Landry Quinn Walker. Illustrated by Eric Jones.
Kid Gravity is a student in a futuristic school, "The Hawking School of Astronautics and Astrophysics."

Disney Jr. Graphic Novels (2006–2007). $3.99.
These are adaptations of the modern Disney films.
Volume 1: *Finding Nemo*
Volume 2: *Lilo and Stitch*
Volume 3: *The Lion King*

Gemstone Books

Ongoing titles:

Walt Disney's Donald Duck Adventures
Walt Disney's Mickey Mouse Adventures
These digest-sized books collect various stories with Mickey Mouse, Donald Duck, Uncle Scrooge, and others. There are 12 volumes of *Mickey* and 21 volumes of *Donald* available for $7.95 each.

Walt Disney's Comics and Stories (2003–). $6.95–$7.99. 635–682+ pages.
Walt Disney's Uncle Scrooge. $6.95–$7.99. 320–371+ pages.
Two monthly prestige format comic books can be purchased for libraries. More than 50 issues of each are available for $6.95 to $7.99, depending on the volume. The stories feature not only the adventures of the well-known characters, but of some of the lesser known characters such as Fethry Duck, Bucky Bug, and Scamp, the son of Lady and The Tramp. Some of the stories are new, some are reprints of older material, and some are translations of stories originally published in Europe. *Uncle Scrooge* is an Eisner award winner for best title for a younger audience.

Collections

Disney Presents Carl Barks' Greatest DuckTales Stories, Volumes 1–2 by Carl Barks (2006). $10.95.
A collection of stories from the 1950s and 1960s. This is on Diamond's list of recommended titles for elementary schools

The Life and Times of Scrooge McDuck (2005). $16.95.
The Life and Times of Scrooge McDuck Companion (2006). $16.99.
In the Eisner-award-winning stories collected in the first book, Don Rosa creates a history of "Uncle" Scrooge McDuck based on clues from the old Carl Barks stories. This volume is also on Diamond's list of recommended titles for elementary schools. The second volume includes additional backstory, and both books have commentary by Rosa explaining the background behind the stories.

Walt Disney's Spring Fever. Written and drawn by various artists (2007). $9.50. A collection of various stories from the 1940s to 1990s, including one by Carl Barks.

Original One-Shots

Walt Disney's Mickey Mouse Meets Blotman and Walt Disney's Mickey Mouse in Blotman Returns by Pat and Carol M. McGreal. Art by Joaquin Canizares Sanchez Gemstone (2005–2006). $5.99.

Mickey travels to a parallel world where Goofy is a Batman-like hero and Mickey is his scruffy sidekick.

Many more collections and original works are being produced.

DK Graphic Readers

Stewart Ross. Art by "Inklink" (2007). $14.99 (hardcover), $3.99 (softcover). **[B]**

Besides their comics-related nonfiction and nongraphic fiction titles (see Appendix B), DK also has a handful of books in comic book format. Their graphic readers are put at level 4 for "proficient readers." The stories take place in different parts of the ancient world, and on the bottom each of the 40 story pages are "Did you know?" facts. Located in the back of the books is additional information about the places in the books along with a glossary that indicates the page on which the word appears. The material in the graphic readers originally appeared in DK's *Tales of the Dead* series, where, in smaller panels, they bordered the pages.

Curse of the Crocodile God (set in Ancient Egypt)
Instruments of Death (set in Ancient China)
The Price of Victory (set in Ancient Greece)
The Terror Trail (set in Ancient Rome)

The Dreamland Chronicles

Scott Christian Sava. Blue Dream Studios (2006–). $19.95. **[B]**. Recommended.

When Alexander Carter was a boy he dreamed of adventures in a magical world. Now as a college student he finds himself going back there, and that the young princess, rock creatures, and fairy that he once played with in Dreamland have aged as well. He doesn't know how he has come back or even if Dreamland is real, but a Dragon is threatening the land, and he's not happy to see Alexander. Two volumes are currently available, with more planned, and those who wish to look at the story, including the parts that have not yet come out, can go to www.thedreamlandchronicles.com.

Ed's Terrestrials

Scott Christian Sava. Illustrated by Diego Jourdan. Blue Dream Studios (2006). $19.99. **[B]**

When three aliens escape from an intergalactic food court they crash-land into the tree house of a young boy named Ed. Can Ed and his new friends help other aliens escape while keeping out of the hands of both mall security and spoiled rich girl Natalie?

Edu-Manga

Digital Manga Publishing. $9.95 each. [**B**]. Recommended.

These educational mangas from Japan tell the lives of several historical figures. Each book has an introduction staring Astro Boy, drawn by Tezuka Productions, in which he and his friends are involved in some activity that leads them to ask their friend Dr. Elefun about the book's subject. Other than this, the characters are not seen, except in a series of questions and answers located either in between certain chapters or at the end of the book. Additional information on the subjects, as well as people with a connection to the subjects, are also included at the end of the books, as are timelines of the subjects' lives as well as world events at the time, and the subjects' connection to Japan is also discussed. Longer than the other graphic nonfiction discussed in this book, the edu-manga titles are still more "docudrama" than a book of facts, and should not be used as the only source in a report. They will, however, teach the reader a great deal about the subject. The Einstein book even explains some of his theories. The books, which are between 140 and 170 pages, are softcovered, unflopped, and rated **A** for for all ages.

> *Edu-Manga: Albert Einstein.* Written by Isao Himuro. Illustrated by Kotaro Iwasaki. (2006)
>
> *Edu-Manga: Anne Frank.* Written by Etsuo Suzuki. Illustrated by Yoko Miyawaki. (2006)
>
> *Edu-Manga: Helen Adams Keller.* Written by Sozo Yanagawa. Illustrated by Rie Yagi. (2005)
>
> *Edu-Manga: Ludwig Van Beethoven.* Written by Takayuki Kanda. Illustrated by Naoko Takase. (2005)
>
> *Edu-Manga: Mother Teresa.* Written by Masahide Kikai. Illustrated by Ren Kishida. (2007)

Electric Girl

Mike Brennan. AiT/PlanetLar (2000–). $9.95–$13.95. [**B**]

Since she was born, Virginia has had electrical powers that are not always in control. And if that's not all, she is the only one who can see a mischievous invisible gremlin named Oogleoog. Between her powers and the gremlin, teenaged Virginia finds herself in all sorts of trouble. Volume 3 is on Diamond's list of recommended titles for middle schools.

Emily Edison

David Hopkins. Art by Brock Rizy. Viper Comics (2006). $12.95. [**T**]

Emily's father was a scientist whose experiment took him to another dimension where he fell in love with and married a woman he had met there. Unfortunately they divorced, and Emily was given into her father's custody, though she visits her mother's world from time to time. Now Emily, who like her mother can fly, must put up with the life of a 15-year-old plus an annoying half-sister (from her mother's world) and a maternal grandfather who wants to destroy the earth so that Emily must live in his world. This original color graphic novel is best for the older tween ages, and is on YALSA's Great Graphic Novels for Teens List.

Fairy Tales of Oscar Wilde

Adapted by P. Craig Russell. NBM (1992–) $15.95 (hardcover), $8.95 (softcover). **[B]**

Artist P. Craig Russell adapts the fairy tale stories of the author of *The Importance of Being Earnest* and *The Picture of Dorian Gray*. Some of the stories are a little odd and may be better for older elementary age youth. Russell has also created graphic novel adaptations of famous operas.

> Volume 1: *The Selfish Giant and the Star Child*
> Volume 2: *The Young King and Remarkable Rocket*
> Volume 3: *The Birthday of the Infanta*
> Volume 4: *The Devoted Friend & the Nightingale and the Rose*

Fantastic Four

Marvel Comics. **[B]**

The "First Family" of the Marvel Universe debuted in 1961. Though others have temporarily joined, the main members have been Mr. Fantastic, his girlfriend/wife the Invisible Girl (later Woman), her brother the Human Torch, and the "ever-lovin blue-eyed" Thing.

> *Marvel Age Fantastic Four* (2004–2005)
> *Marvel Adventures Fantastic Four* (2005–)
>> Part of the *Marvel Age/Marvel Adventures* lines, these all-ages comics are collected in digest size ($6.99 each). These stories are not part of the official continuity, though sometimes adapt older stories. The first *Marvel Adventures* volume is on Diamond's list of recommended titles for elementary schools.

Marvel Age

By Mark Sumerak and various artists.

> Volume 1: *All for One*
> Volume 2: *Doom*
> Volume 3: *The Return of Doom*

Marvel Adventures

> Volume 1: *Family of Heroes*. Written Jeff Parker and Akira Yoshida. Drawn by Carlo Pagulayan and Juan Santacruz.
> Volume 2: *Fantastic Voyages*. Written by Jeff Parker. Art by Manuel Garcia and Scott Koblish.
> Volume 3: *World's Greatest*. Written by Jeff Parker. Drawn by Carlo Pagulayan, Manuel Garcia, and Juan Santacruz.
> Volume 4: *Cosmic Threats*. Written by Justin Grey. Art by Juan Santacruz and Staz Johnson, Raul Fernandez and Jeremy Freeman.
> Volume 5: *All 4 One, 4 for All*. Written by Zeb Wells. Art by Kano.
> Volume 6: *Monsters & Mysteries*. Written by Fred Van Lente. Art by Clay Mann.
> Volume 7: *The Silver Surfer*. Written by Fred Van Lente. Art by Cory Hamscher.

Volume 8: *Monsters, Moles, Cowboys, and Coupons.* Written by Steve Niles. Art by Leonard Kirk.

The first three digests (issues 1–12) are also collected in a hardcover volume.

Fashion Kitty

Charise Mericle Harper. Hyperion Books For Children (2005–). $8.99. **[C]**

In a world of anthropomorphic cats, young Kiki Kittie is hit on the head by a stack of fashion magazines and becomes the super heroine Fashion Kitty. When someone has a fashion emergency, it's Fashion Kitty to the rescue. Some of the approximately 90 pages of the Fashion Kitty books are text with accompanied illustrations, and the rest are in regular comic book format. On some pages in each book readers can cut on the dotted line to "mix and match" fashion styles. Hopefully the children who check them out from the library will refrain from using this feature. These books are best for elementary age.

Fashion Kitty
Fashion Kitty versus the Fashion Queen
Fashion Kitty and the Unlikely Hero

More editions may follow.

First in Space

James Vining. Oni Press (2007). $9.95. **[B]**

A "fictional" nonfiction story about Ham, the chimpanzee who was the first monkey sent into orbit by NASA.

Franklin Richards: Lab Brat

Mark Sumerak and Chris Eliopoulos (2007). $7.99. **[B]**

Franklin Richards is the son of Mr. Fantastic and the Invisible Woman, and in the mainstream comics even has powers. But in these digest-sized all-ages stories, Franklin is just a mischievous little boy, who often gets in trouble while playing with his father's scientific inventions, much to the consternation of his robot nanny/playmate HERBIE. Although superheroes do appear, the adventures of Franklin and HERBIE will remind some readers of *Calvin and Hobbes.*

See also the **Marvel Masterworks and Essential Marvel** entry for the Fantastic Four, as well as the entry for **Abdo Publishing** and **Power Pack**.

Gareth Stevens Publishing

(This is also listed as World Almanac Library.)

Gareth Stevens publishes books on history, biography, and mythology, and the Bank Street series adapts literary classics. The biographies and histories are very simplistic in both art and story, and are also available in Spanish. These should not be used for reports, but are a quick and easy way for a child to learn about a subject. Each is only 32 pages, including the list of suggested reading and Web sites, and there is no index. The graphic mythology books are 48 pages long and include a glossary, index, and a page for further information.. All three series are recommended for grades two through four by the publisher. The Bank Street titles each have three 16-page literary adaptations along with information on the authors. They are recommended for grade three. The books in each series are also on the Accelerated Reader list. For most of these series, libraries have a choice if they wish to catalog/shelve them in the 741s or in the biography or various nonfiction sections. The Bank Street books cost $29.27 (hardcover) or $11.95 (softcover), and the others cost $26.60 (hardcover) to $11.95 (softcover). Additional titles are expected. **[E]**

Graphic Histories

(2006)

> *The Battle of the Alamo.* Written by Kerri O'Hern and Janet Riehecky. Illustrated by D. McHarque.
> *The Battle of Gettysburg.* Written by Kerri O'Hern and Dale Anderson. Illustrated by D. McHargue.
> *The Bombing of Pearl Harbor.* Written by Elizabeth Hudson-Goff and Michael V. Uschan. Illustrated by Guus Floor and Alex Campbell.
> *The California Gold Rush.* Written by Elizabeth Hudson-Goff and Michael V. Uschan. Illustrated by Guus Floor.
> *The First Moon Landing.* Written by Elizabeth Hudson-Goff and Dale Anderson. Illustrated by Guus Floor, Alex Campbell, and Anthony Spay.
> *The Montgomery Bus Boycott.* Written by Kerri O'Hern and Frank Walsh. Illustrated by D. McHargue.

Graphic Biographies

(2006)

> *Anne Frank.* Written by Elizabeth Hudson-Goff and Jonatha A. Brown. Illustrated by Guus Floor, D. McHargue, and Jonathan Timmons.
> *Cesar Chavez* by Elizabeth Hudson-Goff and Kerri O'Hern. Illustrated by D. McHarque.
> *Jackie Robinson.* Written by Kerri O'Hern and Lucia Raatma. Illustrated by Alex Campbell and Anthony Spay.
> *Louis Armstrong.* Written by Kerri O'Hern and Gini Holland. Illustrated by Alex Campbell and Anthony Spay.
> *Nelson Mandela.* Written by Kerri O'Hern and Gini Holland. Illustrated by D. McHargue.
> *The Wright Brothers.* Written by Kerri O'Hern and Gretchen Will Mayo. Illustrated by Rebekah Isaacs and Jonathan Timmons.

Graphic Greek Myths and Legends

Written by Gilly Cameron Cooper and Nick Saunders (2007).

Pandora's Box	*Theseus and the Minotaur*
Perseus and Medusa	*The Trojan Horse*
Odysseus and the Cyclops	*The Twelve Labors of Hercules*

Bank Street Graphic Novels

(2007)

Great Heroes:
    The Adventures of Sherlock
      Holmes
    Don Quixote
    King Arthur
Historical Adventure:
    Around the World in
      80 Days
    A Connecticut Yankee in King
      King Arthur's Court
    The Prisoner of Zenda

Murder & Mystery:
    The Hound of the Baskervilles
    The Legend of Sleepy Hollow
    Macbeth
Science Fiction and Fantasy:
    20,000 Leagues Under the Sea
    Frankenstein
    The War of the Worlds
Travel & Adventure:
    Gulliver's Travels
    Moby Dick
    The Travels of Marco Polo

Go Girl!

Trina Robbins. Illustrated by Anne Timmons. Dark Horse (2002–). **[B]**

Janet Goldman was once the superhero go-go girl. Now her teenage daughter Lindsey has the same flying powers that the she does and is carrying on the family tradition.

    Go Girl! ($15.95)
    Go Girl! Robots Gone Wild ($14.95)

Gordon Yamamoto and the King of the Geeks

Gene L. Yang. SLG/Amaze Ink (2004). $9.95. **[T]**

Gordon Yamamoto is a bully. Each year, he and a friend find a kid in school and put a jockstrap on his head, crowning him "King of the Geeks." This year the "king" was Miles Tanner, but when an alien spaceship gets lodged in Gordon's nose, he finds out that Miles is the only one who can help him. This leads to an understanding between the two and helps them deal with even stranger problems.

Goosebumps

Adapted from the works of R.L. Stine. Illustrated by various artists. Graphix (an imprint of Scholastic). $16.99 (hardcover), $8.99 (softcover). **[B]**

Each volume of this black-and-white series contains three stories from the popular horror series, all with a common theme. The writer/artists for this series include Jill Thompson, Amy Kim Ganter, Kyle Baker, Dean Haspeil, and Ted Naifeh, several of whom have illustrated other books for Scholastic.

    Volume 1: *Creepy Creatures* (2006)
    Volume 2: *Terror Trips* (2007)
    Volume 3: *Scary Summer* (2007)

More volumes are planned.

Grampa and Julie: Shark Hunters

Written and drawn by Jef Czekaj. Published by Czekaj and distributed by Top Shelf (2004). $14.95. **[B]**

Julie tells, as part of her "how I spent my summer vacation" report, of how she and her grandpa went to find Stephen, the largest shark in the world. In their quest, the pair meets Ocean Monkeys, pirates (who among other things pirate software), talking cats, and monsters, and go into space in Gramma's rocket. This funny book is on Diamond's list of recommended titles for elementary schools.

Grease Monkey

Tim Eldred. SF/Humor. Tom Doherty Associates/Tor (2006). $27.95 (hardcover), $17.95 (softcover). **[T]**. Recommended.

An alien invasion has devastated the earth, but a different race of friendly aliens has helped the survivors in many ways, including giving gorillas human-level intelligence. Fifty years later, the battlecruiser Fist of Earth is one of many ships defending the planet, with both a crew both human and a simian (including the commanding admiral). Robin Plotnik is a young mechanic who finds himself working under gorilla mechanic McGimben "Mac" Gimbensky, whose unorthodox manner enrages his superior but appeals to Robin. There is nothing offensive in this 352-page collection, but it would appeal more to middle school aged readers.

Grumpy Old Monsters

Kevin J. Anderson and Rebecca Moesta. Illustrated by Guillermo Mendoza and Paco Cavero. IDW (2004). $13.99. **[B]**

A humorous trade paperback that shows what happens when monsters get old. Dracula, Frankenstein's Monster, the Wolfman, and the others are now residents of the Rest in Peace retirement home, dealing with boredom, nurses, and loneliness. The only high point is visits from young Tiffany Frankenstein. But now her grandfather's castle is being threatened by a greater menace than all of these monsters combined—the developers of the Van Helsing Corporation, who want to tear the castle down and replace it with luxury condominiums. Can the Monsters come out of retirement, escape the home, and save the day?

Hardy Boys and Nancy Drew

These teens have been solving mysteries for the past 80 years, and are now doing it in original graphic novels from Papercutz. The Hardy Boys books are connected to the new "Undercover Brothers" series of paperbacks in which Frank and Joe Hardy are now part of A.T.A.C. (American Teens Against Crime), a secret crime-fighting organization. The first Nancy Drew book, *The Demon of River Heights*, won the 2006 Ben Franklin Award for best graphic novel. The books have a manga style to them, and fashions and technology are modern day with cell phones, iPods, etc. Both series are digest-sized, in color, 96–112 pages, and available in hardcover ($12.95) or paperback ($7.95). **[B]**

Current titles in the series are as follows.

Hardy Boys

Scott Lobdell. Illustrated by various artists.

1. *The Ocean of Osyria* (2005)
2. *Identity Theft*
3. *Mad House*
4. *Malled* (2006)
5. *Sea You, Sea Me*
6. *Hyde & Shriek*
7. *The Opposite Numbers*
8. *Board to Death* (2007)
9. *To Die or Not to Die*
10. *A Hardy's Day Night*
11. *Abracadeath*
12. *Dude Ranch O'Death*
13. *The Deadliest Stunt*

Nancy Drew

Stefan Petrucha. Illustrated by various artists.

1. *The Demon of River Heights*
2. *Writ in Stone*
3. *The Haunted Dollhouse*
4. *The Girl Who Wasn't There*
5. *The Fake Heir*
6. *Mr. Cheeters Is Missing*
7. *The Charmed Bracelet*
8. *Global Warming*
9. *Ghost in the Machinery (The High Miles Mystery Part 1)*
10. *The Disoriented Express (The High Miles Mystery Part 2)*
11. *Monkey Wrench Blues (The High Miles Mystery Part 3)*
12. *Dress Reversal*
13. *Doggone Town*
14. *Slight of Dan*

Harvey Comics Classics

Dark Horse Comics (2007–). $19.95. **[B]**

For decades, Harvey put out child-friendly comics, with such characters as Casper the Friendly Ghost; Richie Rich, the "poor-little" rich boy; Hot Stuff, the "little devil"; Little Dot; and Baby Huey. Now Dark Horse is publishing collections of these older stories.

Volume 1: *Casper the Friendly Ghost*
Volume 2: *Richie Rich*
Volume 3: *Hot Stuff*

More volumes are planned.

Herobear and the Kid: The Inheritance

Mike Kunkel. Astonish Comics (2003). **[B]**

Tyler's grandfather died, and the family inherited his house and butler. Tyler also inherited a broken pocket watch and an old stuffed bear. The watch can tell where danger exists, and how good or bad someone is. When there is danger or evil, the stuffed bear comes to life, grows, and becomes Herobear. The last 50 pages of the book are a "making of" where Kunkel shows off his early work and how he created the comics. The Herobear comic won several awards, including two Eisners for "Best Title for All Ages."

Hikaru No Go

Yumi Hotta and Takeshi Obata. Viz (2004–) $7.95–. **[B]**

A shōnen manga dealing with the Japanese board game Go. Sixth-grader Hikaru Shindo comes across his grandfather's old Go board inhabited by the ghost of an ancient Go master who cannot rest until he achieves the "divine move." He convinces Hikaru to become a Go player, and acts as his tutor so that he can become a championship player. This all-ages title inspired an anime series and has actually increased the popularity of Go among children in Japan and the United States. Less than half of the 23 volumes have been translated as of 2007.

The Imaginaries: Volume 1: Lost and Found

Mike S. Miller and Ben Avery. Art by various. Abacus Comics (2006). **[B]**. Recommended.

When the boy who dreamed him up doesn't create his adventures any more, Super-hero G (who has similarities to a certain DC Comics character) finds himself in "The Imagined Nation," where all imaginary friends end up. Since he won't give up his weakness to the guards at the gate, he has to enter as a "mild mannered reporter" and fights the tyranny of the city's dictator ruler Lady Serenity, the Ice Queen. The book was originally published by Alias.

The Incredibles

Paul Alden. Art by Ricardo Curtis and Ramon Perez. Dark Horse Comics (2005). $7.99. **[B]**

An adaptation of the popular animated film. This is on Diamond's list of recommended titles for elementary schools. **See also** the **Cine-Manga** version.

Iron West

Doug TenNapel. Image Comics (2006). $14.99. **[T]**

Good aliens, evil robots, and Bigfoot, all in the Old West. It's 1898 and all train robber Preston Struck wants to do is get out of town before the law catches up to him. But when the town is invaded by robots bent on taking over the world, he must decide between self-preservation and doing what's right.

Jackie and the Shadow Snatcher

Larry Di Fiori. Alfred A. Knopf (2006). **[C]**

The book is the size of an easy-reader book. Set in the early part of the twentieth century, it is about Jackie, a boy who is always losing things. One day he loses his shadow, and it ends up being found by the Shadow Snatcher, who steals shadows and sews them into a dark quilt to hide himself when he commits crime. Can Jackie get it back?

Jason and the Argobots

J. Torres. Illustrated by Mike Norton. Oni Press (2003). $11.95. **[B]**

In the future, young Jason finds a giant robot in a crevasse near his desert home. What does a kid with a giant robot always do? Save the day. But there is a history behind the robots, which includes aliens and the military.

Volume 1: *Birthquake*
Volume 2: *Machina Ex Deus*

Jet Pack Pets: Let's Make Tracks

Michael Stewart and Garry Black. Amaze Ink/SLG (2005). $14.95. **[B]**

Many of the stories in this book first appeared in the *Disney Adventures* magazine. The three animals, Princess the dog, Bix the cat, and Rocky the turtle, are the pets of Sky City's mayor, police chief, and fire chief. Unknown to their owners, they were given jet packs by Professor Hugo Backfire, which they use to fight villains and monsters as the Jet Pack Pets. Twenty-nine short stories are included.

Jetcat Clubhouse

Jay Stephens. Oni Press (2002). $10.95. **[B]**

Collected from a three-issue limited series and other sources, including *Nickelodeon Magazine*, and based on award-nominated shorts from the television program *KaBlam!*, this title stars Jetcat, an eight-year-old girl superhero. Her friends include mummy Tutenstein (the character appears on a program on the Discovery Kids network) and Oddette, a "weird little Junk Rock kid."

Journey into Mohawk Country

Adapted by George O'Connor. First Second (2006). $17.95. **[T]**

Based on the journal of Harmen Meyndertz van den Bogaert that he wrote when working with the Dutch West India Company in New Netherland, of which New Amsterdam (later New York City) was part of. The journal tells of when he traveled up the North (Hudson) River and into the interior and met with various Mohawk tribes to get trade deals. This book could be cataloged in the 917s instead of the 741s, and is on both Diamond's list of recommended titles for middle schools and YALSA's Great Graphic Novels for Teens List.

Justice League

The major superhero team of the DC Universe, the Justice League was also the star of a popular animated series on the Cartoon Network. These books are for all ages, and most are digest-sized. **[B]**

> *Justice League Adventures* by various writers and artists. $9.95.
> *Justice League Adventures*, Volume 1: *The Magnificent Seven* by various writers and artists. $6.95.

Justice League Unlimited Series

Adam Beechan. Various artists. (2005–). $6.99.

> Volume 1: *United They Stand*
> Volume 2: *World's Greatest Heroes*
> Volume 3: *Champions of Justice*

Justice League Unlimited: Jam-Packed Action

Various writers and artists. $7.99.

This is similar to the animanga type of book.

Kamichama Karin

Koge-Donbo. Tokyopop (2005–). $9.99. [B]

Karin's life is not going so well. She is an orphan living with her aunt, she's not doing well in school, and her cat just died. But when she inherits a ring that lets her become a "little goddess," her life changes. But is it for the better? She soon meets other "little gods and goddesses" and has to deal with new problems. The series ran for seven volumes in Japan, was followed by a sequel series, and had inspired an anime series.

Kampung Boy

Lat. First Second (2006). [T]

Originally published in Malaysia in 1979 under the title *Lat, the Kampung Boy*, the book tells of the life of a young boy growing up on a Malaysian rubber plantation from his birth to the time he goes off to boarding school. This book is a "borderline" graphic novel, more a book with pictures and text. However, it is on YALSA's Great Graphic Novels for Teens List. Lat's story continues in *Town Boy* (2007).

Kat and Mouse

Alex de Campi. Illustrated by Frederica Manfredi. Tokyopop (2006). $5.99. [B]

This is part of Tokyopop's "Manga Readers" line of original OEL manga series for ages eight to twelve. Katherine "Kat" Foster moves with her family to Massachusetts and starts school at the prestigious Dover Academy, where her father is the new science teacher. She soon makes friends with Mee-Seen, aka "Mouse," who helps her find her way around the social strata of her new school (including the popular and spoiled "Chloettes"). But there are mysteries about, including a thief called "The Artful Dodger." Can the team of Kat and Mouse solve the crime and save the day? Each book also comes with a "lab experiment," including how to dust for fingerprints.

> Volume 1: *Teacher Torture*   Volume 3: *The Ice Storm*
> Volume 2: *Tripped*   Volume 4: *Knave of Diamonds*

There may be additional volumes as well.

Kingdom Hearts

Adapted by Shiro Amano. Tokyopop (2005–2006). [B]

These books are adapted from or inspired by the popular video game *Kingdom Hearts*, which mixes well known Disney characters with characters from the video game Final Fantasy. In each chapter, Sora, along with Donald Duck and Goofy travel from world to world battling the Heartless. They encounter Peter Pan, the Little Mermaid, Pinocchio, Hercules, and other Disney heroes, and battle Captain Hook, Jafar, and other villains working for the Heartless. In *Kilala Princess*, Kilala awakens a sleeping prince, but when her best friend is kidnapped, she must visit the worlds of the Disney Princesses—Snow White, Belle, Jasmine, etc.—to rescue her. All four titles are rated **A** for all ages, but only *Kilala Princess* is produced unflopped.

> *Kingdom Hearts: Chain of Memories*. Adapted by Shiro Amano. Tokyopop (2006–2007). Two volumes. $9.99.
>
> *Kingdom Hearts II*. Adapted by Shiro Amano. Tokyopop (2007–2008). Five volumes. $9.99.
>
> *Kilala Princess*. Written by Rika Tanaka. Illustrated by Nao Kodaka. Tokyopop (2007). Four volumes. $5.99.

Korgi (Book One): Sprouting Wings

Christian Slade. Top Shelf (2007). $10.00. **[B]**

This wordless, black-and-white fantasy tells of Ivy, a young member of the woodfolk called Mollies, and Sprout, a young Korgi pup that protects her. Wandering away from Korgi Hollow, they must escape from the troll-like Gallump.

Leave It to Chance

James Robinson. Art by Paul Smith and additional inkers. Image (2002–). $14.95. **[B]**

When the supernatural threatens the town of Devil's Echo, the authorities turn to detective Lucas Falconer for help. His 14-year-old daughter Chance wants to help him, but, worried about her safety, he forbids it. Of course she disobeys him, and with her pet dragon St. George she gets into her own adventures. Three oversized (7" × 10") hardcover collections have been published, the first of which is on Diamond's list of recommended titles for elementary schools. The series has won several awards, including the Eisner for best title for younger readers.

> Volume 1: *Shaman's Rain*
> Volume 2: *Trick or Threat and Other Stories*
> Volume 3: *Monster Madness*

The Legend of Hong Kil Dong: The Robin Hood of Korea

Anne Silbey O'Brien. Charlesbridge (2006). **[B]**

An adaptation of the Korean "Robin Hood" story. The illegitimate son of a powerful minister, Hong Kil Dong studies marital arts, divination, swordplay, magic, and I Ching, and uses his newfound knowledge to help the peasants. The book is partially a hybrid, with a small amount of pages not done in graphic novel style and some narration on other pages. All dialogue, however, is done in word balloons. If cataloging in nonfiction, this book could be placed in the 398s or the 741s.

Legendz

Makoto Haruno. Viz. $7.99. **[B]**

In this four-volume, all-ages manga, mermaids, dragons, werewolves, and other supernatural creatures known as Legendz not only exist but are used by humans in a "role-playing game." There is a related anime and video game for this series.

Lerner Graphic Universe

(2007)

Lerner's Graphic Universe series recounts myths and legends from around the world. Each book contains a 40-page story plus a glossary/pronunciation guide, an "additional reading" list, and an index. The books have multiple chapters and include much of the legends, but not necessarily the complete story. For example, the book on King Arthur goes up only to his receiving Excalibur from the Lady of the Lake, and neither it nor the Robin Hood book goes into the character's final fate. Both the writers and the illustrators have experience working on mainstream comic books. The books are library bound, cost $26.60, and are written on a fourth-grade level, with a fourth-to-eighth-grade interest level. Additional titles are expected. [**B**]

The books in the series are:

Amaterasu: Return of the Sun [A Japanese Myth]. Written by Paul D. Storrie. Illustrated by Ron Randall.

Atalanta: The Race Against Destiny [A Greek Myth]. Written by Ron Fontes and Justine Fontes. Illustrated by Thomas Yeates.

Demeter & Persephone: Spring Held Hostage [A Greek Myth]. Written by Ron Fontes and Justine Fontes. Illustrated by Steve Kurth.

Hercules: The Twelve Labors [A Greek Myth]. Written by Paul D. Storrie. Illustrated by Steve Kurth.

Isis & Osiris: To the Ends of the Earth [An Egyptian Myth]. Written by Jeff Limke. Illustrated by David Witt.

Jason: Quest for the Golden Fleece [A Greek Myth]. Written by Jeff Limke. Illustrated by Tim Seeley.

King Arthur: Excalibur Unleashed [An English Legend]. Written by Jeff Limke. Illustrated by Thomas Yeates.

Robin Hood: Outlaw of Sherwood Forest [An English Legend]. Written by Paul D. Storrie. Illustrated by Thomas Yeates.

Thor & Loki: In the Land of Giants [A Norse Myth]. Written by Jeff Limke. Illustrated by Ron Randall.

The Trojan Horse: The Fall of Troy [A Greek Myth]. Written by Ron Fontes and Justine Fontes. Illustrated by Gordon Purcell.

Yu the Great: Conquering the Flood [A Chinese Legend]. Written by Paul D. Storrie. Illustrated by Sandy Carruthers.

Lerner has also developed a second line, "Graphic Universe Presents Twisted Journeys," a graphic fiction series in the style of the "choose your own adventure" books.

The Life of Pope John Paul II . . . In Comics

Alessandro Mainardi and Werner Maresta. Papercutz (2006). $16.95 (hardcover), $9.95 (softcover). [**B**]

Originally published in Italy, this 100-page biography gives a brief coverage of the life of the late Pontiff, mainly concentrating on his life before becoming Pope.

Li'l Santa Series

Lewis Trondheim. Illustrated by Thierry Robin. NBM (2002–). $14.95. **[C]**

These funny silent books recount the adventures (and misadventures) of Li'l Santa, a miniature version of St. Nick, along with Abominable the Snowman, the Impies, and his other friends. The two books in the series are *Li'l Santa* and the Eisner-nominated *Happy Halloween Li'l Santa*. The frantic and wordless action makes it appealing to elementary age children.

Lions, Tigers, and Bears

Mike Bullock. Illustrated by Jack Lawrence. Image Comics (2006–). Two volumes, $12.99–$14.99. **[B]**. Recommended.

Joey Price was given stuffed animals by his grandmother. The instructions that came with them said that Night Pride, a lion, and a bear and two tigers should be "set around the bed, one at each corner," so that the child could "go to sleep knowing they will protect you through the night." And when the wicked Beasties come out of the closet in the middle of the night, that's exactly what they do. The first volume, *Fear and Pride*, was originally published by Alias, and won the Discovery Youth Prize the Angouleme International Comics Festival.

Little Gloomy . . . It Was a Dark and Stormy Night

Landry Q. Walker and Eric Jones. SLG (2002). $12.95. **[B]**

In this humorous horror book set in the land of Frightsylvania, young mad scientist Simon Von Simon want to get his ex-girlfriend Little Gloomy, the only "normal" girl in the land, back by any means necessary. Can she and her friends, including a werewolf and a small version of a Lovecraftian "Elder God" stop his crazy schemes? The trade collection of this four issue limited series includes sketches and information on how the comic was created.

Little Lulu

John Stanley and Irving Tripp Dark Horse Comics (2005–). **[B]**

Originally created in the 1930s by Marjorie Henderson Buell, Little Lulu was featured in the *Saturday Evening Post*, ads, a daily comic strip, and a comic book series, *Marge's Little Lulu* (1948–1984), which is collected in this series of paperback trade editions. The reprints are in black and white, and each volume has around 200 pages worth of stories. Volumes 1–15 are $9.95. Volumes 16 on are $10.95.

Current volumes are:

Volume 1: *My Dinner with Lulu*

Volume 2: *Sunday Afternoon*

Volume 3: *In the Doghouse*

Volume 4: *Lulu Goes Shopping*

Volume 5: *Lulu Takes a Trip*

Volume 6: *Letters to Santa*

Volume 7: *Lulu's Umbrella Service*

Volume 8: *Late for School*

Volume 9: *Lucky Lulu*

Volume 10: *All Dressed Up*

Volume 11: *April Fools*

Volume 12: *Leave It to Lulu*

Volume 13: *Too Much Fun*

Volume 14: *Queen Lulu*

Volume 15: *The Explorers*

Volume 16: *A Handy Kid*

Volume 17: *The Valentine*

Volume 18: *The Expert*

Additional volumes are planned.

Little Lulu Color Special ($13.95)

A Little Snow Fairy Sugar

Haruka Aoi. Art by BH Snow+Clinic. ADV (2006–). $9.99. **[B]**

In this all-ages manga, 11-year old Saga Bergman, who lives in a small German town with her grandmother, has problems when Sugar, a "Season Fairy" that only she can see, appears. Sugar is an apprentice, and will remain so until she can find "Twinkles." Other fairies are who appear are named Salt, Pepper, Cinnamon, and Basil. Three volumes are currently available.

Little Vampire Series

Joann Sfar. Simon & Schuster (2000–). **[B]**

Translations of the French *Petit Vampire* books, these Eisner-nominated titles feature a small vampire and his human friend Jeffrey. Although the back of the book says that they are for ages ten and up, there are some violent scenes, so librarians may wish to look it over before purchasing for an elementary school library.

Little Vampire Does Kung Fu
Little Vampire Goes to School

The Lone and Level Sands

A. David Lewis. Illustrated by M.P. Mann and Jennifer Rodgers. Archaia Studios Press (2005). $17.95. **[T]**

A hardcover retelling on the story of Exodus, taken from the Bible, The Qur'an, and historical sources. Originally published in black and white, this color version has been nominated for several awards. A reader's group guide for classroom discussion can be found at www.daradja.com/lone_and_level_ sands_rgg.php.

Looney Tunes

DC Comics. $6.99. **[B]**

These digest-sized books collect new stories with the classic Warner Brothers cartoon characters and published in DC's *Looney Tunes* comic book. These books are part of DC's Johnny DC line.

Bugs Bunny, Volume 1: *What's Up Doc?* (2005)
Daffy Duck, Volume 1: *You're Despicable!* (2005)

Lullaby

Mike S. Miller and Ben Avery. Art by Hector Servilla. Abacus Comics (2005–). $14.99. **[T]**

A new look at classic fairy tales Alice, now the Hand of the Queen (of Hearts) trying to find sources of evil and find out more about her past. Among those she meets are Piper, the werewolf Little Red, Jim Hawkins, and Pinocchio, all very different from what we've seen. The book contains violence, and some of the female characters are full figured, so this book is best for middle school readers. The books were originally published by Alias Comics and more are planned.

Machine Teen: History 101001

Marc Sumerak, Mike Hawthorne, and Drew Hennessy. Marvel Comics (2005). $7.99. **[T]**

In this digest-sized trade edition, Adam Aaronson is both a straight-A student and captain of the football team. Then he discovers that he's really a robot and that there are people out to get him. The back of the book recommends it for ages 12 and up, but it should be appropriate for middle school.

Mail Order Ninja

Joshua Elder. Illustrated by Erich Owen. Tokyopop (2006–). $5.99. **[B]**. Recommended.

In this fun, OEL, three-volume manga, Timmy McAllister is a fifth-grader who attends L. Frank Baum Elementary in Cherry Creek, Indiana, a town voted "most vanilla" five years in a row. Timmy is a little nerdy, but his reputation changes when he orders ninja Yoshida Jiro from a mail order catalog. Jiro helps make Timmy popular, much to the annoyance of "stuck-up rich girl" Felicity Dominique Huntington, who has her own evil plans to get back on top. This is part of Tokyopop's Manga Readers line, and is for ages 8 to 12.

Manga Chapters

Tokyopop. $4.99. **[E]**

Tokyopop's Manga Chapters line are digest-sized paperbacks with hybrid stories that are primarily text, but do contain multiple pages in which comics continue the story. *Agent Boo* is a about a fourth-grade girl who becomes a member of an agency that patrols and protects parallel worlds. *The Grosse Adventures* deals with the exploits of the Grosse Brothers, Stinky and Stan. These books contain a number of "fart jokes," but they should be appealing to mid-elementary school boys. The series are all ages, with a reading level between 3.5 and 4.2.

Agent Boo

Alex De Campi and Edo Fuijkschot.

> Volume 1: *The Littlest Agent*
> Volume 2: *The Star Heist*
> Volume 3: *Heart of Iron*

Grosse Adventures

Annie Auerbach.

> Volume 1: *The Good, the Bad, and the Gassy*
> Volume 2: *Stinky and Stan Blast Off*
> Volume 3: *Trouble at Twilight Cave*

Marvel Adventures

Besides the Marvel Adventures collections for the Fantastic Four and Spider-Man (see individual entries), there are other series in the Marvel Age/Marvel Adventures all-ages digests. **[B]**

Marvel Adventures: The Avengers

(2006–) $6.99–$7.99.

One of the major superteams of the Marvel Universe, the membership of the Avengers has included many major and minor heroes. This all-ages digest takes place out of regular Avengers continuity with a team that is different than any seen in the comic book. They fight many established Marvel villains, with many stories having a common link, but still finished in one issue.

> Volume 1: *Avengers Assembled*. Written by Jeff Parker. Illustrated by Manuel Garcia.
> Volume 2: *Mischief*. Written by Tony Bedard. Illustrated by Shannon Gallant.
> Volume 3: *Bizarre Adventures*. Written by Jeff Parker. Illustrated by Juan Santacruz.
> Volume 4: *The Dream Team*. Written by Jeff Parker. Illustrated by Leonard Kirk.
> Volume 5: *Some Assembling Required*. Written by Jeff Parker. Illustrated by Leonard Kirk.

Marvel Adventures: Incredible Hulk

(2007–)

Caught in the explosion of a gamma-bomb, Dr. Bruce Banner becomes the green-skinned, simple-minded Hulk whenever he gets angry or upset. Additional volumes of all titles are planned.

> *Marvel Adventures Incredible Hulk*, Volume 1: *Misunderstood Monster*. Written by Paul Benjamin. Illustrated by David Nakayama. $6.99.
> *Marvel Adventures Incredible Hulk*, Volume 2: *Defenders*. Written by Paul Benjamin. Illustrated by David Nakayama and Steve Scott. $7.99.

Marvel Adventures: Iron Man

(2007–) $6.99–$7.99.

Genius millionaire industrialist Tony Stark was forced to build a suit of high-tech armor to save his life.

> Volume 1: *Heart of Steel*. Written by Fred Van Lente. Illustrated by James Cordeiro.
> Volume 2: *Iron Armory*. Written by Fred Van Lente. Illustrated by Rafa Sandoval.

Marvel Age: Hulk

(2005)

> *Marvel Age: Hulk*, Volume 1: *Incredible*. Written by Mike Raicht. Illustrated by Joe Dodd.

Marvel Masterworks *and* Essential Marvel

Marvel's counterpart to DC's *Archive* and *Showcase Presents* books, though Marvel did it first. The *Masterworks* are hardcovered, in color, usually between 200 and 300 pages, and generally cost between $49.99 and $54.99. The *Essentials* are soft covered, in black and white, more than 500 pages, and generally cost around $16.99. Again, there are times in which a story in the *Masterworks* edition also appears in the *Essential* title. Although there are a few *Masterworks* from the 1940s and 1950s, most *Masterworks* and the *Essentials* reprint stories from the 1960s to 1980s. Some of the earlier volumes of the *Essentials* have been reprinted, but with different content. For example, the first version of *The Essential X-Men*, Volume 2, which came out in 2000, contained *X-Men* issues #120 to #144, whereas the 2005 reprint added *X-Men Annual* #3 and #4. Besides annuals, some of the *Essentials* will also include limited series, one-shots, and even other books into which a story from the collected title has crossed over. Some catalogs will list these books as *Stan Lee Presents the Essential X* or just by "X." **[B]**. Recommended.

Age-appropriate titles include:

Marvel Masterworks: Ant-Man/Giant-Man, Volumes 1–2
Essential Ant-Man, Volume 1

> Dr. Henry Pym has gone through many superpowers and identities over the years. These titles feature his adventures as Ant-Man (with the power to shrink) and Giant-Man (with the reverse ability). The books also feature his partner, the Wasp.

Marvel Masterworks: The Avengers, Volumes 1–7
Essential the Avengers, Volumes 1–6

> "Earth's Mightiest Heroes," with a changing lineup that has included Captain America, Iron Man, Thor, Hawkeye, the Black Panther, and others.

Marvel Masterworks: Captain America, Volumes 1–4
Essential Captain America, Volumes 1–4

> This patriotic hero has been fighting the forces of evil since 1941. These titles collect his Silver Age adventures, but an archive of his 1940s stories is also available.

Marvel Masterworks: Daredevil, Volumes 1–4
Essential Daredevil, Volumes 1–4

> Blinded as a child, attorney Matt Murdock learns that the accident that took his sight also enhanced his other senses and gave him a "radar sense." Combined with his athletic ability, Daredevil fights everything from muggers and gangsters to supervillains.

Essential the Defenders, Volumes 1–3

> Dr. Strange, the Hulk, The Silver Surfer, and the Sub-Mariner are among the heroes that made up this group over the years.

Marvel Masterworks: Doctor Strange, Volumes 1–3
Essential Doctor Strange, Volumes 1–4

> Marvel's "Master of the Mystic Arts" fights evil both on earth and in other dimensions.

Marvel Masterworks: The Fantastic Four, Volumes 1–10
Essential Fantastic Four, Volumes 1–6
Marvel Masterworks: The Human Torch, Volume 1
Essential the Human Torch, Volume 1
Essential Marvel Two-In-One, Volumes 1–2

> Besides the two books containing the team's adventures, collections of the teenage Torch's solo adventurers are also available, along with *Marvel Two-In-One*, which teamed The Thing with a guest star.

Marvel Masterworks: The Incredible Hulk, Volumes 1–4
Essential the Incredible Hulk, Volumes 1–4
Essential Rampaging Hulk, Volume 1
Essential Savage She-Hulk, Volume 1

> Caught in the explosion of a gamma-bomb, Dr. Bruce Banner becomes the green-skinned, simple-minded Hulk whenever he gets angry or upset. Years later, while visiting his cousin, lawyer Jennifer Walters, he is forced to give her a blood transfusion. As She-Hulk, she does not have her cousin's raw power, but she does retain her own mind and intelligence.

Marvel Masterworks: The Invincible Iron Man, Volumes 1–4
Essential Iron Man, Volumes 1–2

> Genius millionaire industrialist Tony Stark was forced to build a suit of high-tech armor to save his life. Now as Iron Man he fights criminals, communist agents, and even pretends to be the bodyguard of his own "playboy" secret identity.

Essential Luke Cage, Power Man, Volumes 1–2
Essential Iron Fist, Volume 1

> Sent to prison for a crime he did not commit, Luke Cage volunteered for an experiment that gave him super strength and rock-hard skin. Breaking out, he set himself up as a Hero For Hire, and later took the name Power Man. After his parents' death, Daniel Rand was raised in the mystical city of K'un L'un, where he was trained in the martial arts. Returning to America, he fights crime and avenges his parents. The two later teamed up for their own joint title, Essential Power Man and Iron Fist, Volume 1.

Marvel Masterworks: The Mighty Thor, Volumes 1–6
Essential the Mighty Thor, Volumes 1–3

> The Norse God of Thunder, Thor was exiled to earth by his father Odin. Sharing his body with that of Dr. Donald Blake, Thor fights criminals, aliens, and the wicked schemes of his half-brother Loki.

Marvel Masterworks: Nick Fury, Agent of S.H.I.E.L.D., Volume 1

> Superspy Nick Fury leads the spy agency S.H.I.E.L.D. against the schemes of the terrorist organization Hydra.

Essential Nova, Volume 1

> Richard Ryder was an ordinary teenager when a bolt from space turned him into Nova, the Human Rocket.

Marvel Masterworks: The Silver Surfer, Volume 1–2
Essential Silver Surfer, Volumes 1–2

> Norrin Radd lived on the planet Zenn-La until the world-devouring Galactus came. Offering to become Galactus's herald in order to save his world, he was imbued with The Power Cosmic and became the Silver Surfer, sentinel of the Space Ways. But when he came to earth the Fantastic Four convinced him to defy Galactus, and for this he was prevented from leaving the planet. Now trapped, the Surfer protects mankind against a host of menaces.

Marvel Masterworks: The Amazing Spider-Man, Volumes 1–9
Essential the Amazing Spider-Man, Volumes 1–8
Essential Peter Parker, the Spectacular Spider-Man, Volumes 1–3
Essential Marvel Team-Up, Volumes 1–3
Essential Spider-Woman, Volumes 1–2

> Perhaps the best-known Marvel character, the *Masterworks* and the first two *Essentials* collect many of his solo adventures, while *Marvel Team-Up* features him with other heroes. Despite having spider-powers of her own, Spider-Woman has no direct relationship with him, but instead fights evil in California. The *Essential* editions collect the entire run of her self-titled series. **See also** the entry for **Spider-Man**.

Marvel Masterworks: The Sub-Mariner, Volumes 1–2

> The son of a human sailor and a blue-skinned Atlantian Princess, Prince Namor, The Sub-Mariner has fought both for and against the surface world.

Marvel Masterworks: The X-Men, Volumes 1–6
Essential Uncanny X-Men, Volume 1/Essential Classic X-Men, Volume 2
Marvel Masterworks: The Uncanny X-Men, Volumes 1–6
Essential X-Men, Volumes 1–8
Essential X-Factor, Volumes 1–2

> Although they've been "hot" for the past 20+ years, there was actually a time in which sales of *X-Men* were so low the book was turned into a "reprint series" and then temporarily cancelled. *Marvel Masterworks: The X-Men* and *Essential Uncanny/Classic X-Men* collects the early run of the series, while the other two books feature the "new" X-Men, including Storm and Wolverine, who starred in the comic after it was revived. *Essential X-Factor* features the original members of the X-Men who formed a new team. Some of the later volumes of *Essential X-Men* and *Essential X-Factor* may be better for middle school readers.

Additional volumes of many of the titles listed will most likely come out.

Megaman NT Warrior Series

Ryo Takamisaki. Viz (2004–). $7.95. **[B]**

This series is based on the popular video game character. In the future the world is peaceful and everyone is connected to the Cyber Network. But there is trouble in paradise as the evil organization World Three are up to no good in cyberspace. Fifth-grade computer wiz Lan Hikari is able to work with an artificial intelligence called Mega-man to save the day. This manga series is rated **A** for all ages, and at least 12 volumes have been published.

Mega Morphs

Sean McKeever. Art by Lou Kang and Logan Lubera. Marvel Comics (2005). $7.99. [**B**]

Comic books based on toys have been around for decades, such as *Transformers* and *Micronauts*. Now, this Marvel all-ages digest collects not only a four-issue limited series but also the mini-comics that came with the Mega Morphs toy line. Tony "Iron Man" Stark has built high-tech robots that amplify the powers and abilities of the heroes that pilot them. Unfortunately, the villainous Dr. Octopus and Dr. Doom have their own plans for the Mega Morphs, so Spider-Man, Captain America, Wolverine, Ghost Rider, and the Hulk must use their personalized machines to stop them.

Mercer Mayer's Critter Kids Adventures

Erica Farber. Illustrated by Mercer Mayer. School Specialty Publishing (2006–). $4.95. [**C**].

A hybrid series for middle-elementary age readers, including those on the highest "beginning reader" level. In this paperback series, the main story is told in text with additional dialogue told with word balloons. In addition, every other page contains a box with a fact about nature, space, or whatever subject the story is dealing with. There is also a vocabulary page.

The Alien from Outer Space	*Octopus Island*
Golden Eagle	*The Prince*
The Jaguar Paw Puzzle	*The Swamp Thing*

The Mighty Skullboy Army

Written and drawn by Jacob Chabot. Dark Horse (2007). $9.95. [**B**]

This black-and-white digest-sized paperback collects Chabots' humorous stories featuring Skullboy, the grade-school-aged (and skull-headed) would-be evil genius. When not dealing with schoolwork (and the kids on the playground), Skullboy hatches his evil schemes working with his less-than-competent minions Unit 1 (a robot) and Unit 2 (a monkey).

Mister O

Written and drawn by Lewis Trondheim. NBM (2004). $13.95. [**B**]

This hardcover French book contains 30 pages, each telling a story divided into a 6" × 10" grid. On each page "Mr. O," a circle with arms, legs, eyes, and mouth, is trying to get over a chasm and failing in a way that has drawn comparisons to the failures of Wile E. Coyote trying to capture the Road Runner and to Charlie Brown trying to kick the football. The book is totally silent, but some of Mr. O's fates make the book better for older elementary and middle school students. In 2007, NBM published the similar *Mr. I*.

Monkey vs. Robot

James Kochalka. Top Shelf (2000). $10.00. **[B]**

The title says it all in this small-sized book. Robots have created a factory that has disrupted the monkeys' jungle and now it's war. The book is low on dialogue, with many panels that are silent or have only sound effects and monkey noises, but it is still better for older elementary and middle school. A sequel, *Monkey vs. Robot and the Crystal of Power*, came out in 2003.

Mouse Guard: Fall 1152

Written and drawn by David Petersen. Archaia Studios Press (2007). $24.95. **[B]**

Widely acclaimed as one of the best comic books of 2006, this collection of a six-issue limited series will appeal to fans of *The Tale of Despereaux*, the *Redwall* series (which has its own graphic novel adaptation), and similar books. The mice have their cities safe from predators, but what happens when they must travel from town to town to trade and sell their wares? It is the job of the sword-wielding Mouse Guard to protect them against snakes, weasels, and other threats. But there is a traitor in the guard, attempting to take control for himself and his own aims. In 2008, a paperback edition of *Fall 1152* was published by Villard Books, and the sequel series, *Mouse Guard: Winter 1152*, was also collected.

Mutant, Texas. Tales of Ida Red

Paul Dini. Illustrated by J. Bone. Oni. $11.95. **[B]**

Back in the 1960s a radioactive comet hit a malfunctioning satellite and the whole thing landed smack on the new Nuclear Power Plant in Mystic, Texas. The cosmic and atomic energies mixed in with the desert's powerful mystic energies, and the people and the animals changed. Now called Mutant, Texas, it's a strange place. Ida Red, who was orphaned as a child and raised by a talking bear, appeared to be normal for a while, but as she gets older, she discovers powers that let her save her friends and her town in this humorous adventure.

Neotopia

Rod Espinosa. Antarctic Press (2004–2005). $9.99. **[B]**

A four-volume color OEL manga series originally published as four limited series. A thousand years into the future, the world has changed. Geography and technology has been altered, humans live in harmony with nature, animals talk, and aliens live and work among them. But there is still danger and evil. Nalyn is a servant, who on the orders of the spoiled Duchess of Mathenia, Nadia, has taken the duchess's place to take care of all the boring aspects of the role. But when war comes, Nalyn must remain in the role and save her people and the world. The books are rated **A** for all ages, but would be enjoyed more by older elementary and middle school readers.

New Alice in Wonderland

Rod Espinosa. Antarctic Press (2006). $14.95. **[B]**

Adapted from the Lewis Carroll story, this is a digest-sized color OEL manga collected from a four-issue limited series. Although the word *new* is in the title, it is the same basic Alice story. This book is on Diamond's list of recommended titles for elementary schools and has an all-ages rating.

Once in a Blue Moon

Nunzio DeFillipis and Christina Weir. Illustrated by Jennifer Quick. Oni Press (2004). $11.95. **[B]**

When she was a child, Aeslin Finn's parents would always read to her from *The Avalon Chronicles*, which told of a far-off fairy land defended by the Dragon Knight and her Prince. But after Aeslin's father died on a business trip, it was the end of the stories. As a teen, Aeslin encounters a strange store that has in it the book's sequel, *Once in a Blue Moon*. Reading it, she suddenly finds herself in the world of the story, now ruled by an evil king, and where her world is nothing but the setting of a popular book. There she gets into adventures and finds out the truth behind her parents. A second book is planned.

Ororo: Before the Storm

Marc Sumerak. Illustrated by Carlos Barberi. Marvel Comics (2005). $6.99. **[B]**

An all-ages digest collection of the limited series, in which young thief Ororo, long before she got her mutant powers and became Storm of the X-Men, must break into a tomb in Cairo.

Osprey Graphic History

A publisher of books on military history, Osprey has also published a series of graphic novels on the Civil War and World War II. Each book is 48 pages ($9.95), in softcover, and includes several pages of text along with the "graphic" story, a glossary, an index, and a list of where to get additional information. Many of the creators have worked in comics including Larry Hama (*GI Joe*) and Doug Murray (*The 'Nam*). The books in this series are also published by Rosen Publishing under slightly different titles, due to an agreement between the two companies. **[B]**

The Osprey titles are:

The Bloodiest Day: Battle of Antietam. Written by Larry Hama. Illustrated by Scott Moore. (2006)

Day of Infamy: Attack on Pearl Harbor. Written by Steve White. Illustrated by Jerrold Spahn.

Deadly Inferno: Battle of the Wilderness. Written by Dan Abnett. Illustrated by Dheeraj Verma. (2007)

The Empire Falls: Battle of Midway. Written by Steve White. Illustrated by Richard Elson. (2006)

Fight to the Death: Battle of Guadalcanal. Written by Larry Hama. Illustrated by Anthony Williams. (2007)

Gamble for Victory: Battle of Gettysburg. Written by Dan Abnett. Illustrated by Dheeraj Verma. (2006)

Hitler's Last Gamble: Battle of the Bulge. Written by Bill Cain. Illustrated by
Dheeraj Verma. (2007)

Ironclads at War: The Monitor vs. the Merrimac. Written by Dan Abnett.
Illustrated by Dheeraj Verma. (2007)

Island of Terror: Battle of Iwo Jima. Written by Larry Hama. Illustrated by
Anthony Williams. (2006)

Surprise Attack! Battle of Shiloh. Written by Larry Hama. Illustrated by Scott
Moore. (2006)

The Tide Turns: D-Day Invasion. Written by Doug Murray. Illustrated by
Anthony Williams. (2007)

The War Is On! Battle of First Bull Run. Written by Dan Abnett. Illustrated by
Dheeraj Verma. (2007)

Owly

Andy Runton. Top Shelf. $10.00. **[B]**. Highly recommended.

This popular, charming, and entertaining series of black-and-white books features the
adventures of a cute little owl and his friends. An all-ages series, Owly has no dialogue,
with any words being sound effects and signs. Any "speech" is as a pictogram. The
Owly series has won many awards, and the first volume is on Diamond's list of recommended titles for elementary schools. This series could be used in classrooms.

Volume 1: *The Way Home & the Bittersweet Summer*
Volume 2: *Just a Little Blue* (2005)
Volume 3: *Flying Lessons* (2006)
Volume 4: *A Time to Be Brave*

Oz: The Manga

David Hutchison. Antarctic Press (2005). $14.95. **[B]**

This digest-sized OEL manga is the most complete adaptation of *The Wizard of Oz* on
this list, containing scenes from the Baum book not found in the other versions. The
book's rating is for teen (ages 13+), but there aren't really any scenes that will be a problem with older elementary and middle school readers.

Patrick the Wolf Boy

Art Baltazar and Franco Aureliani. Devil's Due Publishing (2004–). $10.95–$12.95. **[B]**

Even when he is not in full werewolf form, young Patrick still has wolflike qualities,
including growling, though his parents and everyone else can understand him. His
humorous adventures are told in a series of short stories (some only one page long),
dealing with everything from Patrick in school to his meeting Santa Claus. As of 2008,
four volumes have been published, and more may come out.

Peach Fuzz

Lindsay Cibos and Jared Hodges. Tokyopop (2005–). $9.99. **[B]**

This humorous OEL manga is told from two points of view—nine-year-old Amanda and her pet ferret, Peach. Although Amanda sees Peach as a pet that she can play with and show off (and which her mother sees as a drain on her pocketbook), Peach sees herself as a Ferret Princess, captured and held hostage by the five-headed "Handra." At least three volumes have been produced.

Peanutbutter & Jeremy's Best Book Ever

James Kochalka. Alternative Comics (2003). $14.95. [B]

In this large black-and-white book, Peanutbutter is a cat who "works" for her owner, who understands what she says. Jeremy is a crow who lives nearby. Jeremy is always causing trouble and is often mean to Peanutbutter, but she still considers him her best friend. This book is on Diamond's list of recommended titles for elementary schools, but there is one scene in which Jeremy has a gun that some librarians may wish to look over before purchasing.

Pinky & Stinky

James Kochalka. Top Shelf (2002). $17.95. [B]

Dogs and monkeys have been sent into space, but pigs? Pinky and Stinky are headed toward Pluto, but they crash on the moon. There they encounter some human astronauts, one of whom is quite rude to them. But when there is a conflict between the astronauts and the native moon people, can the porcine pair save the day?

Pixie Pop: Gokkun Pucho

Ema Toyama. Tokyopop (2004–2007). $9.99, three volumes. [T]

Twelve-year old Mayu is just starting middle school when she learns that the boy she once had a crush on, and rejected her, sits next to her in class. But that's not her only problem. After she accidentally drinks the potion of a magical drinks fairy, every times she drinks something she changes. Depending on the temperature, milk makes her shrink or grow, water turns her invisible, pork soup turns her into a piglet, and more. Can love save the day? This manga is rated **T** (for ages 13+), but should be okay for middle school readers.

Plastic Man

Kyle Baker. DC Comics (2004-2006). $14.95. [B]

Since the 1940s Plastic Man has been fighting crime and causing laughs. Kyle Baker's award-winning comic book series is just the most recent adventures.

    Volume 1: *On the Lam*
    Volume 2: *Rubber Bandits*

Pokemon

Viz. [B]

"Got to catch them all!" Even kids and parents who have never heard the words "anime" and "manga" know about Pokemon. It has been a collectable card game, a video game, and both a television show and a theatrical feature.

Some of the all-ages titles include:

All-That Pikachu! Ani-Manga Viz. By Hideki Sonoda. $7.99. (2006)

The Best of Pokemon Adventures: Red. By Hidenori Kusaka. Art by Mato. $7.99. (2006).

The Best of Pokemon Adventures: Yellow. By Hidenori Kusaka. Art by Mato. $7.99. (2006)

Polly and the Pirates

Ted Naifeh. Oni (2006). $11.95. **[T]**

Living in the nineteenth-century San Francisco of an alternate world, young Polly Pringle is attending a "prim and proper" boarding school when she is kidnapped, bed and all, by pirates. They are seeking the treasure of Pirate Queen Meg Malloy, who, as she discovers, Polly has a link to. This leads to several adventures for Polly. Although the back of the book recommends it for ages seven and up, some elements, partly in subtext, make it better for middle school readers.

Power Pack

Marvel Comics. $6.99–$7.99. **[B]**

The Power children—Alex (12), Julie (10), Jack (8), and Katie (5)—were given superpowers by a dying alien, and as Zero-G, Lightspeed, Mass Master, and The Energizer became Power Pack. The stars of their own 1980s series, they have been appearing in a series of four-issue limited series, which are part of the Marvel Adventures line. These comics, which have been collected into digest-sized trade editions with an all-ages rating, have the team alone or meeting other heroes Spider-Man and the X-Men.

As of 2008, the collections are:

Avengers and Power Pack Assemble (2006). Written by Mark Sumerak. Art by Gurihiru Studios. (On Diamond's list of recommended titles for elementary schools.)

Fantastic Four and Power Pack: Favorite Son (2008). Written by Fred Van Lente. Art by Gurihiru Studios.

Hulk and Power Pack: Hulk Smash (2007). Written by Mark Sumerak. Art by various.

Power Pack: Pack Attack! (2005). Written by Mark Sumerak. Art by Gurihiru Studios.

Power Pack Volume 1 (2008). $24.99. Collects the previous threes books into a single volume.

X-Men and Power Pack: The Power of X (2006). Written by Mark Sumerak. Art by Gurihiru Studios.

Spider-Man and Power Pack: Big City Super Heroes (2007). Written by Mark Sumerak. Art by Gurihiru Studios.

Also published in 2008 are the collections of *Iron Man and Power Pack* and *Power Pack: Day One.*

The Powerpuff Girls

DC Comics. $6.95. [B]

Based on the popular Cartoon Network show. Bubbles, Blossom, and Buttercup fight Mojo Jojo and other villains in Townsville. Digest sized.

> Volume 1: *Titans of Townsville*
> Volume 2: *Go, Girls, Go*

President Dad

Ju-Yeon Rhim. Tokyopop. $9.99. [T]

This manhwa deals with high school freshman Ami Wan, whose father has just become president of Korea. She must deal with school and romantic crushes while being in the public eye. A least seven volumes have come out. Although it was originally listed as rated **Y**, it has been re-rated as **T** for early teen.

Prince of Tennis

Takeshi Konomi. Viz (2004–). $7.95. [B]. Recommended.

A shōnen sports manga, the series is about Ryoma Echizena, a new member of the Seishun Academy's tennis team, one of the best around. Much of the series covers his joining the team, his relationships with his teammates and other students, and his team's tournament competition against other schools. Prince of Tennis is rated **A** for all ages. It is not known how long the series will be, but as of January 2008, there were 40 volumes published in Japan (23 translated into English), and more are expected.

Project X Series

Digital Manga Publishing (2006). $12.95. [T]

A "business manga" series from the same publisher that translated the "edu-manga" series. The *Project X* line recounts the history of three successful Japanese business ventures familiar to American readers—Cup Noodles, the Datsun 240Z, and the introduction of 7-Eleven stores to Japan. Each is black and white, between 175 to 200 pages, and includes timelines and photographs. Although these books are rated **A** for for all-ages, the subject matter may not be as interesting to elementary-age readers.

> *Project X: Cup Noodle*. Written and drawn by Tadashi Katoh.
> *Project X: Datsun Fairlady Z*. Written and drawn by Akira Yokoyama.
> *Project X: Seven Eleven*. Written by Tadashi Ikuta. Drawn by Naomi Kimura.

PS238

Aaron Williams. Henchman Publishing (distributed by Dork Storm Press). (2004–). $16.00. [B]. Recommended.

The "school for superheroes" theme has long been used in television, movies, and comics. In collections of this fun comic book, readers see what happens at PS238, an elementary school for super-powered children located beneath a "normal" school. Students include the children of other heroes, aliens, future super-villians, and magical beings. Adventures range from the humorous to dramatic, and even adults will enjoy it, getting a few jokes and references that may go over the heads of younger readers.

Volume 1: *With Liberty and Recess for All*
Volume 2: *To the Cafeteria for Justice!*
Volume 3: *No Child Left Behind*
Volume 4: *Not Another Learning Experience!*

Additional volumes are planned.

Puffin Graphics

With almost 150 pages worth of story, these adaptations of classic works include much more of the original story than most graphic literary adaptations. In adapting the work, the creators, some with a comics background, tell the story with both captions and word balloons. In the case of *Macbeth*, science fiction writer Arthur Byron Cover has kept the Shakespearean dialogue but moved the setting to a distant planet in the far future. Additional pages show how the source material was adapted, including preliminary sketches and storyboards. Combined with the extended story, this information can work well in a classroom environment. Recommended. **[B]**

The books in the series are:

Anna Sewell's Black Beauty. Adapted and illustrated by June Brigman and Roy Richardson. (2005)
Bram Stoker's Dracula. Adapted Gary Reed. Illustrated by Becky Cloonan. (2006)
Jack London's Call of the Wild. Adapted by Neil Kleid. Illustrated by Alex Niño. (2006)
L. Frank Baum's The Wizard of Oz. Adapted and illustrated by Michael Cavallaro. (2005)
Mary Shelley's Frankenstein. Adapted by Gary Reed. Illustrated by Frazer Irving. (2005)
Robert Louis Stevenson's Treasure Island. Adapted and illustrated by Tim Hamilton. (2005)
Stephen Crane's The Red Badge of Courage. Adapted and illustrated by Wayne Vansant. (2005)
William Shakespeare's Macbeth. Adapted by Arthur Byron Cover. Illustrated by Tony Leonard Tamai with Alex Niño. (2005)

Queen Bee

Chynna Clugston. Scholastic Graphix (2005–). $16.99 (hardcover), $8.99 (softcover). **[T]**

Haley Madison is teased in school, and it doesn't help that she has telekinetic powers that she can't control and that cause her great embarrassment. But when she moves with her mother, who works for a teen fashion magazine, to a new town, she reinvents herself. She succeeds in getting in with the popular kids, even becoming "queen bee" of the middle school. But her throne is endangered when a new girl arrives, one who has the same exact abilities. A sequel is planned.

Redwall: The Graphic Novel

Adapted by Stuart Moore and illustrated by Bret Blevins. Philomel Books (2007). $12.99.

An adaptation of the first book in Brian Jacques' popular series of fantasy novels.

Rock and Roll Love

Misako Rocks! Hyperion (2007). $7.99. **[T]**

In this well-reviewed, semiautobiographic original graphic novel, teenage Misako comes from Japan as an exchange student, and while getting used to the United States and her high school falls for Zac, the lead singer in a rock band.

Rosen Publishing

$29.25 (hardcover), $11.95 (softcover). **[B]**. **[C]** for the junior books.

Rosen's nonfiction graphic novels cover a variety of subjects, including history, biography, mythology, and natural disasters. Most of the books are about 48 pages long and include a table of contents, information on the main people, additional information, a glossary, a "for more information" page, and an index. Some of the artists have also worked in comics. The books in the Jr. Graphic Novels are only 24 pages long, and are on a second- or third-grade reading level. Due to an agreement between the two companies, the Civil War and World War II books are the same books that are published by Osprey. The books in the Rosen series can be placed in the 000, 200, 300, 600, and 900 areas of the nonfiction section. Additional titles are expected.

Graphic Battles of World War II

Reading level grade 5. Interest level grades 5–8.

> *The Battle of the Bulge: Turning Back Hitler's Final Push.* Written by Bill Cain. Illustrated by Dheeraj Verma. (2007)
>
> *The Battle of Guadalcanal: Land and Sea Warfare in South Pacific.* Written by Larry Hama. Illustrated by Anthony Williams. (2006)
>
> *The Battle of Iwo Jima: Guerilla Warfare in the Pacific.* Written by Larry Hama. Illustrated by Anthony Williams. (2006)
>
> *The Battle of Midway: The Destruction of the Japanese Fleet.* Written by Steve White. Illustrated by Richard Elson. (2006)
>
> *D-Day: The Liberation of Europse Begins.* Written by Doug Murray. Illustrated by Anthony Williams. (2007)
>
> *Pearl Harbor: A Day of Infamy.* Written by Steve White. Illustrated by Jerrold Spahn.

Graphic Biographies

Reading level grade 5. Interest level grades 5–8.

> *Bob Marley: The Life of a Musical Legend.* Written by Gary Jeffrey. Illustrated by Terry Riley.
>
> *Martin Luther King Jr.: The Life of a Civil Rights Leader.* Written by Gary Jeffrey. Illustrated by Chris Forsey.
>
> *Muhammad Ali: The Life of a Boxing Hero.* Written by Rob Shone. Illustrated by Nick Spender.

Nelson Mandela: The Life of an African Statesman. Written by Rob Shone. Illustrated by Neil Reed.

Oprah Winfrey: The Life of a Media Superstar. Written by Gary Jeffrey. Illustrated by Terry Riley.

Rosa Parks: The Life of a Civil Rights Heroine. Written by Rob Shone. Illustrated by Nick Spender.

Graphic Civil War Battles

Reading level grades 4–5. Interest level grades 3–6.

The Battle of Antietam: "The Bloodiest Day of Battle." Written by Larry Hama. Illustrated by Scott Moore. (2006)

The Battle of First Bull Run: The Civil War Begins. Written by Dan Abnett. Illustrated by Dheeraj Verma. (2007)

The Battle of Gettysburg: Spilled Blood on Sacred Ground. Written by Dan Abnett. Illustrated by Dheeraj Verma. (2006)

The Battle of Shiloh: Surprise Attack! Written by Larry Hama. Illustrated by Scott Moore. (2006)

The Battle of the Wilderness: Deadly Inferno. Written by Dan Abnett. Illustrated by Dheeraj Verma. (2007)

The Monitor vs. the Merrimack: Ironclads at War. Written by Dan Abnett. Illustrated by Dheeraj Verma. (2007)

Graphic Mysteries

Reading level grades 4–5. Interest level grades 3–6.

Atlantis and Other Lost Cities. Written by Rob Shone. Illustrated by Jim Eldridge.

The Bermuda Triangle: Strange Happenings at Sea. Written by David West. Illustrated by Mike Lacey.

Bigfoot and Other Strange Beasts. Written by Rob Shone. Illustrated by Nick Spender.

Ghosts and Poltergeists: Stories of the Supernatural. Written by David West. Illustrated by Terry Riley.

Loch Ness Monster and Other Lake Mysteries. Written by Gary Jeffrey. Illustrated by Bob Moulder.

UFOs: Alien Abduction and Close Encounters. Written by Gary Jeffery.

Graphic Mythology

Reading level grades 4–5. Interest level grades 3–6. (2006)

African Myths. Written by Gary Jeffrey. Illustrated by Terry Riley.

Chinese Myths. Written by Rob Shone. Illustrated by Claudia Saraceni.

Egyptian Myths. Written by Gary Jeffrey. Illustrated by Romano Felmang.

Greek Myths. Written by Rob Shone.

Mesoamerican Myths. Written by David West. Illustrated by Mike Taylor.

Roman Myths. Written by David West. Illustrated by Ross Watton.

Graphic Natural Disasters

Reading level grade 5. Interest level grades 5–10. (2007)

> *Avalanches and Landslides.* By Rob Shone.
> *Earthquakes.* Written by Rob Shone. Illustrated by Nick Spender.
> *Hurricanes.* Written by Gary Jeffrey. Illustrated by Mike Lacey.
> *Tornadoes and Superstorms.* Written by Gary Jeffrey. Illustrated by Terry Riley.
> *Tsunamis and Floods.* By Garry Jeffrey.
> *Volcanoes.* By Rob Shone.

Graphic Nonfiction Biographies

Reading level grades 4–5. Interest level grades 3–6. (2005)

> *Abraham Lincoln: The Life of America's Sixteenth President.* Written by Gary Jeffrey and Kate Petty. Illustrated by Mike Lacey.
> *Alexander the Great: Life of a King and Conqueror.* Written by Rob Shone and Anita Ganeri. Illustrated by Chris Odgers.
> *Christopher Columbus: The Life of a Master Navigator and Explorer.* Written by David West and Jackie Gaff. Illustrated by Ross Watton.
> *Cleopatra: The Life of an Egyptian Queen.* Written by Gary Jeffrey and Anita Ganeri. Illustrated by Ross Watton.
> *Elizabeth: The Life of England's Renaissance Queen.* Written by Rob Shone and Anita Ganeri. Illustrated by Terry Riley.
> *George Washington: The Life of an American Patriot.* Written by David West and Jackie Gaff. Illustrated by Ross Watton.
> *Harriet Tubman: The Life of an African-American Abolitionist.* Written by Rob Shone and Anita Ganeri. Illustrated by Rob Shone.
> *Hernán Cortés: The Life of a Spanish Conquistador.* Written by David West and Jackie Gaff. Illustrated by Jim Eldridge.
> *Julius Caesar: The Life of a Roman General.* Written by Gary Jeffrey and Kate Petty. Illustrated by Sam Hadley.
> *Richard the Lionheart: The Life of a King and Crusader.* Written by David West and Jackie Gaff. Illustrated by Jim Eldridge.
> *Sitting Bull: The Life of a Lakota Chief.* Written by Gary Jeffrey and Kate Petty. Illustrated by Terry Riley.
> *Spartacus: The Life of Roman Gladiator.* Written by Rob Shone and Anita Ganeri. Illustrated by Nick Spender.

Jr. Graphic Novels

$22.50 (hardcover), $9.95 (softcover). **[C]**

Jr. Graphic Biographies

Dan Abnett (2007).

> *Abraham Lincoln and the Civil War*
> *Christopher Columbus and the Voyage of 1492*

George Washington and the American Revolution
Harriet Tubman and the Underground Railroad
Hernán Cortés and the Fall of the Aztec Empire
Sitting Bull and the Battle of Little Big Horn

Jr. Graphic Mysteries

Jack DeMolay (2007).

Atlantis the Mystery of the Lost City
The Bermuda Triangle: The Disappearance of Flight 19
Bigfoot: A North American Legend
Ghosts in Amityville: The Haunted House
The Loch Ness Monster: Scotland's Mystery Beast
UFOs: The Roswell Incident

Jr. Graphic Mythologies

(2007)

African Mythology: Anansi. By Glen Herdling.
Chinese Mythology: The Four Dragons. By Tom Daning.
Egyptian Mythology: Isis and Osiris. By Tom Daning.
Greek Mythology: Jason and the Golden Fleece. By Glen Herdling.
Mesoamerican Mythology: Quetzalcoatl. By Tom Daning.
Roman Mythology: Romulus and Remus. By Tom Daning.

The Sandwalk Adventures

Jay Hosler. Active Synapse (2003). $20.00. [T]

Mara is a follicle mite living with her family and friends on a hair in the eyebrows of a man. This man and his adventures make up the theology of the mites who think of him as "The Fly Catcher." But one day Mara says something and the man hears her. His name? Charles Darwin. Once Darwin realizes that he's not going crazy, he and Mara talk while he takes his daily strolls on his "sandwalk," a path where he liked to walk and think. He tells Mara about the nature of things and explains his theories to her. As in *Clan Apis*, the reader ends up learning while reading, and annotations are included at the end of the book. Given the subject matter, this is best for middle school ages.

Sardine in Outer Space

Emmanuel Guibert. Illustrated by Joann Sfar. First Second Books (2006–). $12.95. [B]. Recommended.

In this French series, young Sardine travels through space aboard The Huckleberry, with the ship's pirate captain, her uncle, Captain Yellow Shoulder, and her cousin Louie. They have many adventures, but mostly foil the schemes of the evil Supermuscleman and his evil minion Doc Krok. There are five volumes currently out, and more may be released.

School Specialty Publishing

$14.95 (hardcover), $6.95 (softcover). **[E]**

The 48-page "stories from history" nonfiction graphic novels contain a informative "cast of characters" list, a multichapter story preceded by several pages of background information, a timeline, a "did you know" fact page, a glossary, an index, and occasional "fast facts" provided throughout the story. The art and story are relatively simplistic, usually with one to three panels per page. The simple dialogue makes the series good for younger readers. Some of the authors have written other history books.

> *The Battle of Gettysburg* by Colin Hynson (2006)
> *The Building of the Great Pyramid* by Colin Hynson (2006)
> *The Discovery of T. Rex* by Dougal Dixon (2006)
> *Elizabeth I and the Spanish Armada* by Colin Hynson
> *Gladiators and the Story of the Coliseum* by Nicholas J. Saunders
> *The Life of Alexander the Great* by Nicholas J. Saunders
> *The Life of Anne Frank* by Nicholas J. Saunders
> *The Life of Christopher Columbus* by Nicholas J. Saunders
> *The Life of Julius Caesar* by Nicholas J. Saunders
> *The Life of Leonardo Da Vinci* by Suzie Hodge
> *Pizarro and the Incas* by Nicholas J. Saunders
> *The Race to the South Pole* by Jim Pipe

Scooby-Doo

Various writers and artists. DC Comics (2003–). $6.99. **[B]**

Part of DC's Cartoon Network/Johnny DC line, these digest-sized paperback trades collect issues of DC's comic based on the popular cartoon. DC's title has run since 1997, but the Scooby gang has appeared in comics since 1970.

> Volume 1: *You Meddling Kids* Volume 4: *The Big Squeeze*
> Volume 2: *Ruh-Roh* Volume 5: *Surf's Up*
> Volume 3: *All Wrapped Up* Volume 6: *Space Fright*

Sea Princess Azuri

Erica Reis. Tokyopop (2006–). $4.99. **[B]**

In this OEL manga, mermaid princess Azuri is put into an arranged marriage to Prince Unagi, leader of the Eel People tribe. But she is in love with a member of the royal guard. What's a girl (or at least a part girl, part whale) to do? The series is rated **Y** (ages 10+) and has at least two volumes.

Shadow Rock

Jeremy Love. Illustrated by Robert Love and Jeff Wasson. Dark Horse (2006). $9.95. **[B]**

Timothy London has moved with his father to the strange New England town of Shadow Rock. But there is a secret in this town, and Timothy, with the help of the ghost of a boy and the girl who is the "white sheep" of the family who controls the town, must find out what it is.

Shrek

Mark Evanier. Art by Ramon Bachs and Raul Fernandez. Dark Horse Comics (2003). $9.95. **[B]**

Set after the first film, Shrek and Donkey must once again rescue Princess Fiona from the forces of the evil and now ghostly Prince Farquad, and they embark on other new adventures. This is on Diamond's list of recommended titles for elementary schools.

The Simpsons

(1994–). $12.95–$14.95. **[B]**. Recommended.

On the air for years, and with a 2007 feature film, the Simpsons appear in books, on merchandise, and, yes, in comic books published by Bongo, and are collected into trades by HarperCollins. These trades collect various Simpsons-related titles, including the main *Simpsons* comic (1993–), the spin-off *Simpsons Comics Present Bart Simpson* (2000–), and the annual *Treehouse of Horror* books (1995–) inspired by the popular Halloween episodes. Each collection collects several issues, and although some stories are set in the "normal" Simpsons world, others are in "fantasy" settings, such as "Bartzan" with Bart as a Tarzan-type character.

The current collected editions are:

Simpsons Comics A-Go-Go
Simpsons Comics Barn Burner
Simpsons Comics Beach Blanket Bongo
Simpsons Comics Belly Buster
Simpsons Comics Big Bonanza
Simpsons Comics Dollars to Donuts
Simpsons Comics Extravaganza
Simpsons Comics Jam-Packed Jamboree
Simpsons Comics Madness
Simpsons Comics on Parade
Simpsons Comics Simps-o-rama
Simpsons Comics Spectacular
Simpsons Comics Strike Back!
Simpsons Comics Unchained
Simpsons Comics Wingding

Big Bad Book of Bart Simpson
Big Beastly Book of Bart Simpson
Big Beefy Book of Bart Simpson
Bit Book of Bart Simpson
Big Bouncy Book of Bart Simpson
Big Bratty Book of Bart Simpson
Big Brilliant Book of Bart Simpson
Bart Simpson's Treehouse of Horror:
   Heebie-Jeebie Hullabaloo
Bart Simpson's Treehouse of Horror:
   Spine-Tingling Spooktacular
The Simpsons Treehouse of Horror:
   Fun Filled Frightfest
The Simpsons Treehouse of Horror:
   Hoodoo Voodoo Brouhaha

More editions are expected.

Sonic the Hedgehog Archives

By various writers and artists. Archie Comics. $7.49. **[B]**

Based on the popular video-game character, this humorous series features Sonic and his friends, including Princess Sally and Antoine, who make up a band of Freedom Fighters opposing the evil Dr. Robotnik. The series is rated **A** for for all ages, and volume one is on Diamond's list of recommended titles for elementary schools. As of 2008 there are six volumes out or announced, and additional volumes are planned.

Spider-Man

Marvel Comics. **[B]** (unless otherwise indicated)

The friendly, neighborhood web-swinger has been one of the symbols of Marvel Comics. Besides the titles in *Marvel Masterworks/Essentials*, the following are some of the more age-appropriate series.

Marvel Age/Marvel Adventures

These digest sized, all-ages book adapt some of the original stories and also create new ones. The digests cost $5.99 to $6.99 each.

Marvel Age: Spider-Man

Todd Dezago and Mike Raicht. Art by various artist (2004–2005).

Volume 1: *Fearsome Foes*   Volume 4: *The Goblin Strikes*
Volume 2: *Every Day Hero*   Volume 5: *Spidey Strikes Back*
Volume 3: *Swingtime*

Many of the individual stories in these trades have been converted into hardcover books by Abdo.

Marvel Adventures: Spider-Man Digests

(2005–)

Volume 1: *The Sinister Six*. Written by Kitty Fross, Erica David, and Jeff Parker. Art by Patrick Scherberger and Norman Lee.
Volume 2: *Power Struggle*. Written by Sean McKeever. Art by Patrick Scherberger and Norman Lee.
Volume 3: *Doom with a View*. Written by Sean McKeever. Art by Mike Norton, Jonathan Glapion, and Norman Lee.
Volume 4: *Concrete Jungle*. Written by Zeb Wells. Art by Patrick Scherberger and Norman Lee.
Volume 5: *Monsters on the Prowl*. Written by Peter David. Art by Mike Norton.
Volume 6: *The Black Costume*. Written by Fred Van Lente. Art by Michael O'Hare and Cory Hamscher.
Volume 7: *Secret Identity*. Written by Chris Kipiniak. Art by Patrick Sherberger.
Volume 8: *Forces of Nature*. Written by Peter David. Art by Pop Mhan.
Volume 9: *Fiercest Foes*. Written by Fred Van Lente with art by Cory Hamscher.

Additional volumes are planned.

Marvel Adventures Spider-Man, Volume One

This oversized hardcover collects the first eight issues of *Marvel Adventures*, which are also in the first two digests. $19.99.

The Mary Jane Books

In the regular Marvel Universe, Mary Jane Watson has been a friend, girlfriend, and wife to Peter "Spider-Man" Parker. In these digests, set in a separate continuity, Mary Jane is in high school, dealing with her friends, boyfriends, and this superhero that has been swinging around. The books have manga-inspired art, are rated 12 and up, and are categorized as "teen romance/comedy." [**T**]

> *Mary Jane*. Written by Sean McKeever. Illustrated by Takeshi Miyazawa (2004–2005). $7.99.
> > Volume 1: *Circle of Friends*
> > Volume 2: *Homecoming*
> *Spider-Man Loves Mary Jane*. All written by Sean McKeever (2006–). $7.99.
> > Volume 1: *Super Crush*. Illustrated by Takeshi Miyazawa.
> > Volume 2: *The New Girl*. Illustrated by Takeshi Miyazawa and Valentine De Landro.
> > Volume 3: *My Secret Life*. Illustrated by Takeshi Miyazawa.
> > Volume 4: *Still Friends*. Illustrated by David Hahn.
> *Spider-Man Loves Mary Jane*, Volumes 1–2 (2007). $29.99 to $39.99. Hardcover collections of the six Mary Jane titles, along with extra material.

Others

> *Spider-Man and the Fantastic Four: Silver Rage*. Written by Jeff Parker. Illustrated by Mike Wieringo (2007). $10.99.
> > Spider-Man the FF must team-up to fight an alien invasion.
> *Spider-Man/Human Torch I'm with Stupid*. Written by Dan Slott. Illustrated by Ty Templeton and various inkers (2005). $7.99.
> > Five new stories covering the relationship between the Spider-Man and the Human Torch over the years. Fun and a bit silly.

Spider-Girl

Set in the near future, the star of *Spider-Girl* is May "Mayday" Parker, the teenage daughter of Peter Parker, the now retired Spider-Man, and his wife Mary Jane. She has inherited her father's powers and has decided to carry on his legacy. While fighting both new and old villains and teaming up with other heroes, May must also deal with the problems of being a high school student and of her parents reluctance over her choice to follow in her father's footsteps. The most successful of Marvel's "MC2" line, the *Spider-Girl* comic was almost cancelled on several occasions, but was rescued by both fan outcry and the sale of the digest-sized trade paperbacks. Although the original comic ended at issue #100, a new series, *The Amazing Spider-Girl*, soon followed. The Spider-Girl books do not have anything objectionable, but there is the occasional mature subject, such as when May discovers that a girl in her class is being hit by her boyfriend. [**T**]. Recommended.

The original series, written by Tom DeFalco with various artists including Ron Frenz and Pat Olliffe, is collected in the following digests ($7.99 each):

Spider-Girl, Volume 1: *Legacy* (2004)
Spider-Girl, Volume 2: *Like Father Like Daughter* (2004)
Spider-Girl, Volume 3: *Avenging Allies* (2005)
Spider-Girl, Volume 4: *Turning Point* (2005)
Spider-Girl, Volume 5: *Endgame* (2006)
Spider-Girl, Volume 6: *Too Many Spiders!* (2006)
Spider-Girl, Volume 7: *Betrayed* (2006)
Spider-Girl, Volume 8: *Duty Calls* (2007)
Spider-Girl, Volume 9: *Secret Lives* (2007)

The digests, which started late in the title's run, have been collecting stories starting from the beginning, and are only about halfway finished, and should have the series completed between Volumes 18 and 20. However, full-sized collections of the new title are also being created, which take place after issue #100.

Second Series

(2007)

Amazing Spider-Girl, Volume 1: *Whatever Happened to the Daughter of Spider-Man?*
Amazing Spider-Girl, Volume 2: *Comes the Carnage*
Amazing Spider-Girl, Volume 3: *Mind Games*

Additional volumes are planned.

Other MC2 Titles

The other short-lived titles from the MC2 line have been collected as digests under the name *Spider-Girl Presents*. They join limited series set in that world, and feature future versions of the Fantastic Four, the Avengers, and other.

Spider-Girl Presents A-Next, Volume 1: *Second Coming* (2006). $7.99.
Spider-Girl Presents Fantastic Five, Volume 1: *In Search of Doom* (2006). $7.99.
Spider-Girl Presents Juggernaut Jr., Volume 1: *Secrets and Lies* (2006). $7.99.
Spider-Girl Presents The Buzz & Darkdevil (2007). $7.99.
Spider-Girl Presents Wild Thing: Crash Course (2007). $7.99.
Last Hero Standing (2005). $13.99.
Last Planet Standing (2006). $13.99.
Avengers Next: Rebirth (2007). $13.99.
Fantastic Five: The Final Doom (2008). $13.99.

Ultimate Spider-Man

(2002–)

Set in a different version of the Marvel Universe, Peter Parker is still in high school, and other characters have different backgrounds. This is the best title in the Ultimate line for tween ages, but librarians may want to examine the series before purchasing. Some of the individual trades have been published in both hard- and softcover, and the series has been collected from the beginning, so more than 100 issues can be read. Brian Michael Bendis has been the main writer for the series, with Mark Bagley and others providing the art. [T]

Volume 1: *Power and Responsibility*
Volume 2: *Learning Curve*
Volume 3: *Double Trouble*
Volume 4: *Legacy*
Volume 5: *Public Scrutiny*
Volume 6: *Venom*
Volume 7: *Irresponsible*
Volume 8: *Cats and Kings*
Volume 9: *Ultimate Six*
Volume 10: *Hollywood*

Volume 11: *Carnage*
Volume 12: *Superstars*
Volume 13: *Hobgoblin*
Volume 14: *Warriors*
Volume 15: *Silver Sable*
Volume 16: *Deadpool*
Volume 17: *Clone Saga*
Volume 18: *Ultimate Knights*
Volume 19: *Death of a Goblin*

In addition, Marvel publishes hardcover editions, titled *Ultimate Spider-Man*, Volume [X], which each collect two of the earlier collections. These cost $29.99 to $39.99.

Spiral-Bound (Top Secret Summer)

Aaron Renier. Top Shelf (2005). $14.95. **[B]**

With a cover reminiscent of a spiral notebook (including a pencil "in" the "metal rings"), *Spiral-Bound* takes place in a world of people-like animals, where, on their summer vacation, an elephant, a dog, and a rabbit (who works for an underground newspaper) have their own adventures, but they all come together when stories of a "monster" in the pond turn out to be true.

Star Wars

Dark Horse has published many stories based on the *Star Wars* films, ranging from tales set thousands of years before Episode One to ones set decades after Episode Six. The most child friendly of these are the *Clone War Adventures*. Beginning in 2004, these stories are set between Episodes Two and Three and are based on the animated series that appeared on MTV. They are original, digest-sized books, with three stories by various authors and artists, and most volumes cost $6.95.

There are many other collections, including the seven-volume *Classic Star Wars: A Long Time Age* (2002–2003 $29.95), which reprints the 1977–1986 Marvel Comics *Star Wars* comic book. Some of the more than 100 other trade collections may be acceptable for middle school students, but it is best to check them prior to purchase. **[B]**

Stone Arch Books

Unlike most of the other "mainstream" publishers who put out graphic novels, Stone Arch's graphic novels are all fiction. The various series—Graphic Sparks, Graphic Trax, Graphic Quest, Ridge Riders, Graphic Revolve, and Graphic Flash—range from very simple books to text/comic hybrids. Each book has a librarian reviewer—Allyson Lyga and Kat Kan among them—and a reading consultant who looks over the book prior to publication and advises them as to any changes that must be made. The more than 50 books are available in hard- and softcover, list a reading level on the back cover, and are generally aimed at a mid-elementary school level. Since each book contains a glossary, discussion questions, and writing prompts, they are ideal for classroom use.

Many of the series also include a link to Internet sites via facthound.com and are on the Accelerated Reader list. Additional titles are expected. **[C]**

Graphic Sparks

(2006–). $21.26 (hardcover), $4.95 (softcover).

The books in the Graphic Sparks line are the easiest line of books, 40 pages long, and generally with a lower word count. Along with a 30-page story, mainly a humorous one, there is information on the creators, a glossary, and further information of an element of the story (for example, *Blast to the Past* has information on dinosaurs). Unless indicated, all of the books listed are written by Scott Nickel and illustrated by Steve Harpster.

> *Backyard Bug Battles: A Buzz Beaker Brainstorm.* Illustrated by Andy J. Smith.
> *Billions of Bats: A Buzz Beaker Brainstorm.* Illustrated by Andy J. Smith.
> *Blast to the Past*
> *The Boy Who Burped Too Much*
> *Curse of the Red Scorpion*
> *The Day Mom Finally Snapped.* Written by Bob Temple.
> *Day of the Field Trip Zombies.* Illustrated by Cedric Hohnstadt.
> *Eek and Ack, Invaders from the Great Goo Galaxy.* Written by Black A. Hoena.
> *Eek and Ack, Ooze Slingers from Outer Space.* Written by Black A. Hoena.
> *Fang Fairy.* Written and illustrated by Andy J. Smith.
> *Jimmy Sniffles* series
>> *Double Trouble*
>> *Dognapped*
>> *A Nose for Danger.* Written by Bob Temple.
>> *The Super-Power Sneeze*
>> *Up the President's Nose*
> *The Monster of Lake Lobo.* Illustrated by Enrique Corts.
> *Night of the Homework Zombies*
> *Robot Rampage: A Buzz Beaker Brainstorm.* Illustrated by Andy J. Smith.
> *Tiger Moth* series. Written by Aaron Reynolds. Illustrated by Eric Lervold.
>> *Tiger Moth, Insect Ninja*
>> *Tiger Moth and the Dragon Kite Contest*
>> *The Dung Beetle Bandits*
>> *The Fortune Cookies of Evil*

Graphic Trax

(2006–). $21.26 (hardcover), $7.95 (softcover).

The next level up, though some volumes have a reading level lower than certain volumes of Graphic Sparx. Each book is 72 pages long and has more words than the Sparx books. The themes of the books include sports, mystery, and adventure. The books in this line were originally published in Great Britain between 2000 and 2003.

> *Aargh, It's an Alien!* Written by K. Wallace. Illustrated by Michael Reid.
> *Archie's Amazing Game.* Written by Michael Hardcastle. Illustrated by Michael Reid.

The *Arf* series. Written by Philip Wooderson. Illustrated by Bridget MacKeith.
  Arf and the Greedy Grabber
  Arf and the Metal Detector
  Arf and the Three Dogs
Hot Air. Written by Anthony Masters. Illustrated by Mike Perkins.
Joker. Written by Anthony Masters. Illustrated by Michael Reid.
Lost: A Tale of Survival. Written by Chris Kreie. Illustrated by Marcus Smith.
The Monster Piano. Written by C. Pitcher. Illustrated by Bridget MacKeith.
Sam's Goal. Written by Michael Hardcastle. Illustrated by Tony O'Donnell.

Graphic Quest

(2006). $22.60 (hardcover), $8.95 (softcover).

The next step up, the Graphic Quest books are more than 80 pages and have more narration in text boxes. Several of the books involve sports (soccer, diving, kayaking), adventure, and mysteries. As with Graphic Trax, most of these books were originally published in Great Britain.

  Abracadabra. Written by Alex Gutteridge. Illustrated by Lucy Su.
  Castaway. Written by C. Pitcher. Illustrated by Peter Dennis.
  Detective Files. Written by Steve Bowkett. Illustrated by David Burroughs.
  Guard Dog. Written by Philip Wooderson. Illustrated by David Burroughs.
  The Haunted Surfboard. Written by Anthony Masters. Illustrated by Peter Dennis.
  The Haunting of Julia. Written by M. Hooper. Illustrated by Maureen Gray.
  Hit It! Written by Michael Hardcastle. Illustrated by Bob Moulder.
  Horror of the Heights. Written by Anthony Masters. Illustrated by Peter Dennis.
  My Brother's a Keeper. Written by Michael Hardcastle. Illustrated by Bob Moulder.
  Raven's Revenge. Written by Anthony Masters. Illustrated by Peter Dennis.
  System Shock. Written by Liam O'Donnell. Illustrated by Janek Matysiak.

Ridge Riders

(2007). $21.26 (hardcover), $6.95 (softcover).

These short, 32-page stories deal with young Slam Duncan and his mountain-bike riding friends The Range Riders and their various adventures. The reading level varies from 1.8-3.3, but the inclusion of text makes this even more of a hybrid. All books in this series were written by Robin and Chris Lawrie, and were illustrated by Robin Lawrie.

Cheat Challenge	*Radar Riders*
Fear 3.1	*Snow Bored*
First Among Losers	*Treetop Trauma*
Paintball Panic	*While Lightning*

Graphic Revolve

(2007) $23.93 (hardcover), $9.95 (softcover).

More than 60-page adaptations of classic stories and novels. Besides the "extras" found in the other series, there is also background on the period in which the book is set.

The Adventures of Tom Sawyer. Adapted by M.C. Hall. Illustrated by Daniel Strickland.

Black Beauty. Adapted by L.L. Owens. Illustrated by Jennifer Tanner.

Frankenstein. Adapted by Michael Burgan. Illustrated by Dennis Calero.

The Hunchback of Notre Dame. Adapted by L.L. Owens. Illustrated by Greg Rebis.

The Invisible Man. Adapted by Terry Davis. Illustrated by Dennis Calero.

Journey to the Center of the Earth. Adapted by Davis Worth Miller and Katherine McLean Brevard. Illustrated by Greg Rebis.

King Arthur and the Knights of the Round Table. Adapted by M.C. Hall. Illustrated by C.E. Richards.

Robin Hood. Adapted by Aaron Shepard and Anne L. Watson. Illustrated by Jennifer Tanner.

The Time Machine. Adapted by Terry Davis. Illustrated by José Alfonzo Ocampo Ruiz.

Treasure Island. Adapted by Wim Coleman and Pat Perrin. Illustrated by Greg Rebis.

Graphic Flash

$23.93 (hardcover), $6.95 (softcover).

A hybrid series in which the amount of text greatly outnumbers the "graphic" content, though when this content does appear it is as part of the story, and not simply illustration. The books also contain background information for the period in which they are set.

Blackbeard's Sword: The Pirate King of the Carolinas. Written by Liam O'Donnell. Illustrated by Mike Spoor.

Fire and Snow: A Tale of the Alaskan Gold Rush. Written by J. Gunderson. Illustrated by Shannon Townsend.

Hot Iron: The Adventures of a Civil War Powder Boy. Written by Michael Burgan. Illustrated by Pedro Rodriguez.

The Last Rider: The Final Days of the Pony Express. Written by J. Gunderson. Illustrated by José Alfonzo Ocampo Ruiz.

Stormbreaker: The Graphic Novel

Adapted by Antony Johnston. Illustrated by Kanako Damerum and Yuzuru Takasaki. Philomel Books/Penguin Young Readers (2006). $14.99. [T]

An adaptation of the popular book by Anthony Horowitz. The other books in the series may also be adapted.

The Strongest Man in the World: Louis Cyr

Nicholas Debron. Groundwood Press (2007). $17.95. [C]

A short biography in graphic novel format of famous Canadian Strongman Louis Cyr (1863–1912), whose reported feats included lifting more than 4,300 pounds on his back. Although the book could be placed in the biography section of the library, it would probably receive more notice in juvenile fiction or 741 sections. This book is best for elementary age readers, and includes an afterword about Cyr.

Stuck in the Middle: Seventeen Comics from an Unpleasant Age

Edited by Ariel Schrag. Viking Juvenile (2007). $18.99. [T]

A graphic novel anthology filled with autobiographical and semiautobiographical stories of what life was like at the middle school age. There is some minor language (the worst words are edited with dashes, e.g., "f—k), and subjects include topics such as menstruation, peer pressure, teasing, and attraction.

Studio Ghibli Library

Viz Comics. $9.95–$9.99. [B]

Japan's Studio Ghibli has produced many of the best-known and highest-grossing anime feature films. Viz has produced a series of unflopped animanga versions of these films. Besides the main story, the books include an appendix that provides a guide to the sound effects that are written in the Japanese phonetic characters called katakana. It first has how the sound is spelled out, followed by the English equivalent. For example, "Do Do Do Do" is the Japanese version of "Vrrroom."

The series that are rated **A** are:

Castle in the Sky   *My Neighbor Totoro*
Howl's Moving Castle   *Spirited Away*
Kiki's Delivery Service

Super Friends

Various writers and artists. DC Comics (2001-2003). $14.95. [B]

These volumes collect the comic book version of the popular 1970s Saturday morning cartoon. Superman, Batman & Robin, Wonder Woman, Aquaman, and various teen heroes in training appear in these child-friendly superhero adventures.

Super Friends!
Super Friends! Truth, Justice, and Peace!

Superman

DC Comics. [B]

One of the best-known comic book characters since his 1938 debut. Besides the *Archives/Showcase* editions, other age-appropriate collections include the following.

Historical Collections

Superman Chronicles, Volumes 1–3. $14.99.
> The earliest Superman stories by his creators Jerry Siegel and Joe Shuster. More volumes are expected.

Collections by Decades

$19.95.

Superman in the Forties   *Superman in the Seventies*
Superman in the Fifties   *Superman in the Eighties*
Superman in the Sixties

Additional

> *Superman: The Greatest Stories Ever Told*, Volumes 1–2
>
> *Superman/Batman: The Greatest Stories Ever Told*

Great Stories Through the Years

> *Superman Adventures*
>> Based on the animated Superman program of the 1990s. They are digest-sized and cost $6.95 each.
>>> Volume 1: *Up, Up and Away!*
>>>
>>> Volume 2: *The Never Ending Battle*

Swan

Ariyoshi Kyoko. DC/CMX (2005–). $9.95. **[B]**

A translation of a 21-volume series that appeared in Japan from 1976–1981. Sixteen-year-old Masumi dreams of becoming a professional ballerina, and her dreams may be coming true. As of 2007, CMX has published 11 volumes. The series is unflopped and rated **E** for everyone.

Sweaterweather

Sara Varon. Alternative Comics (2003). $11.95. **[B]**

A black-and-white book containing short stories, most of which are silent, of talking animals. The book includes cut-out paper dolls with a note that if the reader is "borrowing this book from a library" to make a photocopy instead. One of the more interesting stories with dialogue has 26 panels, each having a consecutive letter either in dialogue or picture.

Teen Titans Go!

J. Torres. Art by various artists. $6.99. **[B]**

Besides the other Teen Titans titles in the *DC Archives* and *Showcase* books, these digest-sized books, part of the Johnny DC kids line, collect issues of the *Teen Titans Go!* comic book, which is based on the popular animated series. Although the cartoon has an anime style to it, the comic has similarities to manga. Each volume collects four issues, and features Robin, the alien Starfire, the mystical Raven, the shape-changing Beast Boy, and Cyborg.

> Volume 1: *Truth, Justice, Pizza!* Volume 5: *On the Move*
>
> Volume 2: *Heroes on Patrol!* Volume 6: *Titans Together*
>
> Volume 3: *Bring It On!* (full-sized for $12.99)
>
> Volume 4: *Ready for Action*

> *Teen Titans: Jam-Packed Action*, Volume 1 (2005). $7.99.
>> An animanga-type digest that takes pictures from the television program.

Tellos

Todd Dezago. Illustrated by Mike Wieringo and multiple inkers. Image Comics. **[B]**

Young Jarek fights beside a Tiger-Man and other allies, including a pirate princess, in this swords, swashbuckling, and sorcery epic. While some the early editions are out of print, the entire story was collected in 2007's *Tellos Colossal*, a hardcover collection that costs $39.99.

Thieves & Kings

Mark Oakley. I Box Publishing (1996–). $13.50–$16.95. **[T]**

A hybrid fantasy series, with pages of comics followed by pages of illustrated text. The teenage thief Rubel gets caught up in an epic adventure that involves endangered princesses, good and evil witches and wizards, magical creatures, reincarnation and more. Five volumes have been published and several more are planned. The amount of reading makes it best for middle school readers.

Time Warp Trio

Jon Scieszka and Amy Court Kaemon. HarperCollins (2006–). $4.99. **[C]**

These digest-sized books adapt the animated series, which in turn adapted the Scieszka books about three boys who travel through time and space.

Volume 1: *Trouble at Joe's House*
Volume 2: *The Seven Blunders of the World*
Volume 3: *Plaid to the Bone*
Volume 4: *Meet You at Waterloo*

Tintin

Hergé. Little, Brown, and Co. Various prices. **[B]**

Famous in Europe and around the world, *The Adventures of Tintin* features adventurous reporter Tintin, his dog Snowy, and various supporting characters. Little, Brown has published translations of many of the titles in both hard- and softcover, as well as three-in-one omnibuses. As discussed in Chapter 3, some of the earlier volumes, most notably *Tintin in the Congo*, which has recently been the subject of controversy, may feature racial and cultural stereotypes. In chronological order, the 24 single *Tintin* volumes are:

Tintin in the Land of the Soviets
Tintin in the Congo
Tintin in America
Cigars of the Pharaoh
The Blue Lotus
The Broken Ear
The Black Island
King Ottokar's Sceptre
The Crab with the Golden Claws
The Shooting Star
The Secret of the Unicorn
Red Rackham's Treasure

The Seven Crystal Balls
Prisoners of the Sun
Land of Black Gold
Destination Moon
Explorers on the Moon
The Calculus Affair
The Red Sea Sharks
Tintin in Tibet
The Castafiore Emerald
Flight 714
Tintin and the Picaros
Tintin and Alph-Art

Tiny Tyrant

Lewis Trondheim. Illustrated by Fabrice Parme. First Second (2007). **[B]**

What happens when a spoiled six-year-old is the all-powerful ruler of a country? The misadventures of King Ethelbert of Portocristo are featured in this humorous French book. Although the title character is six years old, it would better be understood by older elementary and middle school readers.

To Dance: A Ballerina's Graphic Novel

Siena Cherson Siegel. Drawn by Mark Siegel. Atheneum Books for Young Readers (Simon & Schuster) (2006). $9.99. **[B]**. Recommended.

One of the few juvenile graphic autobiographies out there. Siena Siegel tells what made her want to become a ballet dancer, and of her work and training at the School of American Ballet and as member of a company that performed at Lincoln Center in the late 1970s early 1980s. The book was a Robert E. Sibert Award Honor Book, and is on YALSA's Great Graphic Novels for Teens List.

Tokyo Mew Mew

Reiko Yoshida and Miya Ikumi. Tokyopop. $9.99. **[B]**

> *Tokyo Mew Mew*, Volumes 1–7 (2003–2004)
> *Tokyo Mew Mew a la Mode*, Volumes 1–2 (2005)
>> A group of young (11- to 13-year-old) girls have their DNA mixed with that of nearly extinct animals—including a wildcat, a porpoise, and a lion, and form Team Mew Mew to fight alien invaders. The series was also turned into an anime series and is rated **Y**.

Tommysaurus Rex

Doug TenNapel. Image (2005). $11.95. **[B]**. Recommended.

Young Ely's dog Tommy is killed by a car. Helping him cope, his parents send him to visit his grandfather's farm, where he finds a 40-foot tyrannosaurus rex, which he tames, and it becomes his new pet. But the townspeople are unsure about it (at least until all of the positive media coverage), and a local bully is jealous of all Ely's fame.

This is on Diamond's list of recommended titles for elementary schools, though there is some very minor language, and when Grandfather convinces Ely's parents to leave him at the farm for the summer says that they should "go have fun, go have some sex, call me when the summer's over."

Totally Spies

Papercutz. **[B]**

Similar to the Tokyopop cine-manga, this series adapts the popular animated series about three teenage girls from Beverly Hills who are also secret agents. These 96-page digest-sized books are available in both hardcover ($12.95) and softcover ($7.95).

1. The O.P.	*3. Evil Jerry*
2. I Hate the 80s!	*4. Spies in Space*

Ug: Boy Genius of the Stone Age

Raymond Briggs. Alfred N. Knopf (2001). **[C]**

Ug doesn't like how things are made of stone—his bed, the blanket, even the trousers everyone wears. He tries to invent better things, but the other cave people won't go for it. Since everyone in the book wears nothing but stone trousers around their waist, this includes Ug's mother. The fact that she is topless isn't "graphic," but it is apparent. The book is the same size as other children's book by Briggs, including his *Bert* and *Father Christmas* books.

The Ultimate Casper Comics Collection

Ibooks (2005). $14.95. **[B]**

This book collects issues of the 1950s Harvey Comics comic books featuring every-one's favorite Friendly Ghost, Casper. **See also** the entry for **Harvey Comics Classics**.

Universal Monsters: Cavalcade of Horror

Various writers and artists. Dark Horse Comics (2006). **[B]**

This edition collects comics from the early 1990s that adapted the famous Universal Studios horror films *The Mummy*, *Frankenstein*, *Dracula*, and the *Creature from the Black Lagoon*. The monsters resemble their screen counterparts (Dracula looks like Bela Lugosi, for example).

Usagi Yojimbo

Stan Sakai.

This popular, Eisner-award-winning black-and-white series takes place in a world with anthropomorphic animals. In this world's Japan, masterless Samurai Miyamoto Usagi, a rabbit, travels around the land, sometimes working as a bodyguard, and having many adventures. Many of the stories refer to Japanese myths, legends, and historical events, and these are often discussed at the end of the book. Besides multiple Eisner wins and nominations, the series has won other awards, including a Parents Choice Award.

The first nine books are published by Fantagraphics, with the rest by Dark Horse. **[B]**

Volume 1: *The Ronin*
Volume 2: *Samurai*
Volume 3: *Wanderer's Road*
Volume 4: *Dragon Bellow Conspiracy*
Volume 5: *Lone Goat and Kid*
Volume 6: *Circles*
Volume 7: *Gen's Story*
Volume 8: *Shades of Death*
Volume 9: *Daisho*
Volume 10: *The Brink of Life and Death*
Volume 11: *Seasons*
Volume 12: *Grasscutter*
Volume 13: *Grey Shadows*
Volume 14: *Demon Mask*
Volume 15: *Grasscutter II: Journey to Atsuta Shrine*
Volume 16: *The Shrouded Moon*
Volume 17: *Duel at Kitanoji*
Volume 18: *Travels with Jotaro*
Volume 19: *Fathers and Sons*
Volume 20: *Glimpses of Death*
Volume 21: *The Mother of Mountains*
Volume 22: *Tomoe's Story*

Additional volumes will be coming out.

The Vanishers

Chuck Dixon. Illustrated by Andrés Klacik. IDW. **[B]**

Not only are Andy's friends disappearing in front of his eyes, but only Andy can remember that they existed in the first place. Then he sees that another boy in class has also noticed the disappearances. This leads Andy on an adventure involving time travel and killer robots.

Vögelein

Jane Irwin. Fiery Studios (2003–). $12.95. **[B]**. Recommended.

In this wonderful fantasy series, Vögelein is a mechanical fairy created centuries ago. Now she is in New York, where the man who took care of her, winding her when needed, has died. Now she must find a new guardian. The books also cover her early "life," the lives of the people that she encounters, and even real fairies that have become altered by living in the city. Each book has endnotes with additional information. For older elementary and middle school.

> *Clockwork Faerie* (with Jeff Berndt)
> *Old Ghosts*

Wallace and Gromit

Titan Books. $12.95 (hardcover), $8.95 (softcover). **[B]**

Based on the award-winning series of films, these books tell the continued comical adventures of inventor Wallace and his dog. The subtitles of the *Wallace and Gromit* series are:

> *The Bootiful Game*. Written by Ian Rimmer. Illustrated by Brian Williamson.
> *A Pier to Far*. Written by Dan Abnett. Illustrated by Jimmy Hansen.
> *Plots in Space*. Written by Dan Abnett. Illustrated by Jimmy Hansen.
> *The Whippit Vanishes*. Written by Ian Rimmer. Illustrated by Jimmy Hansen.

Warriors Series

Erin Hunter. Adapted by Dan Jolley. Illustrated by James L. Barry. Tokyopop (2007–). $6.99. **[B]**

The first of the OEL mangas in which Tokyopop adapts the works of HarperCollins authors. This series adapts Erin Hunter's *Warriors* series with new adventures featuring the cat Greystripe, a wild cat who is separated from his tribe, and after becoming the "kittypet" of some "twolegs" tries to get back home.

> Volume 1: *The Lost Warrior*
> Volume 2: *Warrior's Refuge*

Additional volumes are planned.

What's Michael

Story and art by Makoto Kobayashi. Dark Horse Comics. $5.95–$8.95. **[B]**

A younger-audience manga about a cat named Michael. In some of the stories he's just a normal cat, and the stories also deal with the humans around him. In others the reader can understand what he and other cats are saying, and in some Michael and the other cats are anthropomorphized, wear clothes, and act like people. There are also some stories that take place in other times and places or feature a vampire called "The Count," who is afraid of cats. Dark Horse recommends the books for ages eight and up. Some of the following may not be available from all sources.

Volume 1: *Michael's Album*
Volume 2: *Living Together*
Volume 3: *Off the Deep End*
Volume 4: *Michael's Mambo*
Volume 5: *Michael's Favorite Spot*
Volume 6: *A Hard Day's Night*
Volume 7: *Fat Cat in the City*
Volume 8: *Show Time*
Volume 9: *The Ideal Cat*
Volume 10: *Sleepless Nights*
Volume 11: *Planet of the Cats*

Whistle!

Daisuke Higuchi. Viz (2004–). $7.99 each, 24 volumes. **[B]**

A shōnen sports manga, the series is about Shô Kazamatsuri who is only on the reserves on his junior high school's soccer team. When he changes schools, everyone thinks he's a great player because of his old school's reputation. But as it turns out, he is not. So he and the new school's other reservists work with one of the best players to improve their skills and prove themselves to the others. The Japanese edition ended at volume 24, and it is likely that this is where Viz will end as well. The title is rated **A** for all ages.

Will Eisner's Literary Adaptations

Will Eisner. NBM Publishing. **[B]**

Comics legend Will Eisner created these short adaptations of *Don Quixote*, *Moby Dick*, and the classic fairy tales.

The Last Knight (2000). $15.95 (hardcover), $8.95 (softcover).
Moby Dick (1998). $15.95 (hardcover), $7.95 (softcover).
The Princess and the Frog (1999). $15.95 (hardcover), $7.95 (softcover).

W.I.T.C.H. Series

Various writers. Disney/Hyperion. $4.99. **[B]**

An Italian fantasy/superhero comic that has appeared in 50 countries in 20 languages, the *W.I.T.C.H.* series gets its name from its five protagonists: Will, Irma, Taranee, Cornelia, and Hay Lin. These teenage girls have been given magical powers, which they use to fight for good. Prior to the graphic novels appearing in the United States, a series of juvenile fiction novelizations have included comic inserts.

Volume 1: *The Power of Friendship*
Volume 2: *Meridian Magic*
Volume 3: *The Revealing*
Volume 4: *Between Light and Dark*
Volume 5: *Legends Revealed*
Volume 6: *Forces of Change*
Volume 7: *Under Pressure*
Volume 8: *An Unexpected Return*

WJHC

Jane Smith Fisher. Art by Kristen Petersen. Wilson Place Comics (2003–). $11.95. **[B]**

This teen comedy features Janey Wells and her friends, who start up a radio station at their high school, New Jersey's Jackson Hill High. Now Janey and the gang at WJHC (Jackson Hill Crowd) have all sorts of adventures in and out of school. Two volumes have been created: *WJHC: On the Air* (2003) and *WJHC: Hold Tight!* (2005). Additional volumes are planned. Volume 1 is on Diamond's list of recommended titles for elementary schools.

The Wonderful Wizard of Oz

Adapted by David Chauvel. Illustrated by Enrique Fernández. Image Comics (2006). $9.99 **[B]**

An additional adaptation of the classic Baum novel. It is in color and adapts most of the story.

The World's Greatest Superheroes

Paul Dini. Illustrated by Alex Ross. DC Comics. $9.95. **[B]**

Between 1999 and 2003, DC put out these oversized, softcover, square-bound graphic novels, written by Paul Dini and painted by Alex Ross. Each book covered a social issue, including crime and hunger. The five volumes are available separately or as a slipcased hardcover.

> *The World's Greatest Superheroes* (2005). $49.99.
> *Batman: War on Crime*
> *JLA: Liberty and Justice*
> *Shazam! Power of Hope*
> *Superman: Peace on Earth*
> *Wonder Woman: Spirit of Truth*

Yotsuba&!

Kiyohiko Azuma. ADV (2005–). $9.99. **[B]**

Yotsuba&! is a translation of *Yotsuba To!* or *Yotsuba and!* as many chapters are titled "Yotsuba and X." Yotsuba, in this case, is a quirky five-year-old girl who has just moved to a new city with her adopted father. Many of her adventures deal with her interactions with the Ayase family next door, especially the three Ayase sisters, whose ages range from college-age to a just a few years older than Yotsuba. The series, which is ongoing, is popular both in Japan and the United States. It has received an Excellence Award at the Japan Media Arts Festival, was on the "best" lists of *Publisher's Weekly* and *The Comics Journal*, and the first volume is on Diamond's list of recommended titles for middle schools.

Zapt!

Shannon Denton and Keith Giffen. Illustrated by Armand Villavert Jr. Tokyopop (2006–). $5.99. **[B]**

This OEL manga series is part of Tokyopop's junior line of books. Twelve-year-old earth boy Armand Jones, the grandson of a Tuskegee Airman, has been recruited into the Pan-Galactic Order of Police, or P.O.O.P. Now he must fight interstellar bad guys while making sure he doesn't get detention in school or grounded at home. The series is rated **A** for for all ages, and is a fun mix of science fiction and humor. Two volumes have been published and a third is planned.

Zorro

Don McGregor. Illustrated by Sidney Lima. Papercutz (2005–). $12.95 (hardcover), $7.95 (softcover). **[B]**

New adventures of this masked adventure who fought against injustice in Old California. These books are digest sized.

Volume 1: *Scars*
Volume 2: *Drownings*
Volume 3: *Vultures*

As long as this list is, it still does not contain nearly all of the age-appropriate graphic novels out there, and more and more are coming out every week. Besides the continuation of the ongoing series, new books—fiction and nonfiction, original works, collections, and adaptations are regularly announced. The sources listed in Chapters 5 and 6 and the sites listed in Appendix C will help you in getting information on the latest titles.

Additional Books and Further Reading

B esides the large number of graphic novels, many books are available that talk about comic books and graphic novels. These include books about the characters, the creators, and even ways to write and draw your own comics. In addition, comic-book characters have been used to teach nonfiction subjects. There are also many examples of juvenile "nongraphic" fiction featuring comic book characters. Finally, books for librarians to read are available that not only further discuss the topic of graphic novels in libraries (and may also include recommended lists), but can also teach librarians more about the subject in general.

Nonfiction

DK Guides

Dorling Kindersley has two kinds of books that incorporate comic book characters. The Ultimate Guides are in a similar style to many of their other nonfiction books, with a mix of text and illustrations. The superhero books, which would generally be cataloged in the 741.5s, cover the history of the characters along with different incarnations, including film and television versions. Several of these books have been updated, often when a new film comes out. Several of the writers and the artists in these books work in the comics industry, and artwork from various comics are reprinted. In addition, some of the animated programs based on comics have their own individual titles. These may be cataloged with other television books in the 782s. The books are acceptable for all ages, but the large amount of text may cause some of the younger readers to only skim it.

The other DK books use DC Comics characters to explain a nonfiction topic. These are for "Level 4" (proficient) readers, and are available in both hardcover ($12.99) and paperback ($3.99), are 48 pages long, and are recommended for ages five to eight. These books can be cataloged in their subject area.

The Ultimate Guides

These cost around $25.00.

> *The Amazing Spider-Man: The Ultimate Guide* by Tom DeFalco
> *Avengers: The Ultimate Guide* by Tom DeFalco

Batman: The Ultimate Guide to the Dark Knight by Scott Beatty
Fantastic Four: The Ultimate Guide by Tom DeFalco
JLA: The Ultimate Guide by Scott Beatty
Superman: The Ultimate Guide to the Man of Steel by Scott Beatty
Wonder Woman: The Ultimate Guide to the Amazon Princess by Scott Beatty
X-Men: The Ultimate Guide by Peter Sanderson

JLA Readers

Aquaman's Guide to the Ocean (2004) by Jackie Gaff
Batman's Guide to Crime and Detection (2003) by Michael Teitelbaum
The Flash's Book of Speed (2005) by Clare Hibbert
Green Lantern's Book of Great Inventions (2005) by Clare Hibbert
Superman's Guide to the Universe (2003) by Jackie Gaff
Wonder Woman's Book of Myths (2004) by Clare Hibbert

Math Made Easy

A new series from DK that uses superheroes to teach math.

Batman: Fifth Grade Workbook
Marvel Heroes/Spider-Man: Second Grade Workbook
Marvel Heroes/X-Men Fourth Grade Workbook
Superman: Third Grade Workbook

Also from DK

The DC Comics Encyclopedia by various writers and artists. $40.00.
Marvel Comics Encyclopedia by Daniel Wallace. $40.00.

Action Heroes

Rosen Publishing (2007). $29.95.

These six, 48-page books tells about six well-known Marvel Comics superheroes. The books cover the background of the character's creation (all six were co-created by Stan Lee) and provide information on the characters abilities, villains, and supporting characters. Comic writers Paul Kupperburg and Danny Fingeroth are among the writers for the series.

The Creation of Captain America by Thomas Forget
The Creation of the Fantastic Four by Eric Fein
The Creation of the Incredible Hulk by Eric Fein
The Creation of Iron Man by Adam Eisenberg
The Creation of Spider-Man by Paul Kupperburg
The Creation of the X-Men by Danny Fingeroth

Comics Book Creators Series

Sue Hamilton. Abdo Publishing. $24.21.

A look at some of the greats of the industry. These 32-page books, which include pictures, diagrams, indexes, and a glossary, are also on the Accelerated Reader list. However, these are on older creators, not those who are currently "hot."

Jack Kirby   *John Buscema*
Joe Simon   *John Romita, Sr.*
Joe Sinnott   *Stan Lee*

Writing and Drawing Books

Some may be better for older readers.

My First Manga Series

Various writers and artists. Digital Manga Publishing.

Nanako   *Shonen Knight*
Ninja Clan   *Various Animals*
Robo Clan

Kids Draw

Christopher Hart. Watson-Guptill. $10.95.

Kids Draw Anime   *Kids Draw Manga Fantasy*
Kids Draw Manga   *Kids Draw Manga Shoujo*

DC Comics Guides

Watson-Guptill. $19.95.

The DC Comics Guide to Inking Comics by Klaus Janson
The DC Comics Guide to Penciling Comics by Klaus Janson
The DC Comics Guide to Writing Comics by Dennis O'Neil

Related Juvenile Fiction

DK Readers

These range from Level 1 to Level 4, and are available in both hardcover ($12.99–$14.99) and paperback ($3.99).

Fantastic Four

Neil Kelly.

Evil Adversaries
The World's Greatest Superteam

Hulk

The Incredible Hulk's Book of Strength by James Buckley
The Story of the Incredible Hulk by Michael Teitelbaum

Spider-Man

Spider-Man: The Amazing Story by Catherine Saunders
Spider-Man: Worst Enemies by Catherine Saunders

Spider-Man's Amazing Powers by James Buckley Jr.
The Story of Spider-Man by Michael Teitelbaum

X-Men

Meet the X-Men by Clare Hibbert
The X-Men School by Michael Teitelbaum

Further Reading

Books on comics, comic's history, and graphic novels in libraries.

Brenner, Robin. 2007. *Understanding Manga and Anime*. Westport, CT: Libraries Unlimited.

Cary, Stephen. 2004. *Going Graphic: Comics at Work in the Multilingual Classroom*. Portsmouth, NH: Heinemann.

Goldsmith, Francisca. 2005. *Graphic Novels Now: Buiding, Managing, and Marketing a Dynamic Collection*. Washington, DC: American Library Association.

Gorman, Michele. 2003. *Getting Graphic: Using Graphic Novels to Promote Literacy with Preteens and Teens*. Columbus, OH: Linworth Publishing.

Gorman, Michele. 2007. *Getting Graphic! Comics for Kids*. Columbus, OH: Linworth Publishing.

Gravett, Paul. 2004. *Manga: Sixty Years of Japanese Comics*. London: Laurence King. (Note: this book contains nudity and graphic images.)

Gravett, Paul. 2006. *Graphic Novels: Everything You Need to Know*. New York: Harper Design International. (Note: this book contains nudity and graphic images.)

Lyga, Allyson A.W. and Barry Lyga. 2004. *Graphic Novels in Your Media Center: A Definitive Guide*. Westport, CT: Libraries Unlimited.

Miller, Steve. 2005. *Developing and Promoting Graphic Novels Collections*. New York: Neal-Schuman.

Nyberg, Amy Kiste. 1998. *Seal of Approval: The History of the Comics Code*. Jackson, MS: University Press of Mississippi.

Pawuk, Michael. 2007. *Graphic Novels: A Genre Guide to Comic Books, Manga, and More*. Westport, CT: Libraries Unlimited.

Pilcher, Tim and Brad Brooks. 2005. *The Essential Guide to World Comics*. London: Collins and Brown.

Weiner, Stephen. 2003. *Faster Than a Speeding Bullet: The Rise of the Graphic Novel*. New York: NBM.

Weiner, Stephen. 2006. *The 101 Best Graphic Novels: A Guide to This Exciting New Medium*, revised ed. New York: NBM.

Online Resources

The Internet can be very helpful to the librarian starting a graphic novel collection, whether it is checking a publisher's Web site to see their upcoming releases, finding vendors, getting reviews, or even getting ideas for classroom activities.

Publishing Companies

Abacus Comics
www.abacuscomics.com
Abdo and Daughters
www.abdopub.com
Active Synapse
www.activesynapse.com
ADV
www.advfilms.com
AiT/Planet Lar
www.ait-planetlar.com
Alternative Comics
www.indyworld.com/
altcomics
Antarctic Press
www.antarctic-press.com
Archaia Studios Press
www.daradja.com
Archie Comics
www.archie.com
Astonish Comics
www.theastonishfactory.com
Barbour Publishing
www.barbourbooks.com
Barron's
http://barronseduc.com
Blue Dream Studios
www.bluedreamstudios.com
Café Digital
www.paulsizer.com

Capstone
www.capstonepress.com
Cartoon Books
www.boneville.com
Dark Horse Comics
www.darkhorse.com
DC Comics
www.dccomics.com
Del Rey Books
www.randomhouse.com/delrey
Devil's Due
www.devilsdue.net
Digital Manga Productions
www.dmpbooks.com
Disney Press
http://disneybooks.disney.go.com/
DK
www.dk.com
Eureka Productions
www.graphicclassics.com
Fantagraphics
www.fantagraphics.com
Fiery Studios
www.vogelein.com/fierystudios/fiery
studios.shtml
First Second
www.firstsecondbooks.com
Gareth Stevens Publishing
www.garethstevens.com

Gemstone
www.gemstonepub.com/disney/
Gossamer Books
www.gossamerbooks.com
Graphix (Scholastic)
www.scholastic.com/graphix
GT Labs
www.gt-labs.com
HarperCollins
www.harpercollins.com
Henchmen Publishing
http://nodwick.humor.gamespy.com/
ps238/
Hyperion Books for Children
www.hyperionbooksforchildren.com/
I Box Publishing
www.iboxpublishing.com
IDW
www.idwpublishing.com
Image Comics
www.imagecomics.com
Lerner Publishing Group
www.lernerbooks.com
Marvel Comics
www.marvel.com
NBM
www.nbmpub.com
Oni Press
www.onipress.com
Osprey
www.ospreypublishing.com
Papercutz
www.papercutz.com

Penguin/Puffin/Viking
http://us.penguingroup.com/
Random House/Alfred Knopf
www.randomhouse.com
Renaissance Press (*Amelia Rules*)
www.ameliarules.com
Rosen Publishing
www.rosenpublishing.com
School Specialty Publishing
www.schoolspecialtypublishing.com
Simon & Schuster/Atheneum Books
www.simonsays.com
Sky Dog Press
www.skydogcomics.com
Slave Labor/SLG/Amaze Ink
www.slgcomic.com
Sterling Publishing
www.sterlingpub.com
Stone Arch Books
www.stonearchbooks.com
Tokyopop
www.tokyopop.com
Top Shelf
www.topshelfcomix.com
Tor
www.tor-forge.com
Viper Comics
www.vipercomics.com
Viz Media
www.viz.com
Wilson Place Comics
www.wjhc.com

Purchasing
Books, comics, and other materials.

Amazon
www.amazon.com
Baker & Taylor
www.btol.com/
Barnes & Noble
www.barnesandnoble.com
Brodart
www.brodart.com and
www.graphicnovels.brodart.com/

BWI
www.bwibooks.com
CBR Comic Shop Locator
www.comicbookresources.com/
resources/locator/
CBR New Comics List
www.comicbookresources.com/
resources/ncl/

DEMCO
www.demco.com

Diamond Comic Shop Locator
www.comicshoplocator.com

Diamond Comics
(main) www.diamondcomics.com
(library page)
http://bookshelf.diamondcomics.com/

Ingram
www.ingrambook.com

Kapco
www.kapco.com

The Master List of Comic Book and Trading Card Stores
www.the-master-list.com/

New Comic Book Release List
www.comiclist.com
This also links to information on reviews, publishers, and comics professionals and is also available via e-mail.

Reviews, Recommendations, Educational Information, and More

Accelerated Reader
www.renlearn.com/store/quiz_advanced.asp

The Beat
http://pwbeat.publishersweekly.com/blog/

Comic Book Awards Almanac
www.hahnlibrary.net/comics/awards/index.html

TComic Book Legal Defense Fund
www.cbldf.org

The Comic Book Project
www.comicbookproject.org

Comic Book Resources
www.comicbookresources.com/

Comic Books for Libraries
http://comicbooksforlibraries.blogspot.com

Comic Books for Young Adults
http://ublib.buffalo.edu/libraries/units/lml/comics/pages

Comic Buyers's Guide
www.cbgxtra.com

Comicon.com
www.comicon.com

Comics in the Classroom
www.comicsintheclassroom.net/

Comics Continuum
www.comicscontinuum.com

Comics Radar
http://comicsradar.com/

Comics Worth Reading
www.comicsworthreading.com/

Friends of Lulu
www.popcultureshock.com/lulu/

Grand ComicBook Database Project (GLD)
www.comics.org

Graphic Novel Reviews
www.graphicnovelreview.com

ICv2
www.icv2.com

Kids Love Comics
www.kidslovecomics.com/

The Librarian's Guide to Anime and Manga
www.koyagi.com/Libguide.html

Library Journal
www.ljdigital.com

Newsarama
www.newsarma.com

No Flying, No Tights
www.noflyingnotights.com

The Pulse
www.comicon.com/pulse/

Recommended Graphic Novels for Public Libraries
http://my.voyager.net/~sraiteri/graphicnovels.htm

Scholastic Make Your Own Graphix
www.scholastic.com/goosebumps
graphix/makeyourown/index.htm

Scholastic Teaching Resources Page
http://content.scholastic.com/
browse/teach.jsp

Scholastic's Using Comics in the Classroom
http://teacher.scholastic.com/
products/tradebooks/boneville_
using_graphic_novels.pdf

The Secret Origins of Good Readers
www.night-flight.com/secretorigin/
SOGR2004.pdf

Sequential Tart
www.sequentialtart.com/

VOYA
www.voya.com

Wizard: The Guide to Comics
www.wizardworld.com

Educational Resources

E-Mail

GNLIB-L

GNLIB-L is a listserv for librarians, dealing with the subject of graphic novels in libraries. The list moved to Yahoo Groups in 2007, but archival material from the Topica board and additional information can currently be found at www.angelfire.com/comics/gnlib/, though this may change in the future.

To subscribe, e-mail GNLIB-L-subscribe@yahoogroups.com, or go to http://groups.yahoo.com/group/GNLIB-L.

PUBYAC

The practical aspects of children and young adult services in public libraries.

To join the list and receive the mailings from PUBYAC, send a message similar the following (no subject necessary):

To: listproc@prairienet.org
Message: subscribe PUBYAC

PW Comics Week

A weekly e-newsletter from *Publisher's Weekly*.

Go to www.publishersweekly.com/subscribe.asp and scroll down to the "e-mail newsletters" section.

YA-YAAC

For young adult librarians.
Send email message to:
listproc@ ala.org
Leave subject line blank
In the body of the message type:
Subscribe YA-YAAC, your first name, last name

YALSA-BK

Book discussion, primarily for young adult titles.
Send email message to: listproc@ala.org
Leave subject line blank
In the body of the message type: Subscribe YALSA-bk, your first name, last name

Usenet

Usenet has long been a place for discussion on comics a graphic novels. Message posters include fans, amateur and professional reviewers, and even comics pros. If you cannot access Usenet through other means, use the googlegroups search engine at www.google.com.

Some of the more popular Usenet Comics groups are:
rec.arts.comics.dc.universe
rec.arts.comics.marvel.universe
rec.arts.comics.marvel.universe.xbooks
rec.arts.comics.misc

Bibliography

"2006 Japanese Manga Market Drops Below 500 Billion Yen." Comipress.com (March 10, 2007). Available: http://comipress.com/news/2007/03/10/1622.

Abraham, Randy. 2007. "Superhero Club Members Work to Create Comic Book. *South Florida Sun-Sentinel*, February 4. People Section, p. 4.

"Accelerated Reader." *Wikipedia* (January 8, 2008). Available: http://en.wikipedia.org/wiki/Accelerated_Reader.

Allen, Erin. 2007. "Graphic Novels Growing Presence in Youth Services." *The Salisbury Post*, September 17. Available: www.salisburypost.com.

Anderson, R.C., P.T. Wilson, and L.G. Fielding. 1988. "Growth in Reading and How Children Spend Their Time Outside of School." *Reading Research Quarterly* 23 (Summer): 285–303.

"Anti-Immigrant Criticism in Denver Extends to Library Fotonovelas." *Library Journal* (August 18, 2005). Available: www.libraryjournal.com/article/CA635920.html.

Aoyama, Yuko and Hiro Izushi. 2004. "Creative Resources of the Japanese Video Game Industry." In *Cultural Industries and the Production of Culture*, edited by Dominic Power and Allen John Scott. New York: Routledge, p. 121.

Arnold, Andrew D. "A Graphic Literature Library." Time.com (November 21, 2003). Available: www.time.com/time/columnist/arnold/article/0,9565,547796,00.html. Accessed: June 27, 2006.

Arnold, Andrew D. "The Graphic Novel Silver Anniversary." Time.com (November 14, 2003). Available: www.time.com/time/columnist/arnold/article/0,9565, 542579,00.html.

Banks, Mike. "Mike Banks of Samurai Comics on Partnering with Libraries." ICv2.com (May 30, 2006). Available: www.icv2.com/articles/indepth/8752.html. Accessed: July 5, 2006.

Beardsley, Nancy. "Graphic Novels Gain Popularity with American Teenagers." Washington, DC: American Library Association (October 19, 2002). Available: www1.voanews.com/article.cfm?objectID=98EDEF8B-C27B-4F9E-B8C1F0D516752029.

Bell, Tom. 2005. "Racy Fluff or Reading Aid?" *Portland Press Herald*, March 14, p. B1.

Bilton, Karen. "Kids Love Comics, Too!" *School Library Journal* (July 2004). Available: www.schoollibraryjournal.com/article/CA429346.html.

Bitz, Michael. 2003. *A Profile of the Evaluation of the Comic Book Project—New York City Pilot*. Cambridge, MA: Harvard Family Research Project. Available: www.gse.harvard.edu/~hfrp/projects/afterschool/mott/cbp.pdf.

Brenner, Robin. 2007. *Understanding Manga and Anime*. Westport CT: Libraries Unlimited.

Brown, John Mason. 1948. "The Case Against Comics." *Saturday Review of Literature*, March 20, pp. 32–33.

Buchanan, Rachel. 2006. "A Case for Comics: Comic Books As an Educational Tool—Part Two." *Sequential Tart*, July 1. Available: www.sequentialtart.com/article.php?id=186.

BWI Public Library Specialists. 2005. *The Public Librarian's Guide to Graphic Novels*. Lexington, KY: BWI.

Byrne, John. "Tricks of the Trade" (January 7, 2004). Available: www.ugo.com/channels/comics/features/johnbyrne_imo/archive_01_07_04.asp.

Cary, Stephen. 2004. *Going Graphic: Comics at Work in the Multilingual Classroom*. Portsmouth, NH: Heinemann.

Cha, Kai-Ming. 2005. "Sports Manga Gets in the Game" *Publishers Weekly*, April 18. Available: www.publishersweekly.com/article/CA525098.html. Accessed: September 11, 2006.

Chabon, Michael. "Keynote Speech 2004 Eisner Awards." Comic-Con International. Available: www.comic-con.org/cci/cci_eisners04keynote.shtml.

Chow, Natsuko. "Comics: A Useful Tool for English as a Second Language (ESL)." Diamond Bookshelf. Available: http://bookshelf.diamondcomics.com/public/default.asp?t=1&m=1&c=20&s=182&ai=37714&ssd=.

Comic Book Legal Defense Fund. Available: www.cbldf.org.

"Comic Books Can Inspire Reluctant and Advanced Readers in Hartford County." 2005. *Harford Schools* 37, no. 5 (January): 1, 11. Available: www.hcps.org/Departments/PublicInformation/HCPS_Newspaper/Archive/2004-05/January2004-05.pdf.

Crawford, Philip. 2004. "A Novel Approach: Using Graphic Novels to Attract Reluctant Readers." *Library Media Connection* 22, no. 5 (February): 26.

Cronin, Brian. "Comic Book Urban Legends Revealed #34." Comics Should Be Good (January 19, 2006). Available: http://goodcomics.blogspot.com/2006/01/19/comic-book-urban-legends-revealed-34.html.

Cronin, Brian. "Comic Book Urban Legends Revealed #39." Comics Should Be Good (February 23, 2006). Available: http://goodcomics.blogspot.com/2006/02/comic-book-urban-legends-revealed-39.html.

Dagg, Emily. 1997. *Graphic Novels in Children's and Young Adult Library Collections*. Seattle, WA: University of Washington.

David, Peter. 1992. "A Convocation of Politic Worms." *Incredible Hulk* 399 (November): 11.

David, Peter. 2006. *Writing Comics with Peter David*. Cincinnati, OH: Impact Books.

DC Comics. 2005. *The Seven Soldiers of Victory Archives*. New York: DC Comics.

de Vos, Gail. 2005. "ABCs of Graphic Novels." *Resource Links* 10, no. 3 (February). Available: www.resourcelinks.ca/features/feb05.htm.

Dobrowolski , Alex. 1983. "The Comic Book Is Alive and Well and Living in the History Class." In *Cartoons and Comics in the Classroom*, edited by James L. Thomas. Littleton, CO: Libraries Unlimited.

Dorrell, Larry and Ed Carroll. 1983. "Spider-Man at the Library." In *Cartoons and Comics in the Classroom*, edited by James L. Thomas. Littleton, CO: Libraries Unlimited.

Eisner, Will. 1974. "Comic Books in the Library." *School Library Journal* 21, no. 2 (October 15): 75–79.

Eisner, Will. 1985. *Comics & Sequential Art*. Tamarac, FL: Poorhouse Press.

Eisner, Will. 2004. "Keynote Address from the 2002 'Will Eisner Symposium.'" *ImageTexT: Interdisciplinary Comics Studies* 1, no. 1. Available: www.english .ufl/edu/imagetext/archives/v1_1/eisner/index.shtml. Accessed: July 25, 2006.

Ellis, Allen and Doug Highsmith. 2000. "About Face: Comic Books in Library Literature." *Serials Review* 26, no. 2: 21–43.

French, Dick. 1942. "Fury in the Philippines." *Military Comics* 11, August. Reprinted in *The Blackhawk Archives* 1: 133.

Gaiman, Neil. "Not Waving but Drowning. Well Waving a Bit" (July 20, 2003). Available: www.neilgaiman.com/2003/07/not-waving-but-drowing-well-waving.asp.

Gertler, Nat and Steve Lieber. 2004. *The Complete Idiot's Guide to Creating a Graphic Novel*. New York: Alpha Books.

Gonzalez, Miguel. 2006. "Good Grief, Charlie Brown! Family Stunned by Porn Comics at Library." *Daily Press* [Victorville, CA], April 12. Available: http://archive.vvdaily press.com/2006/11448553316.html.

Goulart, Ron. 2004. *Comic Book Encyclopedia: The Ultimate Guide to Characters, Graphic Novels, Writers, and Artists in the Comic Book Universe*. New York: HarperCollins.

Grand Comic Book Database. Available: www.comics.org.

"Graphic Novel." Wikipedia (January 12, 2008). Available: http://en.wikipedia .org/wiki/Graphic_novel. Accessed: August 1, 2006.

Gravett, Paul. 2004. *Manga Sixty Years of Japanese Comics*. London: Laurence King.

Hamilton, Edmond. 1963. "The Legion of Super-Monsters!" *Adventure Comics* 309, June. Reprinted 2007 in *Showcase Presents: Legion of Superheroes* 1: 309.

Hamilton, Edmond. 1964. "The Legion's Suicide Squad." *Adventure Comics* 319, April. Reprinted 2007 in *Showcase Presents: Legion of Superheroes* 1: 494.

Harker, Jean Gray. 1948. "Youth's Librarians Can Defeat Comics." *Library Journal* (December 1): 1705–1707.

Harris, Franklin. 2005. "Censored Book Not a Good Start." *The Decatur Daily*, February 10.

Harvey, Robert C. 2001. "Comedy at the Juncture of Word and Image: The Emergence of the Modern Magazine Gag Cartoon Reveals the Vital Blend." In *The Language of Comics: Word and Image*, edited by Robin Varnum and Christina T. Gibbons. Jackson, MS: University Press of Mississippi, pp. 77–78.

Haugaard, Kay. 1973. "Comic Books: Conduits to Culture." *The Reading Teacher* 27, no. 1: 54–55.

Heckman, Will. 2004. "Reading Heroes for a New Generation." *Media Quarterly* (Spring): 3.

Hill, Robyn A., ed. 2002. *The Secret Origins of Good Readers: A Resource Book*. Comic-Con International. Available: www.night-flight.com/secretorigin/sogr2002.pdf.

Hinze, Scott. "The Lowe-Down With Nick Lowe." Comic-Con International (November 6, 2005). Available: www.comicon.com/cgi-bin/ultimatebb.cgi?ubb=get_topic;f= 36;t=004386.

Hosler, Jay. 2000. *Clan Apis*. Columbus, OH: Active Synapse.

"How Comics Can Reach Reluctant Readers." Diamond Bookshelf. Available: http://bookshelf.diamondcomics.com/public/default.asp?t=l&m=l&c=20&s=182 &ai=377=8&ssd=.

Hunt, Jonathan. 2007. "The Trickle-Up Effect: An Interview with David Saylor." *Children and Libraries: The Journal of the Association of Library Service to Children* 5, no. 1: 8–11.

Inge, M. Thomas. 1990. *Comics As Culture*. Jackson, MS: University Press of Mississippi.

"Ithaca Public Education Initiative 2007 Teacher Grants." 2007. *The Ithaca Journal*, January 24, p. 3B.

"Japan Plans 'Nobel Prize of Manga.'" CNN.com (May 23, 2007). Available: www.cnn.com/2007/SHOWBIZ/books/05/22/manga.nobel.ap/index.html.

Jones, Patrick, Michele Gorman, and Tricia Suellentrop. 2004. *Connecting Young Adults and Libraries*, 3rd ed. New York: Neal-Schuman.

Jones, Seth. 2006. "A Gallon of Gas or a Comic? How Rising Oil Prices Affect the Comic Industry." *The Comic Wire*, May 13. Available: www.comicbookresources. com/news/newsitem.cgi?id=7434.

Kavanagh, Barry. "The Alan Moore Interview." Blather.net (October 17, 2000). Available: www.blather.net/articles/amoore/northampton.html. Accessed: August 16, 2006.

Krashen, Stephen D. 2004. *The Power of Reading*, 2nd ed. Westport, CT: Libraries Unlimited.

Kunitz, Stanley J. [As SJK]. 1941. "The Comic Menace." *Wilson Library Bulletin* 15: 846–847.

Kunitz, Stanley J. [As SJK]. 1941. "Libraries to Arms!" *Wilson Library Bulletin* 15: 670–671.

Lavin, Michael R. "The Comics Code Authority" (April 11, 2002). Available: http://ublib.buffalo.edu/libraries/projects/comics/cca.html.

Leonhardt, Mary. 1996. *Keeping Kids Reading: How to Raise Avid Readers in the Video Age*. New York: Crown Publishers.

"Library Cards Get Bonus on Free Comic Book Day." 2006. *Library Journal*, May 11. Available: www.libraryjournal.com/article/CA6333717.html.

"List of Black Superheroes." Answers.com (January 12, 2008). Available: www.answers.com/topic/list-of-black-superheroes.

Long, Tony. 2006. "The Day the Music Died." *Wired*, October 26. Available: www.wired.com/news/columns/0,71997-0.html.

Lyga, Allyson A.W. and Barry Lyga. 2004. *Graphic Novels in Your Media Center: A Definitive Guide*. Westport, CT: Libraries Unlimited.

M., Chris. "The Ebb and Flow of Traditional Superhero Serial Comics." Howling Curmudgeons. Available: http://www.whiterose.org/howlingcurmudgeons/ archives/009843.html. Accessed: August 16, 2006.

MacDonald, Heidi. 2003. "Bookstore Revolution: Graphic Novels Get Their Own Category." *Pulse News*, January 20. Available: www.comicon.com/ubb/ultimatebb .php/ubb/forum/f/36.html.

MacDonald, Heidi. 2004. "Marvel Classics Coming in '05." *Publisher's Weekly*, December 20. Available: www.publishersweekly.com/article/CA488207.html. Accessed: July 11, 2006.

MacDonald, Heidi. 2006. "Manga Alternations/Censorship." *The Beat*, June 26. Available: www.comicon.com/thebeat/2006/06/manga_alterationscensorship.html.

MacDonald, Heidi. 2006. "Meltzer: King of All Media." *The Beat*, September 18. Available: www.pwbeat.publishersweekly.com/blog/2006/09/18/Meltzer-king-of-all-media.

"'Manga is a Problem' and Other Highlights from the ICv2 Graphic Novel Conference." ICv2.com (March 5, 2006). Available: www.icv2.com/articles/home/8313.html. Accessed: July 5, 2006.

"Manga Releases Up 16% in 2007 According to ICv2 Guide." ICv2.com (February 7, 2007). Available: www.icv2.com/articles/news/10034.html.

"Marvel Edits 'Tomb of Dracula' for *Essential Dracula* Reprint." ICv2.com (September 22, 2006). Available: www.icv2.com/articles/news/9357.html.

"Maryland's Comic Book Project Receives Innovation Award." News Release (October 23, 2005). Maryland State Department of Education. Available: www.marylandpublicschools.org/NR/exeres/95DB79BE-780C-49BE-BB6B-78A5321D8DD8.

Maxwell, Arthur S. 1943. *Great Prophecies for Our Time*. Mountain View, CA: Pacific Publishing Association.

McCloud, Scott. 1993. "Comics and the Visual Revolution." *Publisher's Weekly*, October 11, pp. 47–56.

McCloud, Scott. 1994. *Understanding Comics*. New York: HarperPerennial.

McCloud, Scott. 2006. *Making Comics*. New York. HarperCollins.

McTaggart, Jacquie. *The Graphic Novel: Everything You Ever Wanted to Know but Were Afraid to Ask* (handout). Available: www.theteachersdesk.com/. Accessed: January 2008.

Mui, Ylan Q. 2004. "Schools Turn to Comics as Trial Balloon." *Washington Post*, December 13, p. B1.

National Coalition Against Censorship, the American Library Association, and the Comic Book Legal Defense Fund. 2006. *Graphic Novels: Suggestions for Librarians*. Available: www.ala.org/ala/oif/ifissues/graphicnovels_1.pdf.

No Flying No Tights. Available: www.noflyingnotights.com.

Nyberg, Amy Kiste. 1998. *Seal of Approval: The History of the Comics Code*. Jackson, MS: University Press of Mississippi.

Pennella, Brenda. "The POW!-er in the Classroom! A Teacher's Perspective." Brodart.com. Available: www.graphicnovels.brodart.com/teachers_perspective.htm. Accessed: January 12, 2008.

Pilcher, Tim and Brad Brooks. 2005. *The Essential Guide to World Comics*. London: Collins and Brown.

Read, Calvin. 1990. "Picture This: Batman, Popular Syndicated Cartoons and Sophisticated Graphic Novels Have Paved the Way for the Comic's Success in All Markets." *Publisher's Weekly*, October 12, p. 17

Rogers, John. 2006. "Comics Introduce Middle East Superheroes." *The Cincinnati Enquirer*, May 13.

Rogers, John. 2006. "Mideast Conflicts—Pow! Zap! Blam!—Resolved." *The New Journal*, May 13.

Rosen, Judith. 2006. "Comic Shops Turn to Book Distributors for Graphic Novels." PW Comic Week. *Publisher's Weekly*, July 18.

Rowe, Peter. 2006. "Invasion of the Comic Fanatics." *Union-Tribune*, July 16. Available: www.signonsandiego.com/news/features/20060716-9999-1n16comicon.html. Accessed: July 17, 2006.

Russell, Michael. "History of Comic Books Part II." Ezine Articles (December 17, 2005). Available: http://ezinearticles.com/?History-of-Comic-Books—Part-II&id= 114701. Accessed: July 28, 2007.

Serchay, David S. 1998. "Comic Book Collectors: The Serial Librarians of the Home." *Serials Review*, 24 no. 1: 57–70.

Serchay, David S. 2004. "But Those Aren't Really Books! Graphic Novels and Comic Books." In *Thinking Outside the Book: Alternatives for Today's Teen Library Collections*, edited by C. Allen Nichols. Westport, CT: Libraries Unlimited.

Swain, Emma. 1983. "Using Comic Books to Teach Reading and Language Arts." In *Cartoons and Comics in the Classroom*, edited by James L. Thomas. Littleton, CO: Libraries Unlimited.

Talbot, Bryan. 2007. *Alice in Sunderland: An Entertainment*. Milwaukee, OR: Dark Horse.

Thomas, James L., ed. 1983. *Cartoons and Comics in the Classroom*. Littleton, CO: Libraries Unlimited.

Thompson, Don and Dick Lupoff. 1998. *The Comic-Book Book*, revised ed. Iola, WI: Krause Publications.

Trelease, Jim. 2001. *The Read Aloud Handbook*, 5th ed. New York: Penguin Books.

Twiddy, David. 2007. "Pictures Causing Problems." *The Gazette* [Cedar Rapids–Iowa City, Iowa], January 14, p. 5L.

"Using Comics and Graphic Novels in the Classroom." *The Council Chronicle* (September 2005). Available: www.ncte.org/pubs/chron/highlights/122031.htm. Accessed: October 16, 2006.

Varnum, Robin and Christina T. Gibbons, eds. 2001. *The Language of Comics: Word and Image*. Jackson, MS: University Press of Mississippi.

Weiner, Stephen. 1996. *100 Graphic Novels for Public Libraries*. Northampton, MA: Kitchen Sink Press.

Williams, Gweneira and Jane Wilson. 1942. "They Like It Rough: In Defense of Comics." *Library Journal* (March 1): 204–206.

Worthy, J., M. Moorman, and M. Turner. 1999. "What Johnny Likes to Read Is Hard to Find in School." *Reading Research Quarterly* 34 (Jan–Feb–Mar): 12–27.

Wright, Ethel C. 1943. "A Public Library Experiments with the Comics." *Library Journal* (October 15): 832–835.

Yang, Gene (uncredited). "History of Comics in Education. Comics in Education (2003). Available: www.humblecomics.com/comicsedu/history.html.

Zimmerman, Thomas. 1954. "What to Do About Comics." *Library Journal* (September 15): 1605–1607.

"ZOIKS! Comic Books Offer a Key to Literacy Says UOFW Prof." 2007. News Release. January 18. University of Windsor, Ontario, Canada.

Title, Series, Creator, Character, and Publisher Index

Note: For the titles in this index, I have listed both the series name and the subtitles of the original volumes. For example, for *Marvel Age Spider-Man:* Volume 1: *Fearsome Foes*, both *Marvel Age Spider-Man* and *Fearsome Foes* have entries. Subtitles are listed with their series in parenthesis. Titles from the nonfiction publishers and Stone Arch are also listed in this manner.

Due to space limitations, in cases where parts of a series start with the same word and are found on the same page and nowhere else in the book, then their entries may be combined. This includes the individual *Archives/Showcase Presents* books from DC and the *Essential/Masterworks* books from Marvel. In addition, some titles listed within the book or in Appendix B may be listed by title or creator only or not at all.

Subject Index

Page numbers followed by the letter "e" indicate exhibits; those followed by the letter "f" indicate figures.

A

Accelerated Reader (AR) List, 63, 64e, 127, 148, 159, 178, 212, 226, 231
Adaptations and licensed properties
    from film and television sources, 31–33, 51, 156, 165–167, 172–173, 182, 183, 207, 211, 215
    film, radio, and television based on comics and graphic novels, 67, 68e–70e, 70
    from literary sources, 30, 31–33, 63, 64, 87, 88, 89, 90, 91e, 101, 103e, 107, 113–114, 148, 152, 155, 156, 157, 176, 179, 197, 201, 202, 213–214, 221, 222
    literary works based on comics and graphic novels, 63, 64, 97
Adults and graphic novels, 46, 53, 87, 91, 99e, 114, 115, 131, 132
Advance, 176
African-American comic characters. *See* Black comic characters
ALA. *See* American Library Association
Altering stories
    to improve, 14
    to make age-appropriate, 47, 142
    for translation, 49
Amazon.com, 80, 230
American Library Association (ALA), 132
    conferences, 66e, 94–95
    YALSA, 66, 90e, 94, 153, 155, 164, 172, 175, 183, 184, 218, 232
Amerimanga. *See* Manga
Angoulême International Comics Festival, 53, 187
Animanga. *See* Manga

Anime, 44, 46, 47, 51, 76, 79, 80, 87, 88, 98, 115, 123, 153, 157, 182, 184, 185, 199, 215, 218, 227
    anime and manga clubs, 96, 123
    See also Manga
Annuals, 9
AR List. *See* Accelerated Reader List
Asian comic characters, 38, 40, 41, 153
Awards
    historical, 95e
    winners, 76, 87, 90, 94, 95e, 102e, 152, 153, 158, 164, 173, 180, 181, 185, 197, 198, 218, 219, 222, 231
    See also individual awards

B

Baker & Taylor, 76, 78, 230
Ballantine, Ian, 61
Balloons, 6, 7e, 12, 20
Bandé dessinée. *See* French comics
Barnes & Noble, 47, 79, 80, 94, 230
Beat, The, 231
Belgian comics, 51, 53, 88, 107
Bibz, 76
Big Little Books, 4, 63
Binding, 111
Biographies. *See* Graphic nonfiction
Black comic characters, 38–40
Book Wholesalers, Inc. *See* BWI
Booklist, 76, 93
Bookmarks, 120–122, 124
Books based on comic books. *See* Adaptations and licensed properties
Books with comic-based themes, 28, 64
Books-A-Million, 79
Bookshelf format, 11
Bookstores, 77, 79, 80, 91, 94, 111. *See also individual stores*
Booktalking, 123

About the Author

David S. Serchay is a youth services librarian for the Broward County (Florida) Library System, where he is on the graphic novel selection committee, and has been reading comic books all of his life, with a personal collection of more than 25,000 comics and graphic novels. He has previously written about the subject for *Library Journal, Serials Review, Florida Living, Animato!*, and Comics Source, and the upcoming *A Librarian's Guide to Graphic Novels for Adults*. He also contributed to the "Comic Book" section of *Magazines for Libraries*, has lectured on the subject of graphic novels and libraries, provided indexes for the Grand Comic Book Database, and wrote a chapter on graphic novels for *Thinking Outside the Book*. He lives in Coral Springs, Florida, with his wife, Bethany, and can be reached at davidserchay@yahoo.com.